D0930361

This study combines an analysis of the argumentative complexities of Romans 1–8 with the presentation of modern theories of how meaning arises and functions. These theories (especially as represented by the semiotics of Umberto Eco) shed important light on two central questions raised by Paul's method: why does he reason so persistently about matters which depend ultimately on supernatural enlightenment, and why, where he does, are his arguments often so unclear and so hard to reduce to logical consistency? To both questions new answers emerge.

SOCIETY FOR NEW TESTAMENT STUDIES

MONOGRAPH SERIES

General Editor: Margaret E. Thrall

82

WRESTLING WITH RATIONALITY IN PAUL

Wrestling with rationality in Paul

Romans 1–8 in a new perspective

JOHN D. MOORES

Formerly Lecturer in Italian,
University College London

CAMBRIDGE
UNIVERSITY PRESS

Published by the Press Syndicate of the University of Cambridge
The Pitt Building, Trumpington Street, Cambridge CB2 1RP
40 West 20th Street, New York, NY 10011–4211, USA
10 Stamford Road, Oakleigh, Melbourne 3166, Australia

First published 1995

Printed in Great Britain at the University Press, Cambridge

A catalogue record for this book is available from the British Library

Library of Congress cataloguing in publication data

Moores, John D.
Wrestling with rationality in Paul : Romans 1–8 in a new
perspective / John D. Moores.
   p. cm. – (Monograph series / Society for New Testament Studies: 82)
Includes bibliographical references and indexes.
ISBN 0 521 47223 7
1. Bible. N.T. Romans I–VIII – Criticism, interpretation, etc.
2. Faith and reason – Christianity.   3. Enthymeme (Logic).   I Title.
II. Series: Monograph series (Society for New Testament Studies): 82
BS2665.2.M66   1995
227′.1066 – dc 20   94–15199   CIP

ISBN 0 521 47223 7 hardback

CE

To the memory of my mother and father

Nothing can credibly be proposed as the language of faith which cannot honestly be defended by the person who speaks.

Harmony comes into being through love mediated by language.

G. Ebeling

Pauline theology . . . circles round in ever new attempts to bring out the saving significance of the Cross. It is a theology of the Word because it is only through the word of the Cross that Jesus's death remains present, remains grace, remains promise and covenant; and it is the work of the one who is risen to let this word manifest itself in preaching, in the sacraments and in the Christian life.

E. Käsemann

CONTENTS

ix

ACKNOWLEDGEMENTS

I owe an immense debt of gratitude to Professor Leslie Houlden of King's College London, without whose encouragement I would never have brought to completion the London University thesis on which this book is based, and without whose kindly strictures it would never have been publishable.

Where the linguistic dimension of the work is concerned I am deeply appreciative of the ready and reassuring help I have received from Professor Giulio Lepschy of Reading University.

Among numerous other friends who have given me the benefit of their comments and corrections, I would particularly like to mention Mr Mohan Uddin who has read and re-read the text with unfailing patience and care, as well as Miss V. Petrassi, Mr S. Q. K. Underwood and Mr T. Barnes whose collaboration in checking proofs and other details has been invaluable.

I have been constantly aware, in pursuing this enquiry, of how much I owe to the seminars at the London Bible College which first opened my mind to modern hermeneutical and technical approaches to biblical study.

My indebtedness to Professor Eco is evident in the study itself. It arises entirely from the powerful impact upon me of his published writings (in welcome accord with my life's long-standing orientation towards Italian stimuli). I have not sought his approval of my application of his theories or his confirmation of my construal of them. The responsibility is mine if I have misused them.

May I finally add how grateful I am to Dr Thrall and the Society for New Testament Studies for the privilege of being allowed to contribute to their Monograph series.

ABBREVIATIONS

ET	English translation
ETL	*Ephemerides Theologicae Lovanienses*
EvTh	*Evangelische Theologie*
ExT	*Expository Times*
FRLANT	Forschungen zur Religion und Literatur des Alten und Neuen Testaments
FS	Festschrift
GTA	Göttingen Theologische Arbeiten
HBT	*Horizons in Biblical Theology*
HCHC	Hermeneia – A Critical and Historical Commentary on the Bible
HNT	Handbuch zum Neuen Testament
HTKNT	Herders theologischer Kommentar zum Neuen Testament
HTR	*Harvard Theological Review*
ICC	International Critical Commentary
Int	*Interpretation*
JBL	*Journal of Biblical Literature*
JSNT	*Journal for the Study of the NT*
JSNT SS	*Journal for the Study of the NT*, Supplement Series
JTS	*Journal of Theological Studies*
LB	*Linguistica Biblica*
LN	J. P. Louw and E. A. Nida: *Greek–English Lexicon of the NT, Based on Semantic Domains*, 2nd edn, 1989 (NY, UBS)
LSJ	H. W. Liddell and R. Scott: *A Greek–English Lexicon* (revised and augmented by H. Stuart Jones and R. McKenzie), 9th edn, 1940 (Oxford, Clarendon)
LT	Lieux Théologiques
LXX	Septuagint
MKEK	Meyers kritisch-exegetischer Kommentar über das Neue Testament
MM	J. H. Moulton and G. Milligan: *The Vocabulary of the Greek Testament*, 1930 (London, Hodder)
MNTC	Moffatt NT Commentary
MT	Masoretic Text
NEB	New English Bible, 1970 (Oxford UP)
Neot	*Neotestamentica*
NICNT	New International Commentary on the NT
NIGTC	New International Greek Testament Commentary
NovT	*Novum Testamentum*

NovTS   Supplements to *Novum Testamentum*
NTD   Das Neue Testament Deutsch
NTS   *New Testament Studies*
PLJP   E. P. Sanders, *Paul, the Law and the Jewish People*, 1985 (London, SCM)
PPJ   E. P. Sanders, *Paul and Palestinian Judaism*, 1977 (London, SCM)
Presb   *Presbyterion*
RB   *Revue Biblique*
Rhet   *Rhetorica*
RSV   Revised Standard Version of the Bible, NT 2nd edn 1971, OT 1952
SB   H. L. Strack and P. Billerbeck: *Kommentar zum Neuen Testament aus Talmud und Midrash*, 1926–28 (Munich, Beck'sche)
SBLDS   Society of Biblical Literature Dissertation Series
SE   *Studia Evangelica*
Sem   *Semeia*
SJT   *Scottish Journal of Theology*
SNTSMS   Society for NT Studies Monograph Series
SNTU   *Studien zum Neuen Testament und seiner Umwelt*
ST   *Studia Theologica*
StB   Stuttgarter Bibelstudien
TDNT   *Theological Dictionary of the NT*, ed. G. Kittel and G. Friedrich (ET), 1964–76 (Grand Rapids, Eerdmans)
Theol   *Theology*
TNTC   Tyndale NT Commentary
TPINTC   Trinity Press International NT Commentaries
TQ   *Theologische Quartalschrift*
TS   U. Eco, *A Theory of Semiotics*, 1976 (Bloomington, Indiana UP)
TSG   U. Eco, *Trattato di semiotica generale*, 10th edn 1987 (Milan, Bompiani)
TZ   *Theologische Zeitschrift*
UCr   H. Cremer: *Biblico-theological Lexicon of NT Greek*, ET from German edn of W. Urwick, 4th edn 1895 (Edinburgh, Clark)
WBC   Word Biblical Commentary
WGTh   *Greek–English Lexicon of the NT*, ET (revised and enlarged) by J. H. Thayer of Grimm's Wilke's *Clavis Novi Testamenti*, 4th edn 1901 (Edinburgh, Clark)

WMANT   Wissenschaftliche Monographien zum Alten und Neuen Testament
WUNT   Wissenschaftliche Untersuchungen zum Neuen Testament
ZNW   *Zeitschrift für die Neutestamentliche Wissenschaft*
ZTK   *Zeitschrift für Theologie und Kirche*

THE LAYOUT OF THIS STUDY AND THE APPROACH BEHIND IT

For Paul the truth of the gospel of Christ was not to be understood by dodging the logical riddles with which it confronts us. He does not speak as if the illumination guaranteed by the Holy Spirit dispenses with the need for reflection. Rather he speaks as if, sharpened and directed by the Holy Spirit, the human capacity for exercising critical judgement plays a formative role in our grasp of the gospel. In addressing those who, in different ways according to their differing backgrounds, had to face the difficulties such a perspective entails, Paul, impelled by the urgency of his message, was unaccommodating.

'The attempt to understand the logic and argumentation of Paul must give a Greek a headache,' V. Grönbech once observed (in *Paulus Jesu Christi Apostel*). And certainly to the mind shaped by the Socratic tradition, his manner of reasoning could scarcely fail to occasion perplexity of reader response. It was not his aim to stimulate detached intellectual enquiry in anything like the Socratic spirit. He assumes in his readers a core of conviction in which an answer to every question lies latent. And yet, if his approach is thus out of line with the Greek tradition, it is no less out of line with the OT tradition. In his concern with explanation, verification, substantiation, though it may be questionable how much there is of the Greek philosopher, there is certainly much of the Greek rhetorician with his philosophical background. Paul's propensity for applying to the data of divine revelation a technique of syllogistic appraisal is clearly part of his Greek inheritance, and if his use of it is such as to give a Greek a headache, his Jewishness can hardly have failed to ensure it meant headaches for him too. But if it did he seems to have thrived on them.

This study focusses on Romans 1–8, an area pervaded by argument which is nothing if not intricate and tangled. Commentators have given much attention to cultural influences and situational motivation in the attempt to account for its awkwardnesses. Necessary and valuable as such researches eminently are, I believe that they involve a risk of falsifying the tune Paul is playing; for he introduces his arguments as representing a source of blessed encouragement. At any rate, that is how I would propose we should construe Paul's attitude. It is a construal which colours all my considerations, and is the goal towards which they all tend – as its role in drawing my discussion to a conclusion in Chapter 5, sections 4–5, displays. Towards this proposal, which gives my study its direction, the build-up is essentially a vindication of the intellectual substance of Paul's argumentation. It is a vindication founded on a somewhat innovatory approach to Pauline rationality.

I have been led to it by viewing Paul against the background of semiology, the science of signs – perhaps, better, of *signification* or *sign-production*. Though I see this as giving to my study a new and distinctive slant, let me say at once that the final outcome I have to report is more a matter of envisaging a promising line of investigation than of being able to offer results. The promise is that afforded, as I believe, by the new analytical tools of 'fuzzy logic': promise of a more conceptually penetrating dissection than has hitherto been feasible of some of the issues that figure most prominently in Paul's argumentation, in particular those surrounding his use of the terms δίκαιος, νόμος and θάνατος. As to what this might involve, I give as much elucidation as my level of competence permits in Chapter 5, section 3. That section thus provides the immediate foundation on which I base my proposal regarding the 'encouraging' tenor of Paul's 'tune'.

I do not settle upon 'fuzzy logic' as the best source of promise without having first reviewed other approaches to Pauline argumentation that developments in the science and philosophy of language in the twentieth century might seem to commend. And Chapter 5, section 2, reflects my concern to take account of the scope such approaches may offer, notably those emanating from the ambit of aesthetics, existentialism and deconstructionism. Into a related category Chapter 1, sections 2–4, may also be seen to fall, where I deal with the 'rhetorical' and 'sacred' dimensions as they impinge on Pauline discourse.

It is, however, the way that general semiotics has led me to where I stand that I am principally concerned to expound as fully as possible in this study. And it is to this exercise that I apply myself right at the very beginning of Chapter 1, section 1. Attention there centres at once on a nucleus of semiological theory which is to dominate all my references to the subject: that constituted by the typology of semiosis elaborated by Umberto Eco. I see in his findings a striking relevance to the Pauline propensity for logical argumentation. The method by which I move towards vindicating the latter springs from this relevance, for in the principle of signification which – among the various modes into which he classifies sign-productivity – Eco identifies by the term 'Recognition' we can, I believe, see both the reason why argumentation is indispensable to Paul and why it gets him into difficulties. Section 1.1 illustrates the applicability of Eco's semiological typology to Paul's apprehension of the significance of the Crucifixion. The persistence with which intractable logical issues are pursued by him can then be linked to specific tendencies inherent in the particular semiological mechanism (Recognition) which is involved. Later in the chapter (1.5) I show how these tendencies and the impasse to which they bring the deductive process (on which Recognition nevertheless depends) are manifested in Paul's argumentative persistence.

The central body of my study then deals with the technical phenomenon which is the most conspicuous outcome of this persistence, syllogistic reasoning formulated enthymematically – that is to say, elliptically, without a full display of the syllogistic components. That Paul's argumentation may often not be clear, that it may involve insidious shifts of meaning, that its motivation may be difficult to perceive (and that the influence of cultural and situational factors complicates and confuses the issues as much as it sheds light on them) are all features which become amply apparent as Chapters 2–4 of my study work their way through the argumentation of Romans 1–8 highlighting the incidence of the enthymematic element, and bringing out the perplexingly wide varieties of effect with which it becomes associated (Chapter 2), the differing ways in which it arises (Chapter 3), and the changing levels of importance which it assumes (Chapter 4).

I do not pretend that the semiological background against which I would view these complexities disposes of the problems to which they give rise. I do, however, contend that it does much to set them in a fundamentally positive light, not only because it shows them as inevitable rather than self-induced (of an essentially healthy, not idle, irrelevant or incidental origin), but because they emerge as tangles in which illuminatory potential is as much to be cherished as obscurity regretted or excused. They emerge in a light compatible with their having inspired in Paul an optimism and a confidence to be shared with others as blessings. It is indeed a function of semiology to show that communicativity does not depend on 'clarity' of one kind only; it shows, for example, that rational inconsistency or inexactitude is not incompatible with expressive immediacy. These are issues I pursue in 5.1 – but only, in the end, to affirm that the promise which I can see in recourse to 'fuzzy' logic deflects me from tackling Pauline reasoning on any such basis. In fact, it convinces me that the most fruitful approach to the rational element in Paul, particularly – but not only – in Romans 1–8, is to expect the communicative energy inherent in objective argumentative substance to be the *main* source of illuminatory potential in the tight corners where Paul's logic lands him.

1

ENTHYMEMATIC SEMIOSIS IN PAUL

1.1 A semiotic perspective for the study of Pauline argument. Umberto Eco's 'typology of modes of sign-production'.

'It is very difficult to imagine an imprint that mentions a referent without the mediation of a content.' This is a comment which the semiologist Umberto Eco is prompted to make in relation to the significance which Robinson Crusoe reads into the human footprint which he comes upon on the island where he is shipwrecked.[1] The message may be spelt out thus: 'There is at least one other human being on this island in addition to me.' The referent which the imprint, by virtue of its form, 'mentions' is 'human being', but the 'mention' does not come about for Crusoe on this occasion without the mediation of a content which the words 'human being' alone do not adequately represent. He does not think 'human being' except as 'a particular human being who must be my fellow inhabitant on this island'.

This example illustrates one mode of the operation which Eco defines as 'sign-production'. It is the mode which he refers to as 'Recognition'. It is the first of four modes into which he distinguishes 'sign-production'. The others are Ostension, Replica and Invention.[2] It is a feature of Eco's general theory of semiotics that the object of semiological study should be understood not as the sign itself but as the production of signs.[3] It is his belief that it must be a theory which embraces all the forms in which sign-production can occur.[4] Its products, he considers, are more properly identified by the term 'sign-function' than 'sign'.[5] It is a further feature of his theory that 'sign-production' embraces not only intentional but also unintentional signs.[6] The Crusoe example is a case in point. The 'production' of the sign in such a case – the process whereby the imprint becomes 'sign-functional' – arises with the act of recognition. Eco's definition of 'Recognition' is, in fact, as follows: 'Recognition occurs when a given object or event, produced by nature or human action (intentionally or unintentionally), and existing in a world of facts as a fact among facts, comes to be viewed by an addressee as the expression of a given content, either through a pre-existing and coded correlation or through the positing of a possible correlation by its addressee.'[7]

The crucifixion of Jesus Christ is an event which was produced by human action and which exists as a fact in a world of facts. These – whatever doubts some may have or have had on the subject – were undoubtedly the terms on which it was recognised by Paul of Tarsus as the expression of the content which he read into it through the correlation which he posited between the event and that content. That the action, as understood by Paul, has a dimension which makes 'human' an epithet of questionable adequacy, and that the complexity which invests the intentionality of its occurrence is of a uniqueness that lies outside anything Eco was concerned to accommodate, does not prevent his definition of 'Recognition' from fitting the sign-receptive experience of Paul as aptly as it does that of Robinson Crusoe.

Eco's definition of Recognition, as I have just quoted it, may not seem to account adequately for his inclusion of Recognition under the heading 'sign-production'. The 'coming to be viewed' of an event or object in a certain light is not naturally or obviously to be equated with the view having been 'produced' by anyone. (And to call the viewer the 'addressee' sounds decidedly odd.) But, as Eco sees it, when an object or event is recognised as having a certain meaning – as being, that is, the expression of a certain content – it is as if (a) the one who recognises the meaning had had his attention drawn to it, or (b) as if recognising it had involved its being represented to him, or (c) had entailed an appeal being made to his creative judgement. 'The object or event', as he puts it, 'must be considered as if it had been produced by ostension, replica or invention.'[8]

Paul first sees the Crucifixion as speaking to himself. This is Recognition. But it speaks as something he has been shown and that he can show to others. If Crusoe had had a fellow castaway with him, he could have shown him the footprint, and – without his having said anything – his companion would have understood the message to be 'Look, we are not the only human beings on this island.' From Recognition we pass at once to Ostension.[9] And there is a sense in which Paul considers that the Crucifixion is an event which, once it is shown, speaks.[10] But even if the significance of the Crucifixion may be considered as essentially complete the moment the identity of the victim is grasped (i.e. that he is the Son of God), to any but those who had been with him personally or had enjoyed a unique illuminatory experience like Paul's, it would need pointing out and spelling out.[11] Even Paul has understood the meaning revealed to him by spelling it out, representing it to himself. And here we move into the ambit of Replica.

The term 'replica' is used by Eco to cover that category of sign which is distinguished by its repeatability. A sign that has the form of an object or an event existing in a world of facts is by its nature unrepeatable. Intentional communication largely operates by means of artificial signs which depend for their functioning on the reproduction of the convention.[12] The English word 'book' means what the body of English speakers agrees it to mean. Repetition is both the mode and the source of its sign-productivity. Words are by no means the only form that repeatable signs can take, but they are the most common, and are notable particularly for the capacity to explicate the meaning latent in other types of sign-production (*some* others, that is: not all – as Eco characteristically insists, whatever had previously been claimed);[13] words explicate what is recognised in Recognition and what is displayed in Ostension. Through repetition they represent the meanings which as a result of the sign-productive process come to be recognised in or imparted to objects or events.

The meaning of a footprint in the sand seems to be best construed as something that represents itself to Crusoe in words. And so it is with the meaning of the Crucifixion to Paul. In both cases the communication of the meaning by means of ostension can be seen as implying a verbal content, even if, at least in the case of Crusoe, it can do without any words actually being uttered aloud. In the case of Paul silent ostension is not feasible – with far-reaching consequences for the involvement of the mechanism without which semiosis could not occur at all: Coding.

The meaning of an object or event is something we decipher, and to decipher we need to know and apply the appropriate code. Decoding is a matter of correlating forms with meanings. Coding is the principle by virtue of which objects or events are correlated as 'expression' to 'content'. It is the principle on which words depend for their meaning.[14] Where expression is verbal the correlation with content is fundamentally arbitrary and is brought about by coding which operates at various different levels.[15] It is ultimately rooted in the manipulation of expression units composed of elements which depend for meaning entirely on the combinations in which they figure.[16] For example, 'book' exists as a sign-function in its own right. It can also contribute to the sign-functional value of a propositional unit such as 'That book is red'. But whereas the meaning of the proposition is the sum of a series of sign-functional contributions the nature of each of which can be separately identified and explained, the meaning of the word 'book' is not the aggregate of what the orthographic elements b, o, o, k, of which it is made up, can be separately explained as contributing.[17] The coding on which the combination of elements like these depends for its operation is coding at its most rigorously artificial.[18] Replica, then, is a semiotic mode in which a great deal of the coding involved is arbitrary. However, where Replica occurs non-verbally (as in the case of conventional signs, on the road, in public buildings, etc.) the convention may contain a 'motivation' that makes it less than entirely arbitrary and to some extent self-explanatory. For instance, the sign ⚢ is chosen to indicate access to a provision intended for women because its appearance has some correlation to the circumstances of being a female. Where sign-production arises through Recognition or Ostension, the correlation, though it may enjoy the status of a convention in some cases, never involves wholly arbitrary coding. In the case of an imprint the code is established by experience, and experience provides all that is necessary to crack it.[19] The range of experience enjoyed by an 'addressee' may indeed determine whether or not, and according to what principle, he or she is in fact 'addressed' by the sign-productive potential of the situation. As women come to wear skirts less and less, a child of today may need to be taught a convention before being able to interpret the ⚢ which experience would formerly have sufficed to decode.

Whether the code which enabled Paul to 'recognise' the meaning of the Crucifixion was a code provided by experience alone, it is effectively impossible for us to say. The Recognition certainly depended on a code which, through the experience of a moment of privileged insight, invalidated at a stroke the code that had served him hitherto. By the terms of the invalidated code to the formation of which the whole of Paul's earlier experience had contributed, he had read the crucifixion of Jesus as the fitting punishment of an impostor who had blasphemously claimed to be the Son of God whose coming the Hebrew Scriptures had foreseen.[20] Under the new code formed with dramatic suddenness as an integral part of his conversion experience, he read the same event as God's sacrifice of his Son in mysterious fulfilment of all (and more than all?) that the Hebrew Scriptures could be seen to foreshadow concerning his coming. The writings of Paul abundantly display his anxiety that the meaning he thus saw in the Crucifixion should be adequately spelt out. But their volume scarcely seems to square with his resolve to know nothing among the Corinthians except Jesus Christ and him crucified, a declaration which is consequently often regarded as a mere tactical device to be seen strictly in relation to the dangers of over-reliance on intellect or of empty shows of eloquence.[21] I would argue that it should be taken more seriously.

The key factor in the disclosure experience of Paul's conversion is identified by Paul himself as his having seen the risen Jesus. The new code is determined by the evidence that he who was crucified had indeed risen from the tomb and was alive for ever. Paul's identification of the victim of the Crucifixion as the Son of God, and the particular connotative dynamic which the title 'Son of God' carries for Paul (as well as all the soteriological implications that he draws from it) arise from the code having its origin in the evidence of Paul's own eyes (albeit those spiritually opened for him by miraculous means). I see myself here as following assertions in Paul's own letters (Gal 1:12–16; 1Cor 9:1; 15:8).[22] If it is thought that I make insufficient allowance for the teaching he received from other Christians, I would still say that whatever part such teaching may have played in his act of recognition, a unique focus on the risen victim of the Crucifixion remains characteristic of, and central to, his experience.[23] However, Eco affirms that 'all sign-functions depending on replica, ostension and recognition articulate given units in order to produce more complex texts'.[24] Paul cannot grasp what he has 'recognised' without the mediation of a verbal text. And he cannot communicate what he has grasped without relaying the verbal text as it has articulated itself for him.

The experiential background to the sign-productive event of Paul's recognition of the significance of the Crucifixion is one in which the experience of a revelatory confrontation with the resurrected victim impinges on a network of attitudes and of beliefs drastically reshaping and expanding it. And therefore, whilst the code governing the Recognition is provided by a single sudden experience, at least six distinct core statements seem to inhere in the content of the Recognition as Paul must, even initially, have spelt it out to himself for it ultimately to produce the flood of more complex texts that it does.

1   A man is crucified.
2   That man is the son of God.[25]
3   God gave him up to be crucified.
4   It was for us that God gave him up to be crucified.
5   This is the extent of God's gift to us.
6   The measure of the gift is the measure of God's love.

For the meaning of what Paul points to in the Crucifixion to be communicable to others certainly no fewer than these six propositions are necessary. Its decoding cannot begin to come about in terms of less textual elaboration than this. But perhaps no more elaboration than this is necessary for enough text-productive energy to have been sparked off to generate, without further boosting, the total result with which the teaching of Paul confronts us. Already, however, the minimum textual elaboration needed to give effect to the initial decoding dynamic of Paul's encounter with the Risen One depends necessarily on the special codificatory mechanisms by which verbal communication operates. These quickly multiply and diversify (as we shall see in 1.4) as more and more explicatory texts, flooding Paul's channels of outgoing transmission, amplify the basic textual nucleus. Nevertheless the acts of sign-production that make up Paul's teaching are all ultimately instances of Replica effecting Ostension by explicating Recognition; the myriad sign-productive tokens of which his discourse is composed serve always, directly or indirectly, in diverse ways, to articulate the single sign-productive event which the Resurrection led him to decode as the Crucifixion of the Son of God. Once this is taken duly into account, many problems to which the idiosyncrasies of his discourse give rise are alleviated, not the least those surrounding his propensity for introducing arguments to support his statements. The present study attempts to demonstrate this.

1.2   Pauline argument and the rhetorical dimension of his discourse. Two lines of approach: the classical and the 'new'.

Paul's use of argument can roughly be said to take two forms: they are (1) appeals to Scripture; (2) appeals to reason. Only (2) comes within the scope of what I have just been saying and what I am proposing to say.

There seems to be a fairly wide consensus of opinion today that it is in the rhetorical dimension of Paul's discourse that we have the context which determines the role played by his appeals to reason. How vital a role it is to be accounted will be a problem inseparable from how positively or how negatively his rhetoric is viewed. How indeed it should be viewed has been the object of much discussion in recent times. The discussion has pursued two rather different approaches according to whether it is the ancient or the modern understanding of rhetoric that is being brought to bear on the issue. Whichever is to the fore, a certain diffidence seems to prevail about facing the proposition that rhetoric is an essentially fraudulent mode of discourse. And yet it has been current for almost as long as 'rhetoric' has denoted a genre, and has been given a new lease of life in some of the most recent waves of twentieth-century speculation (Eco being an accomplice in this). Understandably it is something of a stumbling-block to Paulinists, who are very inclined to pass it over altogether. It is a proposition that cannot be ignored.

In Plato's *Gorgias* the admired teacher of rhetoric, amid the reassuring flattery of his pupils, is pressed mercilessly by Socrates to explain what rhetoric is, and in attempting to do so passes from one ineptitude to another. Granted the patent insufficiency of defining rhetoric as being concerned with discourse unless the end to which discourse tends is also clarified, Socrates penetrates right to the core of the issue when Gorgias agrees that rhetoric is concerned with discourse tending to persuasion. Is the persuasion it brings about (Socrates asks) a persuasion arising from belief or knowledge? Gorgias cannot escape from the admission that it is the former and not the latter.[26]

With its origins in the fifth-century democracy of Syracuse and the practical exigencies of property litigation, it is not surprising that Greek rhetoric should have pursued above all else the aim of inducing belief: expediency dictated its methods. The elaborate techniques which it evolved and codified from Corax to Isocrates testify to the vigour and exclusiveness of this concern. Its ethical rating fluctuated. In the context of the Sophists, who despaired of knowledge, its status could not be the same as in the context of philosophers who pursued it, albeit without hope of definitive conclusions.

In the former context the *power* of rhetoric predominates over other considerations:[27] in that of concern with knowledge the issue of its *legitimacy* will stand out. It becomes possible through Aristotle, in fact, to distinguish the earlier practical conception of rhetoric, culminating in that of the Sophists with their emphasis on the aims and methods of the speaker, from his philosophical rhetoric, where the focus shifts to the value of rhetoric for the hearer. The scholastic rhetoric of later times, notably that of the Romans, though it felt the influence of both kinds in various ways, at various times, and to varying degrees, actually owes its character less to Aristotle than to his predecessors.[28] It is from this pattern of development that the kinds of question arise which Kennedy notes as constantly recurring:

> What is the relationship of the art or discipline called rhetoric to the art or discipline called dialectic, the art of reasoning? What is the relationship of rhetoric to oral speech in contrast to writing? What relative weight of importance at different stages in the history of classical rhetoric is given to each of the factors in the speech act – the speaker, the speech itself and the audience? What is the relationship of classical rhetoric to political and legal institutions? To poetics and literary history? To religion, in particular to Christianity and the Judaeo-Christian rhetorical tradition?[29]

The rhetoric I have focussed on is 'primary rhetoric', that is the rhetoric of public speaking, above all in the court of law and – as time went on – in the political assembly as well. Kennedy's list reflects the existence of a secondary rhetoric, the rhetoric recognised as present in forms of communication which are not primarily rhetorical, or are rhetorical but not public, and written instead of oral.[30] Aristotle noted the analogy between rhetoric and painting or sculpture. Rhetoric was seen to be an art. Conversely, art in general involves both qualities and techniques akin to those of rhetoric. In either there is an appeal to feeling, and the means by which it is made is form.

It is from such considerations as these that a twentieth-century methodology of rhetorical criticism in literature has drawn its impetus. This methodology is also, however, firmly based on the view that all human communication has a rhetorical element. All human communication makes some direct appeal to the feelings through the medium of form. It is a question of degree. Kennedy notes the difference between an ordinary telephone directory, where the rhetorical factor is as nearly absent as it is possible for it to be, and the Yellow Pages where it plays a prominent role.[31] It could perhaps be said that the basic principle on which the modern rhetorical methodology seeks to function is that an essential aspect of all artistic phenomena is missed unless due account is taken of the rhetorical factor. Or, to put it another way, the dynamic of persuasion is a fundamental factor in all artistic activity; a new depth of insight into its products is afforded by approaching them in the light of this realisation.

The principle has been and is being widely upheld and exploited as a basis for literary criticism both in England and elsewhere, but whether it is a principle by means of which rhetoric can be shown to be a useful category in the specific area of biblical criticism is an issue fraught with many complications.[32]

These arise for two opposite reasons. They arise because rhetoric is in one sense closer to, and in another more remote from, biblical as opposed to literary discourse. Just how far and how close will depend on what precise view is taken of the nature and status of biblical writings, or of that particular part of them which is under consideration. Yet, in any view of them that sees them as divinely inspired (in whatever sense or measure), it can be said that they are distinguished from other forms of persuasive communication in that their persuasiveness is plainly advertised as not depending ultimately on argument accessible to the human reason or on techniques that lie within the inherent resources of human language.[33] Nevertheless it is now widely held that a rhetorical approach can be useful in biblical studies, and also that it should be such as not to lead merely to a penetration of the substance of the biblical writings that gets no further than their literary qualities.

The application to biblical studies of an approach that involves rhetoric in a sense that moves towards this requirement goes back to a 1968 address of Muilenberg's.[34] He was led to it as a means of overcoming the limitations by which he felt the criticism of biblical texts had become bound through the hegemony of form criticism, the methods of which he nevertheless considered to have borne valuable fruit and which he saw himself as supplementing rather than supplanting. He saw form criticism as undervaluing the personal and unique element in biblical writing and as being too averse to biographical and psychological interpretations of them and the relating of them to their particular historical context. He defined his own concern as being to exhibit 'the structural patterns that are employed for the fashioning of a literary unit', and to discern 'the devices' by which the parts are 'formulated and ordered into a unified whole' – an apparatus he would call 'rhetoric', and the methodology that examines it 'rhetorical criticism'.[35]

Reviewing the effects of Muilenberg's example, Wuellner sees many of his followers as 'victims of the fateful reduction of rhetorics to stylistics, and of stylistics in turn to the rhetorical tropes or figures', and he cites Schökel and Alter as exemplifying this. 'Rhetorical criticism', he says, 'has brought us to a crossroad where we must choose between two competing versions of rhetorical criticism: the one in which rhetorical criticism is identical with literary criticism, the other in which rhetorical criticism is identical with practical criticism'; and in clarification of the latter he quotes from Eagleton: it means reading and interpreting texts 'as forms of *activity* inseparable from the wider social relations between writers and readers'.[36] Simple words, but behind them lie some very radical notions indeed. This is reflected in another quote which he uses to indicate what he sees as the fruitful way to understand rhetoric in the context of biblical criticism. It is from Booth: 'Rhetorical study is the study of use, of purpose pursued . . . for the sake not of pure knowledge but of further (and improved) practice'. And he glosses it by adding, 'rhetorical criticism is taking us beyond hermeneutics and structuralism to post-structuralism and post-hermeneutics'. It takes us 'to the "social aspect of language which is an instrument of communication and influence on others"'.[37] And the last quote is from Perelman and leads to the real root of his thinking, for Perelman is the source of a view which uses rhetoric as the model for a total restructuring of philosophical thought in the wake of existentialism. He may be seen, in fact, as having played a major role in articulating and promoting a new trend in the area of its relevance for literature, and indeed in pushing ideas in the direction which has led to Derrida and post-structuralism.

Perelman himself says he introduced his 'New Rhetoric' to the world in 1949.[38] The name represented what Zyskind describes as Perelman's 'rediscovery of rhetoric, evolved from his concern over the finding he reached about values in his first essay on justice: that there was no basis of logical necessity or experiential universality for judgements of value'.[39] It was thus the law that led him back to the ancient genre to which juristic exigencies had first given rise. Perelman sums up the essence of this rediscovery thus: 'the rhetorical perspective makes it possible to understand the philosophical enterprise itself better, by defining it in terms of a rationality that transcends the idea of truth and understanding the appeal to reason as a discourse addressed to a universal audience'.[40] This is the outcome of an immensely subtle, rigorous, exhaustive (in fact, life-long) meditation, which it would be rash for me to assume I can do more than begin to understand. And yet Perelman himself would be the first to acknowledge that judgement cannot be delayed, and the question I feel cannot not be asked is: What does it all add up to if not that there is no objective truth but only what people can be persuaded to believe? Zyskind uses some very disconcerting words in comparing Aristotle's solution to that of Perelman, who 'tends as much as possible to assimilate feeling into the quality of thought itself, thickening it with an extra dimension'. Clearly everything turns on the 'thickening', and he never really does much to reassure us, relating the 'marge d'appréciation' Perelman sees in all decision-making to its 'irrational core'. This is likened to the rejection by Socrates in Plato's *Phaedrus* of Lysias' maximising of pleasure and utility in favour of the coherence and order of a 'psychagogic rhetoric of the living word'.[41] It seems to me more like a return to the faith of the Sophists in a persuasion arising from belief and not knowledge, which is precisely what Socrates in the *Gorgias* was holding up to ridicule. It surely involves a renunciation of anything like Aristotelian confidence in the value of rational reflection on ultimate reality.

How far such a critique of objectification in philosophy as is represented by Perelman's 'new rhetoric' (where 'ontology . . . becomes . . . a proposal submitted to an audience, not a structure being imposed from objective determinations of reality') can be relevant to the confidence which a writer such as Paul held in his message as a revelation of ultimate truth clearly remains very much open to debate.[42] Nevertheless, it is the precise desire of Wuellner that rhetorical criticism of the Bible should take account of such far-reaching philosophical implications, and it is his complaint that it seldom does so. Conscious authorial preoccupation with rhetoric by no means facilitates the modern analyst's maintenance of a clear distinction between a new notion of rhetoric and the conceptions entertained in antiquity regarding what constituted its parameters. In Paul the uncertain extent of such conscious preoccupation both invites and confuses the analysis of his writings from the rhetorical angle.[43]

1.3   Intentionality in Pauline rhetoric. Differing estimates and the assumptions they entail concerning Pauline persuasiveness.

'Verbis enim utitur et figuris multis Graecam doctrinam redolentibus, nec sine arte ratiocinatur': thus Melanchthon, who, given the air of Greek learning which pervades Paul's choice of words and figures, along with the studied expertise of his argumentation, was confident that a close adherence to the rules of classical rhetoric was mandatory for Paul.[44] Nor does it seem at all to have perturbed Melanchthon that this at once raises the question of what Paul was doing thus expressly implementing techniques that stood in such an equivocal relation to the pursuit of truth. However, doubts on this score may well have been present in the mind of Augustine, who also noted the rhetorical qualities in Paul's style, but was less explicit about their intentionality.[45] If indeed such doubts are apposite, the question is certainly not dodged by one very important and convinced present-day exponent of a rhetorically based analysis of Pauline texts, H. D. Betz; he faces it promptly and squarely as soon as he embarks on what constitutes the most extended and exhaustive attempt so far undertaken to demonstrate the applicability of rhetorical analysis to Paul, his commentary on Galatians. I will outline the reasoning of his introduction, much of the material of which also appeared as an independent study ('The literary composition and function of Paul's letter to the Galatians', 1975).

'Modern scholarship', Betz says, is still 'under the spell of the myth of Paul the non-thinker'.[46] Indeed, in Germany, where the view goes back to Nietzsche, who saw in Paul the logic of hatred, there was (originally at least) division on the issue of Paul's rationality. But in the cooler climate of the later twentieth century Betz sees only 'agreement' that Paul's letters are at any rate 'confused', disagreement being confined to whether the confusion is caused by emotional disturbance, 'Diktierpausen', or Rabbinic methodology. Of the inadequacy of such attitudes Betz reckons he has found the clearest possible demonstration in what happens when Galatians is construed as belonging to the category of the apologetic letter and is analysed in the light of the criteria applicable to that genre: it reveals itself to be highly skilful and coherent.[47] But by definition the apologetic letter belongs to rhetoric; and rhetoric relies on the art of persuasion, the home and source of which is the court of law, where the skill which makes people believe something to be true (by demonstration, persuasive strategy, psychological exploitation of the audience) matters more than truth itself. The effectiveness of the art of persuasion depends on the naïveté of the hearer. 'Rhetoric works only as long as one does not know *how* it works.' Its use is therefore highly questionable from the start, but its use in Paul appears even more questionable when we realise that *no* kind of rational argument can possibly defend his position. Moreover, 'as his strategy of defense he has chosen to defend the gift of the Spirit to the Galatians' – a most hazardous, if not indeed absurd, enterprise.[48] Betz analyses Paul's argument. In brief it runs as follows.

You the Galatians have come (a) to regard yourselves as people of the Spirit, as (b) free from this evil world with its repressions, its social, religious and cultural laws and conventions. You have (c) overcome the 'ignorance of God' and barbaric superstition. You are the 'avant-garde' of a 'New Creation'. All this adds up to the substance of your 'makarismos'.

Those to whom Paul was writing had come to doubt the validity of these things, probably as a result of the 'end of the initial enthusiasm and of problems with the "flesh"'. 'When "transgressions" had occurred in their community they found themselves unprepared to deal with them. Paul's opponents, however, had the means which seemed adequate and effective: Torah and Circumcision.' Paul is counter-attacking.

The strategic advantage of his method is that the *factum* to be defended was identical with the experience of the 'jury', so Paul, where questions regarding the Spirit are concerned, can appeal to the 'jurors' as experts. In agreeing with him they would not feel humiliated. This is the covert strategy. The overt strategy is, throughout the body of the letter, rational. Paul speaks as theologian, 'one who is able to handle irrational phenomena in terms of rational thought' – throughout the body of the letter.[49] But then there are the prescript and the postscript. And to these Betz attaches exceptional importance, on account of the curse contained in the first which balances the blessing contained in the second. As a result, he observes, there is the stark implication that reading the letter 'automatically' produces 'judgement'.[50] It will confront the reader with the choice: salvation or damnation. Its acceptance will bring the one, its rejection the other. A repetition is thus brought about of the original situation of the Galatians when initially confronted by Paul with the gospel. Paul thus creates what in the technical categories of antiquity would count as a 'magical' letter, in order to convert a piece of apologetic rhetoric into an instrument dependent on and invested with supernatural power. But if in this sense it is a magical letter, it is also by the same token, Betz adds, a 'heavenly' one.[51]

How does this stand in relation to the 'new' concept of rhetorical criticism? In the view of Wuellner it does not go far enough. It merely applies historical criteria of discernment to a Pauline letter and leaves it at that. However, most of the other work that has been done on Paul in the name of rhetorical criticism also falls short in Wuellner's view, either on similar grounds or for various other reasons. As a way of putting things on a more satisfactory footing he himself set about testing Kennedy's 'classical model of rhetorical criticism' against 1Cor 9.[52]

The result is an application of the new rhetoric to Pauline writing which is characterised by the fact that it bypasses, or superimposes a new classification on, the classification which is arrived at by dint of a critical method based on adherence to historical notions of genre, even those of rhetoric itself. This was already very clearly seen to be the effect of his approach in his earlier study on 'Paul's rhetoric of argumentation in Romans'. He refers in that to the 1970–75 seminar of the Society of Biblical Literature on the letters of Paul conducted by Nils Dahl, and it is clear that much interesting work on Paul lies hidden in unpublished papers presented there. The seminar upheld the conviction that the 'holistic approach, based on the literary method of critical study of ancient epistolography, could not account for the variety of Paul's letters'. This led Dahl, in a 'monograph-sized' paper on Galatians, to consider relating that letter to the rhetorical genre rather than the literary, but not to pursue the issue of *which* rhetorical genre, the step which Betz then so confidently took when he classified it as apology. This was the background against which Wuellner formulated his view that 'the best way to approach a piece of argumentation' is by asking 'to what sort of judgement it is ultimately directed'.[53] And it is the question which embodies for him the difference between studying what he describes as the 'argumentative situation', likening this to the 'deep structures' of the structuralists, as against the surface situation to which he sees Betz and Dahl as limiting themselves.

Whatever doubts may be entertained about the theoretical foundations of Wuellner's attitude, his 'new' rhetorical approach does elude the questionable assumption, commonly tacit in historically based rhetorical criticism of Paul, that his links with the 'old' rhetoric

are a factor of determinative significance (even demonstrable efficacy) in his discourse.[54] Paul's impact, in fact, can surely not have
been either much like that of rhetoric on the jury in the Sicilian
law-court where rhetoric was born, or like that on the connoisseurs
of oratory in Imperial Rome where rhetoric later atrophied. And
modern concern with rhetoric in Paul must allow for the indifference shown to it by the earliest of Paul's commentators.

This, it is true, may have been primarily the effect of his own
disclaimers of concern with, or skill in, the use of linguistic artistry.[55] That such practicality of aim left him no room for literary
considerations as first-century Greece understood them was a view
largely endorsed by the positivist scholarship of the last century.
Overbeck, for example, did not see any New Testament writings as
eligible for inclusion in 'Literaturgeschichte' as German scholars of
the period had come to conceive it. They constituted no more than
an artless substitute for the spoken word ('kunstlose und zufällige
Surrogat des gesprochenen').[56] Deissmann, in the early twentieth
century, supported this view, with particular stress on its validity for
the Pauline letters, of which he formed an estimate based on the new
foundation of a vast body of recently discovered utilitarian Greek
correspondence, of Egyptian provenance, ranging over a wide
period of relevant time, some of it displaying remarkable affinities
with both the tone and the content of the non-didactic material in
Paul. This evidence led Deissmann to recommend a precise distinction between the letter and the epistle, and to exclude Paul's writings
from the latter category, since not designed with posterity in mind
but only the particular persons to whom they were addressed. Paul's
occasional attempts at the more formal and systematic treatment
characteristic of the true epistle serve only all the more clearly to
display, according to Deissmann, the limitations of his aims and
ability.[57] Norden, in his *Antike Kunstprosa* of 1909, confirms the
general spirit of most of this, but sees a danger of our underestimat-
ing the literary character of even utilitarian correspondence in
ancient Greece, and counts Paul's letters as at least a step nearer to
Hellenistic literary tastes than Acts. But not much. (And Hebrews
he sees as going further than anything authentically Pauline.) Paul
was not as uninfluenced by rhetoric as his disclaimers imply. These
have to be taken as a reaction to the utterly exorbitant value placed
on rhetoric in Paul's world. In fact many of the 'old friends' of
Greek rhetoric figure prominently in his style; but his Greek could
scarcely do greater violence to the genius of the Greek language, and

his handling of the period is generally, though not uniformly, clumsy – the same being already true for most of his contemporaries. (The periods of Ephesians, however, he considers too trying even to be Pauline; thus they provide ample proof of its inauthenticity.)[58] What Norden says carries all the more weight because he is far from indifferent to the positive potential of the unpolished and alien style he finds in Paul. There are in fact moments – he goes so far as to affirm – where it restores to the Greek language a dynamic power it had lost for centuries, that of the inspired eloquence of the seer in ecstatic union with his divinity.[59] How, Norden muses, it must have struck hearers accustomed to the foolish babbling of the Sophists. This comment, however, following on the reference to the inspired seer, seems to show that it is where Norden hears the echo of the spoken words of Paul that he sees merit in the style. It is an orientation that he inherits from Overbeck. It is also the orientation of the young Bultmann in his 1910 study entitled *Der Stil der paulinischen Predigt und die kynisch-stoische Diatribe*, a work where the gleaning of echoes of Paul's oral style is hailed by the author as the welcome outcome of the enterprise.

Paul emerges from Bultmann's study as without concern for the reputedly appropriate trappings of discourse. And his alien visage shows. Yet the mantle of the Greek orator hangs about him.[60] Paul's style is thus seen as something basically natural to him, the appreciation of which is not to be achieved by dissecting its relation to conventions, but only by seeing any such relation against the background of his preaching, and then listening to the distinctive features revealed by that perspective. What Bultmann would have thought of the discoveries of Betz and today's other champions of rhetorical criticism we can only surmise. He certainly did not envisage the structural links with traditional rhetoric they would be so confident in displaying. Whether the 'new' rhetorical approach broadens the basis of discussion in a way that could be harmonised with his criteria seems doubtful.

Bultmann was conscious of working without an adequate foundation of research into many aspects of the epistolographical background.[61] The efforts that have since been made (e.g. by Aune or J. L. White) to remedy the deficiency in this area have amply shown the complexity and elusiveness of its relevance. Aune is led by his study of this background to favour a decidedly circumspect approach to the application of rhetorical categories to epistolary material.[62] His work, however, presents affinities with the concern of the 'new rhetoric' for the definition of the argumentative situation (the focus Wuellner defined; see *supra* p. 18). White harks back quite specifically to the initiative of Dahl and his seminar, and when he sums up Paul's position with the statement 'the religious nature of the epistolary setting, acting in conjunction with the apostle's own creativity, gave formal expression and recognizable identity to Paul's letters',[63] behind it lies the combatively 'new' rhetorical methodology of Funk, on whom he had drawn at the outset of his study to convey the position in which the epistolary genre stands for Paul: 'the letter opens onto the debate over the nature of the new reality, and the norms whereby it is to be ordered'.

The regard paid in White's words to the religious factor brings out the special situation of Paul vis-à-vis all rhetoric, be it the old or the new, the epistolary or the forensic, the unconscious or the artificial; and it is a healthy reminder that failure to keep this in the foreground risks rendering all analysis of Paul's appeals to reason irrelevant.

1.4 From the rhetorical to the sacred dimension. Coding levels in Paul. The role of the enthymeme.

Ancient rhetoric invited its audience to reflect on probabilities, and consider what was the most reasonable deduction. The rhetorician was concerned to induce a particular construction on evidence which was susceptible of more than one interpretation. Whatever the state of Paul's feelings towards particular groups of addressees, his use of rhetorical argumentation is never an invitation to them to weigh the gospel evidence on the probability scales. This being so, can inferential deduction, where employed by him, be any more than a means of endorsing a construction which they do not, in fact, see themselves as questioning? It can be, and often is, a means of clarifying corollaries; but beyond that domain does it, in reality, ever set any serious store by its own persuasiveness? We are confronted with a particularly complex version of a problem which Kennedy sees in all rhetoric which has the communication of the gospel as its role. It is a problem in the unravelling of which he relies much on the term 'radical'. In 2 Corinthians he sees unusual interest in the fact that 'it shows Paul's consciousness, and his manipulation, of two different kinds of rhetoric, the radical (basically sacred) rhetoric of authority and the rhetoric of rational argumentation'.[64] What Paul is doing reflects what is happening in different ways throughout most of the New Testament. For example, comparing the gospels from this angle, he says: 'John's gospel is radical Christian rhetoric in its demand for immediate and direct response to the truth, but John makes far more demands than Mark on his readers in approaching the truth they are to perceive. He uses the forms of logical argument not so much as proof, as does Matthew, but as ways of turning and reiterating the topics which are at the core of his message.'[65] The general perspective which Kennedy sees as emerging from his New Testament study is one where 'premises . . . are supported, at least in a formal sense, by human reasoning', because 'a process was underway of recasting expressions in enthymematic form' – expressions, however, which are of 'sacred' origin, and the reasoning remains formal.[66]

Meticulous though Betz was in pursuing the complexities surrounding Paul's use of rhetorical argument, he did not see Paul as going about his work of persuasion in anything like the same spirit of reliance on these methods as that which governed the approach of the classical rhetorician. For Paul the power of the letter lies in the truth of what he is saying and his authority to proclaim it as such. 'What I am saying to you will damn or bless you according to whether you accept it or reject it, exactly as happened with my original proclamation of the gospel.' I would say that this is a fair account of the message for the Galatians that Betz reads into the letter, and that it explains his use of the word 'automatic' in defining what Paul sees as the mode by which his letter functions. It explains, further, why he sees fit to enlist the term 'magical'. It might seem advisable to avoid using the term in this context, but it helps to make his point, and the analogy with the parlance of pagan categorising neatly and arrestingly indicates the over-ruling of the normal potentialities of human discourse by a power beyond and above it, such that there can be no doubt about the validity of the instrument which Paul's letter is seen thus to constitute.

Bultmann, too, despite his concern to catch the accents that are most characteristic of Pauline argumentation, makes a point of stipulating that Paul does not employ such argumentation because he thinks arguments are needed to overthrow false attitudes. These have been already overthrown by God in the act he has performed for man's sake, 'Gottes Tat am Menschen'. It is this which determines man's position, not the words of Paul.[67]

For all the disparity in the environment of their thinking and the consequent differences in their perspective and method, it is axiomatic for both Bultmann and Betz that Paul is using argumentation to endorse a fact which in no way depends on his words for its validity to be made manifest. Betz, however, seems to see Paul's words as being more vitally instrumental in activating the power of what God has done in Christ than Bultmann does. And Betz also thinks that Paul himself saw his words as constituting this vital instrument.[68]

Paul's role as spokesman of God, and its implications for the mode and effectiveness of his argumentation, is frequently the object of attention in the work of Young and Ford on 2 Corinthians, and not only with regard to its relevance for its original audience. 'Paul's appeal for recognition by the Corinthians in those particular circumstances long ago demands from readers of all time the same response. We are challenged by the text to make the same judgement: Was this man the spokesman of God as he claimed? Did he know what he was talking about? Or was he mad?'[69]

The position which results from focussing on Paul from the angle illustrated by such related observations as these of Betz, Bultmann, Kennedy, Young and Ford is one in which rhetoric does not so much cease to be a determinative force, as prove to be a force the determinative nature of which is entirely determined by the status of the one who is employing it. There are clear affinities with the scenario envisaged as ideal by the more idealistic current that colours rhetorical tradition to a varying degree and depth from Aristotle onwards: the vision of an orator making capital out of the unimpeachability of his own character for the purpose of promoting justice and the rule of truth. Kennedy notes the parallel, accentuated by the ambiguities inherent already in the Aristotelian vision itself, and inseparable from any actual instance of approximation to it in a practical context:

> It was obviously Aristotle's intention to encourage the use of logically valid proof in oratory. Greek oratory is certainly far more logical than the arguments to be found in the Bible, but even Greek oratory, especially in contexts other than a law-court, contains strong subjective elements. An audience is regularly asked to make a judgement or take an action on the basis of values which they hold. . . . It is very commonly the case that logical arguments are introduced into a speech only to support details or to give an appearance of reason or to justify a decision which is in fact

made largely on the basis of ethos or pathos. The same is almost always the case in religious discourse, because the premises of argument are usually based on a scriptural authority or personal intuition, enunciated in sacred language. Matthew and Paul make extensive use of the *forms* of logical argument, but the *validity* of their arguments is entirely dependent on their assumptions, which cannot be logically and objectively proved. To a non-believer they may seem totally invalid.[70]

This is a parallel that seems to help us to grasp how we should view the disquietingly ambiguous role of rational argument in Pauline rhetoric. It would highlight as crucial that we take account of the ethos Paul is claiming for himself, and thereby suggest that our problem is essentially that of establishing the place, function and value of argument in a sacred text, and that within this framework both concern for and disdain for genuine dialectical cogency can probably co-habit quite fittingly and harmoniously, and that the power of Paul's rhetoric is not of a kind that is to be measured by either attitude. This perspective, however, brings with it the whole complement of problems surrounding what a sacred text is and whether the letters of Paul should or should not be considered as falling within this category either as he saw them or as we see them.

'The question, "what is a sacred text?" is one of those that tend to go unasked because we think we know the answer. Once asked, it turns out to be mischievous and subversive.'[71] So says Detweiler, identifying as the crucial feature of sacred discourse the fact that it 'restricts the free play of response' in the reader. In effect, the reader 'expects the sacred text to delimit his freedom of interpretation, and he submits to it with varying degrees of compliance'. The restriction resembles the restriction which is part of a reader's response to any kind of material – fiction, journalism, history, a scientific paper, etc. 'In no case will he be totally open to the text, but he will always distinguish between what is "real" . . . and what is . . . a product of imaginative projection.' The difference where a sacred text is concerned is the difference between 'a willing suspension of disbelief' and 'an intensified act of believing in the message of the text against the evidence outside of it in the reader's world'.[72] The letters of Paul certainly posit a peculiarly programmed reading, but are the terms of the programme comparable to those specified for sacred texts by Detweiler?

This we shall discover by examining the agents of the programming. And they are none other than the codes on which semiosis depends. Paul establishes a clear decoding requisite without which those whom he is addressing cannot correctly apprehend his meaning. It consists in the triple endowment of (1) their nature as a nature transformed by the Holy Spirit (at work within them), (2) their identity as those who have become identified with Christ, and (3) their minds as minds opened to the truth of the Gospel. Paul's discourse, in short, presumes its addressees to have at their disposal a code which nothing other than the experience of Christ which he and they share together (as those who have recognised the meaning of the Crucifixion) will suffice to supply.

Detweiler distinguishes between a 'willing suspension of disbelief' and 'an intensified act of believing in the message of the text against the evidence outside of it in the reader's world'. Obviously Paul is not admitting that he is calling for anything like the latter. Quite the reverse. He is treating his readers as though they cannot question what he is saying, because the meaning 'God loves us' that he had recognised in the Crucifixion is borne out in the experience of all who have shared in this recognition. Paul is expressly excluding the possibility that there is any evidence in his readers' experiential world that militates against belief. This could, however, be the very quintessence of rhetorical guile. It could be almost exactly the 'covert strategy' identified by Betz in Galatians. Paul boosts the flagging confidence of his converts by appealing to them as 'experts' in matters regarding the Spirit. 'Dissimulating the contradictions that exist, reconstructing on the imaginative plane a relatively coherent discourse, which offers a horizon to which those concerned can relate what they "know from experience", via representations shaped on real connections and inserted into an artificial unity of connections': could this be what Paul is doing? It sounds very like what Betz claims him to be doing. Instead, I am translating from a left-wing political writer's account of the brain-washing techniques by which the world of today manipulates us.[73] The kind of thing that is envisaged occurs often in advertising. 'Save 20% on a new carpet!' is blazoned across the window. The passer-by is induced to deem as applicable the argumentative context: 'The standard price of the carpet is £x. We are offering it at £x − 20%. You save.' Instead the argumentative context that may well be the proper one is: 'The carpet you have at home will last for many years yet. Money spent on a new one today that could be earning interest in the bank for many years to come is the reverse of a saving. The only circumstances in which you could be construed as saving 20% would be if a new carpet is a truly urgent necessity.'

This is a technique of fraudulent persuasion which may be called 'code-switching'.[74] Its users in such a case are employing it knowingly. Sometimes a collective self-deception may be involved. Newspapers sell on the interest readers unfailingly feel in the spectacle of the rich and 'blue-blooded' engaging in tasks like washing the dishes or making their own beds. 'Look, they are really just like us!' is the reasoning with which such wonders are met. But the fact that it is *as* wonders that they are viewed betrays the very opposite conviction to be the psychological reality behind the interest aroused. Columnist and reader alike may well be the victims of the same crossing of the wires: each deluded, the former is no less convinced than the latter by the reasoning whose cross-coded lure is what gives a fillip to the newspaper's sales.[75]

If a speaker says, 'You know what I say to be true because you all feel it', he could (A) be doing this precisely because he knows that they do not. However, (B) he and they may all be committed alike to a single unreasoned stance. He could also of course (C) be talking good sense. Betz seems to think that in Galatians Paul can be identified as representing (A), not through any underhandedness of motive but out of concern to foster the response that will be for the good of his readers. If we are to see Paul, either there or elsewhere, as fitting into Detweiler's perspective of the way religious texts function, we would have to identify his approach as a case of (B).

The code-switching involved in either (A) or (B) is facilitated by the fact that the arguments are not fully spelt out, or even spelt out at all. Such a technique corresponds to that which in the rhetoric of antiquity was the enthymeme. A great many of Paul's arguments belong demonstrably to this category, whether by design or unconsciously (which it is, however, eludes us, and depends in part on the degree to which rhetoric was a conscious mode with him). Eco sees the enthymematic principle as one which naturally, and very generally, comes into play in all forms of communication where persuasion dominates the motivation.[76] The enthymeme, which, however conducive it may be to it, by no means always abets the complex process of code-switching, does always highlight in a particularly notable way the superimposition of one code upon another which is a pervasive feature of sign-production.

Although the 'expression' constituted by the footprint on

Crusoe's island is at once mediated by the 'content' 'another inhabitant of the island', two codes have had to come into operation to make this possible: the code which through experience enables Crusoe to recognise the imprint of a human being, and the code which through inferential deduction leads him to read human being as 'fellow inhabitant of the island'. Much is then made by Defoe of the further reading 'danger', which Crusoe's knowledge of cannibalism leads him to torment himself with, though his pious mind regrets that he cannot deduce 'blessed fellow mortal, source of life-transforming companionship'. The act of recognition thus involves, from the very first moment of its occurrence, a content dependent on the supplementation and superimposition of codes.[77]

To designate such supplementation and superimposition the term 'over-coding' is often used. A wide variety of factors supplies the extra codes. (Extra coding can sometimes take an institutionalised form, as when 'How-do-you-do?' is received not according to the code by which it first becomes meaningful but according to a conventional extra code which supplants the first – a 'sub-code', it may be called.) Conversely it may happen that instead of codes crowding in on one another, codes have to be discovered or invented for meaning to be generated. This contingency can be termed 'under-coding'.[78] It is perhaps, therefore, appropriate to designate as 'under-coding' the process which prevents us from being able to say what music means, whilst nevertheless insisting that it can and must make sense. It belongs to a category of sign-production where sense does not depend on codes provided by anything outside the music itself. They are the product of relationships which the elements of the medium set up by themselves among themselves: tensions, resolutions, progressions, developments, etc. It is only in terms of such abstractions that music can be said to have meaning (though it is capable of conveying something less abstract by analogy). The meaning is an invention unique to music. An analogous process is at work (in less obvious ways) in all artistic activity. This gives rise to Eco's fourth category of sign-productive mode: Invention.[79] It may be that Pauline argumentation acquires (by rather a roundabout route) properties of this kind. They are by no means incompatible with verbal discourse, even if music is their most distinctive embodiment. It is their presence which distinguishes poetic discourse from non-poetic discourse. But I will delay further consideration of this until a survey of the enthymematic factor in a substantial portion of Paul's work has given me some examples to refer to. My primary aim here in discussing coding *levels* is simply that of making clearer what is involved in the choice of explanations that presented itself to us as we reflected on that factor in Paul's discourse which is his confidence in the experiential proof that his addressees had of the veracity of his doctrine.

What in fact we find ourselves having to choose between are three different patterns of 'over-coding'. If instead of (A) or (B) we were to follow explanation (C), and take Paul as being essentially reasonable where he treats his addressees as co-beneficiaries of good concrete evidence for their shared conviction, then the over-coding is exactly that represented by his own clearly manifested decoding requisite (the 'triple endowment' to which I have referred), an over-coding in which there is no 'strategy' and which arises out of confidence in a real match between the experiential foundations guiding both parties to the transmission. The reasons for attributing the 'strategies' of the rhetorician to Paul's arguments, or for associating them with the blinkered states of mind that surround the 'sacred' text (and thus raising the sign-productive process involved to a level of much more elaborate 'over-coding'), may lie in the eagerness of scholars to approach the subject with the greatest possible 'critical' detachment. However, the matter and tone of Paul's arguments themselves have probably been the main reason why so many who are less than extreme in their 'critical' scruples have not felt he can just be taken at his word. He argues too much as one wishing his addressees to view the situation with a rational eye, whilst focussing them in fact on those propositions which his arguments can be made to confirm (and not always to confirm without some blurring of the issues). The pervasiveness of the enthymematic factor contributes to this effect. Premises are constantly being taken for granted where it is far from easy to identify precisely what they are. I believe it is possible, however, to see this state of affairs as stemming from causes more natural, more inevitable, than the 'rhetorical' or 'sacred' perspectives envisage, and as something both to be welcomed and excited by. This comes about if we move away from the models which those perspectives offer to the one I am drawing from Eco's theory of sign-production.

1.5   Consequences of a semiological perspective. The crisis of rationality in Paul.

The letters of Paul constitute the type of discourse in which, by means of Replica, Recognition is explicated. Replica thus performs the office of Ostension. Paul has recognised the meaning of the Crucifixion. His writings are all a pointing to what is involved in, and what follows from, this meaning, which his readers too are presumed to have recognised through the mediacy of his earlier efforts or those of other agents of evangelical ostension. It is for him a meaning which, in being recognised, leaves nothing as it was before. That he and his hearers have ample experience of this is something presumed even where his letters are at their most reproachful and censorious. It is nevertheless a meaning which has to be spelt out to be understood. It is a meaning that does not cease to need constant reiteration, clarification, elaboration, reconfirmation. This inevitably involves recourse to reason. When explication figures as the agent of that sign-productive mode which is Recognition, demarcation problems arise over the jurisdiction of reason which are as inescapable as they are baffling. It is clear that Recognition occurs only insofar as what has been recognised can be spelt out. (This does not in any way cease to be true because spelling-out may be difficult or remain irreducibly imprecise.) Recognition is, therefore, nothing until spelt out. Recognition is governed by explicability. However, it is also clear that spelling-out is only spelling-out if it remains within the boundaries of what has been recognised. Explication is, in this sense, subservient to Recognition. This is never more so than when the code governing the recognition is experiential. So that, although the spelling-out of the content of what has been recognised relies on reason, once the content recognised is spelt out, only such further reasoning as is compatible with the established content of the Recognition can be tolerated. The very object of recognition which it has been instrumental in explicating deprives it of its autonomy. Somewhere there is a boundary. Pauline discourse is poised on this boundary.

Reason is operative from the outset in Paul's recognition of the meaning of the Crucifixion. It is, however, common for Recognition to occur without its intervention. There is a smell which I recognise as meaning that something is burning, and no discursive thought is mediator. It is not very different when Crusoe recognises the mark in the sand as a human footprint. Discursive thought comes into play only when he considers (as for a moment he does and at once rejects) the possibility that it might not be human. The conclusion that it proves the island to be inhabited and that that represents a danger involves a larger input of deductive thought. The bitter irony that the human footprint should spell menace not blessing, and the abortive hope he manages for a while to entertain of overturning the danger message (by proving to himself that it was his own print) bring its meaning into the full glare of analytical observation. The notoriety of Jesus ensured that his crucifixion had from the start meant for Paul more than 'a man crucified', rather as the footprint at once acquired emotive connotations for Crusoe. But 'a blasphemous impostor rightly liquidated' might well have been where its sign-productivity rested for Paul had not a shattering content replacement changed the meaning to 'crucified Son of God'.

Whether this meaning was apprehended by Paul with the immediacy that the mark in the sand is apprehended by Crusoe as human footprint depends on too many sublime imponderables to be open to assessment. But the expansion of meaning represented by 'crucified Son of God, risen and alive for evermore' and the inference following from it, 'God's love for us is unbounded', involve an input of deductive thought that takes meaning in a couple of leaps from the sphere of what is understood before reason intervenes to that which goes infinitely beyond its reach. How much Paul considered the explicative operation to have been guided, determined or integrated, either by the teaching he received from the church or by secondary personal revelations or by special insights imparted by the Holy Spirit (distinct from the understanding integral to the continual experience of its transforming power) are areas in which his own words do not convey an altogether unitary picture. In effect his explication forms a tightly connected derivative chain of ideas so that teaching and revelation subsequent to the initial determinative insight are neither to be excluded nor to be deemed crucial. Indeed, even if certain passages in Paul are viewed as dependent on pre-existing credal or hymnic formulations, and if these include a certain amount of doctrinal matter with which Paul in earlier times would have been personally credited, the tightness of the conceptual whole to which they contribute is unlikely to be anything but his. We do not need to know how much of what he recognised came in an initial onrush of insight and how much by more gradual means. The fact is that his understanding of the gospel emanates outwards from a central core of recognition. The object of that recognition is Jesus as 'crucified Son of God, risen and alive for evermore'. Even as we pass from that to 'God's love for us is unbounded' we have passed from explication proper to corollary. And from this it is only a step to grappling with interrogatives: why God's gift to us was necessary; why it is the most beneficial of all possible gifts; and, if 'sin' provides the answer to these, then what implications does that have for 'righteousness' (and its source) presses for explanation. And Paul cannot *not* know the answer to the interrelated questions arising out of the last: What does Christ crucified mean for the value of law-obedience? What does it mean for the privileged position in which God placed the Jews? At this point the relationship between Recognition and explication becomes problematical. Reason, which has been the channel of great depths of meaning in the explicatory process, now begins to display its independence and generate propositions that conflict with each other, and with those already established. Those who obey the commandments of God must please him more than those who do not. If we say we can please God we belittle his love as the sole source of all blessing. Paul is not deterred, and enters the minefield with the flag of reason held high. However, the fact that, two thousand years on, controversy can still spring up afresh as to how precisely he negotiated it suggests that it is something more than our imperfect knowledge of the circumstantial background that renders the tracing of his path thus perennially debatable. In fact there is plenty of internal evidence that it is something more, in the frequent ambiguities of his terminology, and perhaps above all in his constant re-workings of the same arguments. If Paul had reasoned less, his reasoning would have been clearer. But to reason less would have been to allow that logic may, at a certain point in that communicative process which is the explication of Recognition, become its own impediment, especially where – as with him – expression and content are correlated by a code in which the experiential factor is irreplaceable. It would have been to come through the minefield in one piece, but at the expense of having sacrificed his banner. As it is the banner comes through rather badly tattered. For Paul continues to pursue a logic that will accommodate the content of his Recognition and all its entailments.[80]

Sometimes, it is true, the result is a logic so wayward that we might wonder whether Paul is not just ironically exposing the irrelevance of logical argument. At other times it seems more as though his logic has the function of merely lending the air of logical demonstrability to what is essentially affirmation which he is not really concerned about being able to support. More often, however, he argues as if he sees in the persuasive weight of logical deduction an authority that he must show his statements to possess. In the highly enthymematic manner of arguing which he adopts, all these outcomes find a place. But if we analyse carefully the logical structures that can be seen to lie behind his enthymemes and consider them in the light of the semiological perspective I have been outlining, his appeals to logic will be seen to be not so much gratuitous and culture-specific as symptomatic of his indomitable intellectual persistence. To clarify with greater precision the role and status with which this invests them is the aim with which I now proceed first to scrutinise (in Chapters 2 to 4) the relevant evidence in Romans 1–8, and then to explore further (in my closing chapter) the theoretical perspective, and to relate it to what that scrutiny brings to light. The scrutiny itself constitutes an independent investigation into those aspects of Pauline argumentation which are brought into focus by searching out the enthymeme according to its traditional definition (that which relates it strictly to the syllogism). As should by now be clear, I see my method throughout this study as standing in an essentially lateral relationship to rhetorical criticism in either its 'new' or its historical applications. I do, however, purposely use as criteria in Chapters 2–4 principles of logical analysis which have their origin in antiquity and cannot have failed to impinge on both the dialectical and the rhetorical strains in Paul's writing; and in order that the aspects which this analytical exercise brings out may be focussed upon without prejudice, it is only after Chapter 4 has completed the exercise that I shall introduce further reference to how seeing these aspects in semiological perspective expedites their evaluation (see *infra* p. 130). I likewise go no further towards accommodating the advances of twentieth-century logical and linguistic theory than the avoidance, through a limited application of modern propositional breakdown techniques, of some of the irrelevancies which attend insufficient penetration below the surface structure of verbal communication.

2

VARIETIES OF ENTHYMEMATIC EFFECT IN ROMANS 1–4

2.1 The character of the enthymeme. Identifying enthymemes.

There is no other Pauline letter in which inferential argument figures more prominently than it does in Romans. Much of this argument takes the form of immediate deductive inference, where each conclusion is drawn from a single premise.[1] Often these two-part units occur in sequence so that the conclusion of one forms the premise of the next. But conclusions involving two premises also often occur, and the resulting process of mediate deductive inference introduces the argumentative structure which is that of the syllogism. The surface structure of Paul's discourse, however, is not normally syllogistic but enthymematic, the syllogistic argument which underlies his statements remaining only partly expressed, and what is expressed being often expressed obliquely.

'If God be for us, who can be against us?' is an oblique way of arguing that given God's support we are invincible. It takes as read the premise that God is invincible. Compare the principle behind Goneril's words to Lear: 'As you are old and reverend, you should be wise.' They assume the premise that the old are wise. The illustration was among those used by H. W. B. Joseph, who made a number of extremely important points regarding the enthymeme, which nothing in subsequent developments in logical theory has rendered less valid:

> An enthymeme . . . is not a particular form of argument, but a particular way of stating an argument. The name is given to a syllogism with one premise – or, it may be, the conclusion – suppressed. Nearly all syllogisms are, as a matter of fact, stated as enthymemes, except in the examples of a logical treatise, or the conduct of a formal disputation. It must not be supposed, however, that we are

the less arguing in syllogism, because we use one member of the argument without its being explicitly stated. Syllogism is an act of thought, and if, in order to perform this act, we need to recognise in thought all three propositions, we are arguing syllogistically, whether we enunciate the whole syllogism or not.[2]

These latter observations need particularly to be noted in the context of the present study, because while there must always be a risk, in reconstructing Paul's logic, of making him say what he does not say, it is a risk that has to be run (and is not avoided by such as are most scrupulous in not adding to what he says).

Nevertheless the fact that an author's expressive mode is enthymematic need not be a matter deserving of any special note, so clearly implicit may the missing elements be in the light of what the context makes explicit. The enthymematic character of the mode in which reasoning is presented is, in fact, something which quite often can perfectly appropriately remain unperceived by both the one who formulates it and the recipient for whom it is designed.[3] It may be no more than this. But it may be much more. It may be used in a way which is both highly self-conscious and clearly motivated. The user may even exploit the imbalance between his awareness of its enthymematic character and the unawareness on the part of the recipient. Such variation will depend on the nature of each particular case: how much, for example, it is natural to leave implicit; how much can safely be so left; how much anything left elliptical may function differently by being so left.

If all is not instantly clear, the recipient may be made to think and to focus more attentively on the factors involved precisely because something has been taken for granted.[4] On the other hand, brevity makes for impact, and the rhetoricians of antiquity were quick to perceive how over-explicitness engenders tedium and inattention in the average listener.[5] They were also quick to perceive the advantages of focussing attention on that which was most likely to persuade or move, passing over that which was not.[6] As a result a tension arose between the proof which the syllogism had been so carefully designed by the logicians to safeguard and the persuasion for which its enthymematic presentation gave scope to the rhetoricians. In effect, enthymematic argument seems often not to be concerned with the pursuit of truth at all, but instead to be merely making use of the opportunity which *seemingly* logical argument offers for blurring the truth.[7]

The relations between classical rhetoric and the writings of Paul are difficult to clarify, but the connection between truth and logic was a matter of concern to him; just what kind of concern and how radical it was can nowhere be better judged than in his enthymemes. The analysis on which I am about to embark is concerned with, and motivated by, the importance of the role they play in the first eight chapters of Romans.

I shall first take a somewhat cursory look at Romans 1–4, where the enthymematic factor figures in ways that serve to display something of the variety of effect which it promotes. I shall then scrutinise more attentively Romans 5–7, where the enthymemes are such as to raise interesting questions regarding the purpose and status of their implementation. I will reserve my most detailed analysis for Romans 8, where the imperious sweep of Paul's ideas leaves argument (and the enthymemes that carry it) significantly but untypically upstaged.

It is obvious that the enthymeme must by its nature be an elusive object. It is often hidden or barely perceptible, at least until it is looked for. Inevitably it thus also follows that one who looks for enthymemes must be prepared to find that he has chased a phantom, or at least to be left wondering. They can easily be missed and they can easily be imagined to exist where they do not. In fact, whether a given instance should or should not be construed as an enthymeme is a subtle matter. At a very simple level, Barker asks concerning the argument 'This is red, therefore this is coloured', 'Is this an enthymeme, with the suppressed premise "Everything red is coloured", or is the argument complete as it stands, with its principle of inference being that from "x is red" we may infer "x is coloured"?' And he decides: 'The latter answer is the better one. The principle that being red entails being coloured is so obvious and uncontroversial (in most contexts of discussion) that it is better to regard this as the principle according to which the argument proceeds, rather than as a premise.'[8] Both the examples I quoted just now (the Pauline and the Shakespearian) offer subtle grounds for questioning of this kind, a questioning which, though in no way undermining the fundamental criterion affirmed by Joseph, may complicate our application of it (compare my later remarks on the Pauline instance in chapter 4.3 *infra*).

It is traditional to classify enthymemes according to which element of the underlying syllogism is left implicit. Where it is the major premise the enthymeme is of the first order; where it is the minor premise the enthymeme is of the second order. It is also possible for the conclusion to be left implicit, in which case the enthymeme is of the third order.[9] It may occasionally be useful to employ this classification.[10] If I do, it will be based on the practice to which I shall conform of calling 'minor' the premise which contains the term that figures as subject in the conclusion of the syllogism. This practice, usual since the Middle Ages, avoids a decision having to be made regarding the relative importance of the premises, as Aristotle originally intended.[11] The complications into which this led him proved awkward, however.[12]

In the kind of discourse where the enthymeme is most frequent, the pattern of implications is often too loose for any classification of enthymemes by order to be feasible. For example, more elements may have to be supplied than a single premise, and much rewording of what is expressed may be needed to produce the constituent parts of a syllogism.[13] And alongside the further possibility of more than one integration being viable, an enthymeme may look back for its integration to material other than that which is closest at hand, or even forward to things which have not yet been said. Much discretion may be needed, and disagreement is to be expected. Copi draws up a clear general standard of practice.[14] Jevons notes some interesting examples.

The traditional application of the term ἐνθύμημα does not follow the sense in which Aristotle originally applied it.[15] Kennedy counts it among Aristotelian concepts that by (or through) Quintilian 'were watered down or restated in terms more congenial to the teachers of the sophistic tradition or the writers of handbooks'.[16] Hamilton, in an extensive survey of the earliest post-Aristotelian applications of the term, observed that it was 'used by the oldest commentators on Aristotle in the modern qualification'.[17] Today it is also given a wider application, and the principle involved is clarified by calling enthymemes 'telescoped inferences' as Schipper and Schuh do.[18]

More often than not connective particles or formulae signal the presence of deductive inference and the possible presence of enthymemes. By far the most common of these links is γάρ, in Romans as in all the Pauline writings. It is, however, such a common word and serves so many purposes – on occasions it seems merely to provide a link which is virtually neutral – that it is as likely to confuse as to aid interpretation. Frequently ὅτι and οὖν are the conveyors of inferential deduction, though, particularly with the former, explanation or cause may be all that is conveyed. The same is true of the less frequent ἄρα. The consequences to which διό normally points may well be the fruit of deduction, as may equally well be the case with διὰ τοῦτο and ὥστε. Particles or formulae which follow the grounds (premises) of any logical deduction they may convey (e.g. οὖν, ἄρα, διό, διὰ τοῦτο, ὥστε) are likely to appeal to a wide (and perhaps irreducibly indeterminate) field of subject matter for the integration of their premises. This is almost regularly the case when they stand at the beginning of a new section or paragraph, as they commonly do. Conversely, particles that follow the conclusion which they convey and herald the premises on which it is based (e.g. γάρ, ὅτι, διότι) will normally make explicit some part of their logical foundation immediately. Special problems attend formulae such as διὰ τοῦτο, which is capable of referring forward as well as back (as is διότι outside the NT).

Conditional sentences might well seem to provide the most appropriate form for the presentation of syllogistic argument. They are far from being the most prevalent where this presentation is enthymematic. They are not even the most lucid. A hazard can, in fact, arise through this type of construction being sometimes a mere device to express co-ordination or equivalence. For example, 'if we are sons, we are also heirs' may mean either (a) 'it can be inferred that those who are sons are heirs' or (b) 'to say we are sons is the same as saying we are heirs', or merely (c) 'we are truly both sons and heirs'.

Generally speaking, however, enthymemes are less easily overlooked in a language as fond of link words as Greek than in one where unsignposted juxtaposition of the constituents in a logical argument is as common as it is in English. However, in Greek too, mere juxtaposition does at least have to be anticipated.

2.2 The 'power of the gospel'. The enthymematic factor in Romans 1:16–17. Reconstructing the logic of debatable meanings.

The first case I shall consider in Romans 1–8 lies on the fringe of the enthymematic; but to the extent that it may be seen as lying on that fringe, it is paradigmatic for the place of reasoning in Pauline discourse. Its occasion is his statement in 1:16 concerning the power of the gospel. This statement prompts at once a supporting argument duly signposted as such by a γάρ (1:17a):

> δικαιοσύνη γὰρ θεοῦ ἐν αὐτῷ ἀποκαλύπτεται ἐκ πίστεως εἰς πίστιν.

The formula καθὼς γέγραπται then introduces further support in the shape of scriptural quotation (1:17b): ὁ δίκαιος ἐκ πίστεως ζήσεται.

In the second edition of the RSV (1971) the proposition in 1:17a is rendered thus: 'For in it the righteousness of God is revealed through faith for faith.' If, for now, we let this rendering serve as a convenient provisional basis on which to converse in English about the passage, we appear to be confronted by an argument which embodies four elements: God's righteousness; the revelation of this righteousness; the vehicle or mode of the revelation; and the receptive faculty to which the revelation is directed.

The argument thus compounded contributes to a pattern of reasoning the surface structure of which is as follows: 1:17a carries the premise from which Paul deems it legitimate to infer the conclusion represented by his statement regarding the gospel in v. 16, namely: 'The gospel is the power of God for salvation to everyone who has faith, to the Jew first and also to the Greek.' Only the clause containing the marker γάρ is specifically cast in the role of premise to this conclusion, but if we inspect the relation in which its terms stand to those of the conclusion, we see at once that by itself it is not a premise adequate to justify the inference which the conclusion draws from it.

It is not adequate because it does not make clear how from the four elements embodied in it the conclusion is to be derived. At least four questions arise:

1. Is it because the *righteousness* of God is revealed?
2. Is it because it is *God's* righteousness that is revealed?
3. Is it because this righteousness is *revealed*?
4. Is it because the requisite for the revelation to be received, and the channel by which it is received, are *faith*?

We have, in fact, to supply a second premise. This second premise that we have to supply is actually the major premise of the syllogism which results. I will attempt to draft the four syllogisms which correspond to the four interrogatives just listed:

Syllogism 1

A   MAJOR PREMISE (*supplied*)
Righteousness is the key to salvation.

B   MINOR PREMISE (explicit in text, and tailored to correspond with assent to the *first* of the interrogatives listed above)
The gospel reveals **righteousness**.

C   CONCLUSION (drawn by Paul)
     The gospel is salvific.

Syllogism 2

A   MAJOR PREMISE (*supplied*)
     The **righteousness of God alone** is the key to salvation.
B   MINOR PREMISE (explicit in text, and tailored to corres-
     pond with assent to the *second* of the interrogatives listed)
     The gospel reveals a **righteousness which is that of God**.
C   CONCLUSION (drawn by Paul)
     The gospel is salvific.

Syllogism 3

A   MAJOR PREMISE (*supplied*)
     The **revelation of God's righteousness** is the key to salvation.
B   MINOR PREMISE (explicit in text, and tailored to corres-
     pond with assent to the *third* interrogative listed)
     The gospel yields the **revelation of God's righteousness**.
C   CONCLUSION (drawn by Paul)
     The gospel is salvific.

Syllogism 4

A   MAJOR PREMISE (*supplied*)
     It is the **faith integral to the revelation of the righteousness of
     God** that is the key to salvation.
B   MINOR PREMISE (explicit in text, and tailored to corres-
     pond with assent to the *fourth* interrogative)
     The gospel (and only the gospel) can (but may not always)
     occasion the **faith integral to the revelation of God's right-
     eousness**.
C   CONCLUSION (drawn by Paul)
     The gospel is potentially salvific. (It depends on faith.)

A syllogism is built around three terms, 'two' – to quote Joseph's
formulation – 'which form the subject and predicate of the conclusion, and one with which each of the former is brought into relation
(in the way of subject and predicate) in one of the premises. The
subject and predicate of the conclusion are called respectively the
minor and the major terms: the term common to the two premises is
called the middle term.'[19] The figure ἐνθύμημα owes its designation
to the need for consideration and judgement which it entails.[20] The
enthymematic dimension in Romans 1:16–17 arises from the

uncertainty with which Paul's wording leaves us over what we should identify as the middle term of his syllogistic reasoning. My analysis should have served to set the problem clearly in relief (the middle terms of the syllogisms being represented by the words in heavy type in the propositions). However, in three of the syllogisms from which we have to choose, the problem is merely how Paul reaches his conclusion. The fourth introduces uncertainty over what the extent of his conclusion is. Does he consider his argument to have proved merely that the gospel saves, or is the fact that it saves only those who have faith an essential part of what he is claiming to have demonstrated? Would it be logical to claim what is in effect a limitation of the power of the gospel as an essential part of the proof of its power? But why, it may be asked, are such choices necessary? Can the gospel be the power of God for salvation unless all four syllogisms stand simultaneously – unless, that is, (a) faith comes into operation; unless (b) its operation has a revelatory dimension; unless (c) what is revealed through faith is righteousness; unless (d) the righteousness is of God? In response to this three observations seem relevant.

1.   If all righteousness is of God, then (d) is superfluous to the logic: *(d) states a fact which combines with (c) to form a single dialectical constituent.*

2.   Faith would not avail if it were not a channel for right-eousness. Righteousness would not impinge on man without the operation of revelatory faith as its channel. Paul may well – did certainly – intend to draw attention to the channel whereby right-eousness impinges on man. However, the fact that the gospel *can* mediate the righteousness that it *does* mediate is sufficient to prove it effective. Ultimately it is only on righteousness that Paul's argument for the salvific efficacy of the gospel must rest. *The crucial factor is (c).* Faith is not *why* but *how* the gospel is a power for salvation (at any rate faith taken in the sense it has most usually been taken – but I will postpone consideration of that for the moment).

3.   Paul, however, may not so much be wishing here to prove *that* the gospel is a power for salvation as to point either to *how* it saves (i.e. that its *method* is revelation and that the *channel* of revelation is faith) or to *what* does the saving (i.e. that it is right-eousness and that righteousness is of God). Thus *in effect (a), (b)*

and (d) could be his main objects of concern regardless of the status they may occupy in the hierarchy of inferential cogency.

And we have a guide. The quotation from scripture that completes v. 17 has the air of confirming and clarifying what has been said, and hence might be expected to resolve precisely the kind of problem we are confronted with. But it remains too closely in line with the spirit of enthymematic discourse, and points in the direction of the key factor without making an unequivocal statement. Nevertheless, although in this case the pointer provided is far from unambiguous, the example of Luther has inevitably promoted the construal which sees it as confirming the 'faith integral to the revelation of righteousness' as the middle term of Paul's syllogising, and the qualification 'it depends on faith' as integral to what his argument has proved.

Dunn discusses at length the complex problems surrounding both the import of the quotation in its original context and the intent with which Paul was employing it. The Masoretic Text, he says, 'clearly has in view the *zadiq*, the righteous man. At the time of Paul this would be understood to be the man who is a faithful member of the covenant, who fulfils the obligations laid upon him by the law of the covenant as a loyal Jew; namely, faithful observance of and devotion to the law as the ideal of Jewish piety.'[21] However, the four different forms in which the quotation is known to us – MT, LXX, Paul (Romans 1:17 and Galatians 3:11), and Hebrews 10:38 – offer conflicting indications as to whose the πίστις/*emunah* referred to is. Ziesler sums up the situation thus: 'The LXX probably means "the righteous will live by my (i.e. God's) faithfulness", or else possibly "the righteous will live by faith in me". The Hebrew means that the righteous will live by faithfulness (to God).'[22] The omission of the possessive adjective which causes the discrepancy (LXX ἐκ πίστεώς μου, as against MT *be'emunato*) is considered by Dunn to be conscious and deliberate. It is, he says, Paul's wish

> to give πίστις his own, or its particularly Christian force ('trust in'), in a way which ran counter to the generally understood meaning of the MT form; that is, to free πίστις from the interpretation usually put upon it by virtue of the MT's 'his'. When πίστις is understood as 'trust', better sense can be made of *both* the chief alternative text forms: that is to say, for Paul the counterpart of God's faithfulness

is not man's *faithfulness* (at any rate as understood within Judaism), but *faith*, his trust in and total reliance upon God.[23]

Dunn therefore sees as 'unreal' the division which still prevails among commentators over whether ἐκ πίστεως should be taken with ὁ δίκαιος or with ζήσεται (yielding the alternatives: 'he who through faith is righteous shall live' or 'the righteous shall live by faith'); the issue being whether, in Ziesler's words, 'those who are already righteous will live by faith', or 'faith is the way to righteousness'. This issue ('real' or 'unreal') clearly affects the emphasis of Paul's logic.[24]

If Paul were quoting Habakkuk for the sake of the meaning 'those who are already righteous will live by faith', then it would be to identify 'righteousness' as the middle term of his syllogistic reasoning (its relation to faith figuring as supplementary explanation). If instead his quote is prompted by the meaning 'faith is the way of righteousness', then its function would be to identify 'faith' as his middle term (the predicate concerning righteousness figuring as the supplementary contribution). The contrast is that which obtains between Syllogisms 1 and 4 in my presentation of the different possible centres of emphasis in Paul's argument. Let me re-present them so as to bring out this aspect.

Syllogism 1 (middle term: 'righteousness')
A Righteousness is the key to salvation.
B The gospel reveals righteousness (namely, the righteousness which consists in having faith).
C The gospel is salvific.

Syllogism 4 (middle term: 'faith')
A Faith is the key to salvation.
B The gospel can occasion faith (namely, the faith which affords access to righteousness).
C The gospel is potentially salvific. (It depends on faith.)

The interpretation through which Dunn sees the 'unreality' of this 'either/or' as being exposed stands on a foundation of recent work on the concept of righteousness in Paul which brings out a relationship between faith and righteousness not fully appreciated in earlier criticism.

Dunn notes: 'Not least important is the fact that the ἐκ πίστεως of the Hab 2:4 quotation is probably intended by Paul to be understood with an ambiguity which embraces both God's faithfulness and man's faith.'[25] He notes this when dealing with the obscurities of ἐκ πίστεως εἰς πίστιν in 1:17a. These lead him to wonder whether it should not 'be considered more fully than do most commentators whether Paul intended the ἐκ πίστεως to refer to God's faithfulness and only the εἰς πίστιν to man's faith'. And he stresses the extent to which the faithfulness of God is an integral theme of Romans 'as part of the theme of God's righteousness', and that 'the righteousness of God can be defined quite accurately as "God's covenant-faithfulness"'.[26]

To say – as I did earlier – that 'faith' is not *why* but *how* the gospel constitutes 'power for salvation' becomes less easy when 'faith' is part of a context where it responds to that aspect of God's righteousness which is his faithfulness. In fact we are confronted with a simultaneous emphasis on both faith and the faithfulness of God (equated with the righteousness of God). And thus, from my original range of four syllogisms, a combination of Syllogism 2 and Syllogism 4 has come about which carries with it more than a suggestion that they add up to the same thing. However, this has come about only by dint of equivocation between πίστις = faith (that of man) and πίστις = faithfulness (that of God). From the logical point of view the 'ambiguity' with which (according to Dunn) ἐκ πίστεως may be intended by Paul can scarcely fail to compromise the inferential solidity of his argument.[27] It is well to remind ourselves that where equivocation enters into syllogistic reasoning the result can be insidious, as Joseph illustrates with the example: 'It is the business of the state to enforce all rights: a judicious charity is a right: therefore it is the business of the State to enforce a judicious charity.'[28] The ancient example he notes is also worth quoting: 'Finis rei est illius perfectio: mors est finis vitae: ergo mors est perfectio vitae.' In its dependence on the double meanings of *finis* (end/fulfilment) and *perfectio* (completion/perfection), the latter defies translation. If we construe Paul to be using the Habakkuk quote in order to clarify himself as intending to make the statement 'The gospel is the power of God for salvation because in it the πίστις [= faithfulness] of God is revealed to the πίστις [= faith] of man', then the structure of the reasoning behind it could be identified as:

Fallacious Conflation of Syllogisms 1 and 4

A   Righteousness (= faithfulness = πίστις) is the key to salvation.

B   The gospel occasions faith (= πίστις ≠ faithfulness).

C   The gospel is salvific.

The equivocation, of course, remains disguised only while the
pseudo-middle term involves a conflation of the inferential emphasis
represented by Syllogism 1 with that of Syllogism 4. For the conflation to extend to the emphasis represented by Syllogism 2, either
the equivocation must be viewed as blatant (and Paul's concern here
with logic seen in terms of nonchalance, disdain, or rhetorical
exploitation), or the relation between God's faithfulness and man's
faith has to be seen in a real and profound sense as constituting a
union. That their relationship is not a simple matter is indicated by
Paul's use of the verb ἀποκαλύπτεται to denote the process by
which they enter into relation with each other.

In my formulation of Paul's reasoning in terms of the emphasis
represented by Syllogism 4, I referred to the faith involved as 'the
faith integral to the revelation of righteousness', and with the word
'integral', I fully appreciate that I enveloped its role in a thick
semantic haze. Words from Fitzmyer, however, help to account for
and vindicate my doing so. 'The basis of the Christian experience'
('a new union with God') is 'an ontological reality that is not
immediately perceived by man's conscious faculties.' Faith is best
defined in terms of the function it performs in integrating 'his
psychological activity with the ontological reality within him'.[29]
'Integration' also accommodates the very precise reason Käsemann
sees for Paul's use of the term ἀποκαλύπτεται: 'The gospel is the
power of God because in it the divine righteousness breaks into the
world as eschatological revelation.'[30] Thus we find Paul's argument
assuming a pattern where the middle term of his syllogistic inference
emerges not as it is determined by the emphasis displayed either in
Syllogism 2 or in Syllogism 4, but as it is determined by the emphasis
displayed in Syllogism 3, yet in such a way as to draw into its ambit
the middle terms of 2 and 4 as well, bringing about their union with
each other and with itself. At any rate this is what happens if, as
Käsemann (endorsed by Stuhlmacher) claims, the righteousness of
God is precisely and specifically his saving power.[31] For once the
revelation of the righteousness of God is rendered operative by
faith, salvation is a necessary consequence. The 'why' and the 'how'

of the gospel's power are merged. The righteousness which is revealed through faith is not something apart from faith, but something to which faith is as integral as it is to its revelation.

I have called this a 'cursory' look at the enthymeme in Romans 1–4, and I venture no further into such a difficult area. My aim has been to show how Paul's logic is inescapably bound up with the matters I have been considering, and how in the light of them the enthymematic character of his discourse in Romans 1:16–17 emerges as attributable, not to indifference to logical rigour or abuse of logic, but to profundities of meaning which human reason and language have extreme difficulty in encompassing.

Although we may need (as E. P. Sanders concludes) to allow for a more flexible understanding on the part of Paul of the concept of the righteousness of God than that attributed to him by Käsemann and Stuhlmacher, they mark a radical break with older approaches.[32] That the break was decisive is now little contested, and the discussions of earlier times regarding whether the genitive of δικαιοσύνη θεοῦ is subjective or objective, and whether πίστις is 'fides qua' or 'fides quae', are considered to be largely irrelevant.[33] They led to much more clear-cut choices between different placings of inferential emphasis.[34] However, to the extent that they tended to read Romans 1:16–17 as designed above all to emphasise the role of faith in salvation, they also tended to divest that emphasis of any inferential character. To affirm that the gospel is the power of God for salvation because faith in it ensures salvation is less to argue *why* it saves than to state *when* it does. The 'how' of salvation remains distinct from the 'why'. To the extent that the 'why' is seen to reside in the communication to man of a righteousness which is not his, through the operation of a response compounded of comprehension, trust and acceptance: to that extent an 'inferential' dynamic exists. And the choice confronting the interpreter is whether Paul is motivated to set up the argument he does in Romans 1:16–17 more by concern to demonstrate the power of the gospel, or more in order to point to what brings its power into operation. Insofar as his aim is considered to be the latter, he cannot be reckoned to be engaging the enthymeme. Insofar as his aim is considered to be the former, he can. The conclusions which have come to prevail in present-day criticism blur any such choice, and with that the scope of the enthymematic factor also. In consequence it figures as an altogether more pervasive presence. It figures more pervasively, but more elusively – more elusively, however, because of the greater depth and subtlety of the concepts of which it is seen to be compounded. The enthymeme would be a less appropriate instrument in such circumstances if it were amenable to fully explicit analysis and integration.

Romans 1:16–17 constitute a moment of exceptional density of reasoning. As the discourse moves towards and into chapter 2, it descends to a plane where the issues lie more within the grasp of human reason, and where enthymematic suggestion is less abstruse and involves logic less resistant to explicit integration.

2.3   Those who are 'without excuse'. Those referred to in 1:20. The one addressed in 2:1. The enthymeme as innuendo.

The enthymematic argument of Romans 1:16–17 is very soon followed by more reasoning that admits of the same definition.[35] It arises in the course of 1:18–21 when Paul pronounces men to be ἀναπολογήτους in the face of God's anger at their attitude towards the truth. And it arises because the fact of their inexcusability, which is introduced as a consequence of their faulty relation to God's provident ordering of things, is at the same time a rating for which Paul offers logical justification by stressing two factors: (a) the evidence of God's existence which is built into the universe; (b) man's failure to glorify him accordingly and be grateful.[36] For these to spell inexcusability two stages of implicit syllogistic deduction have to be envisaged:

> *Stage 1*
> A   MAJOR PREMISE
>   Once God is recognised he requires worship and gratitude.
> B   MINOR PREMISE
>   God made himself recognisable to man in the created universe.
> C   CONCLUSION
>   Man should worship and give thanks to God.
>
> *Stage 2*
> A   MAJOR PREMISE
>   Not to worship and give thanks to God is inexcusable.
> B   MINOR PREMISE
>   Man failed to worship and give thanks to God.
> C   CONCLUSION
>   Man is inexcusable.

In both syllogisms the major premise has had to be supplied; in the first the conclusion as well. It might perhaps be contended that part of what being God entails is that worship and thanksgiving are owing to him, and that there is no real need to envisage syllogistic structures in which that figures as a supplied premise. Paul is merely taking it for granted that where God has recognisably manifested himself we must necessarily concede that not to honour him is inexcusable. And it is probably fair to acknowledge that Paul's mode of presentation here does little more than exemplify the economy that characterises everyday speech and the natural enthymematic tendency that this promotes. Be that as it may, deductive inference next occurs in 2:1 with the only other occurrence in Paul of the word ἀναπολόγητος. This repetition, prefaced by a διό, seems to suggest that what has come between is all to be taken as an elaboration of the logical support given to that earlier inference. But Man's state is now such that he is 'past-excusing', 'beyond' rather than 'without' excuse, and the syllogism implied is:

A MAJOR PREMISE
   No one who sins can escape God's condemnation (hence all sinners are condemned).
B MINOR PREMISE
   God has given all men over to sin (hence all are sinners – all are condemned).[37]
C CONCLUSION
   You (being a man) cannot escape condemnation.

Paul's words constitute an enthymeme consisting only of the conclusion διὸ ἀναπολόγητος εἶ, ὦ ἄνθρωπε. Three additional words, πᾶς ὁ κρίνων, which complete his proposition, serve instead to introduce another argument. Whether we read 'you who pass judgement, whoever you are' or 'if, whoever you may be, you pass judgement', the object of proof to which the διό relates at once shifts from being man in an unqualified sense to the man 'who passes judgement'. And thus arises an awkwardness (not untypical of Paul), in that the διό seems to be at the same time a reference back to 1:21–32 *and* an anticipation of the γάρ clause which follows the κρίνων and supplies the reason why the man who passes judgement is ἀναπολόγητος, namely that he will be passing judgement on sinners such as he himself inevitably is.[38] And thus ἀναπολόγητος applies to him on two counts: (a) because he is man, (b) because, as

such, he rashly presumes to pass on others the judgement he himself
falls under. And this gives rise to a situation that calls for closer
consideration.

Count (b) is spelt out so fully by Paul as to provide all the
elements necessary to a fully explicit syllogism:

> MAJOR PREMISE: You condemn all those guilty of sins
>   abc.
> MINOR PREMISE: You are guilty of sins abc.
> CONCLUSION: You stand self-condemned.

The argument is incontrovertible and, in its completeness, entirely
unenthymematic – at any rate on the surface. But if we are to dispel
the sense of awkwardness that arises from the double justification of
ἀναπολόγητος we have to interpret the tone of Paul's ὦ ἄνθρωπε
πᾶς ὁ κρίνων as conveying the sense 'and it is precisely in order to
address myself to you who set yourself up as a judge that I have been
saying all this'. And many commentators would read much more
between the lines than that – no less than some such message as:

> *You who are a Jew judge non-Jews as unable to escape God's
> condemnation because they are outside the Law, and think
> you can do this because, as a result of God's favour towards
> his chosen people the Jews, you are within the Law; but, in
> fact, since you are sinners no less than the rest of mankind,
> you cannot escape condemnation, but instead incur it under
> the terms of the very law which you see as furnishing you with
> the means of escaping from it.*[39]

And this projects us briskly into the ambit of the enthymeme. A
syllogistic pattern of argument is implied of the type which a
speaker arguing enthymematically envisages for the sole purpose of
displaying its falsity. He sets up a kind of 'Aunt Sally'. It is a typical
feature of the diatribe style. The argument envisaged here (read by
Paul into the mind of his addressee) runs:

A MAJOR PREMISE
   Those to whom God has shown special favour by disclosing
   to them his law can judge as being under his condemnation
   those to whom he has not shown such favour.
B MINOR PREMISE
   To the Jews alone he has shown special favour in this way.

C CONCLUSION

He who is a Jew can judge non-Jews as being under God's condemnation (i.e. unable to escape his wrath), and, by the same token, count himself as being enabled to escape it.

In this way, Paul's πᾶς ὁ κρίνων acquires the force of an innuendo along the following lines:

> *I say πᾶς ὁ κρίνων – I say anybody who passes judgement, but you know very well who I have in mind and it is you who think salvation is for Jews alone.*

Taken thus, Paul is seen as preparing the way by such innuendo for what he makes explicit in 2:17.

There is no doubt that from that point in the chapter the addressee of his discourse is the one 'who calls himself a Jew'. But the phrase in itself contains no clue as to whether it effects a restriction or merely a clarification of the category of the hearer towards whom Paul's words are directed. Not so long ago reading the Jew into 2:1 would have come up against the kind of view represented by Leenhardt, who considered that, seen as a paragraph addressed to the Jew, Romans 2:1–11 'would interrupt the flow of a discourse on mankind . . . for the apostle indisputably returns to the theme of the natural man at v. 12. Moreover in several particulars it would duplicate what is said of the Jews from v. 17 onwards.'[40] These very particulars, on the other hand, convince F. Watson that the paragraph must be meant for Jews.[41] And today the problem may be to justify talking merely of 'innuendo' in the eyes of interpreters who, whilst perhaps not following Sanders in the boldest of his conclusions, incline to suspect with him that the whole text of Paul's letter from 1:18–2:29 owes its character to having been originally a synagogue sermon.[42] The connection with Jewish material perceptible in the theme of Israel committing the sins of the Gentiles had already been made by Nygren.[43] But there are still those who see at least ambivalence in the opening verses of Romans 2. 'It is probably a Jewish interlocutor whom Paul has primarily in mind . . . though at this stage the discussion relates more to a difference determined by response to what is known of God, which to some extent cuts across the more clearcut ethnically determined Jew/Gentile distinction.'[44] It is quite possible to see an ambiguity in the text – but an intentional one, not due to complexity or subtlety in the point Paul is making, but designed to make it strike home more effectively by striking in an underhand manner. But on whom would Paul intend the technique to work? On any of his actual addressees (if the cap should fit – as it certainly would according to the hypothesis of Watson)? The spirit of the diatribe signals that we must be prepared for all to be illustration – illustration aimed at bringing out the falseness which the gospel of Christ reveals in Jewish notions of privileged status. We cannot infer that Paul's Roman readers are being asked to acknowledge that any of *them* makes the mistake of thinking that as a Jew he is not touched by sin, but only to see what a disastrous mistake the Jew makes who does so. Paul brings this out by talking *as if* he were berating one who entertained such false confidence. Much of the logic in Romans is aimed at the demolition of false beliefs as such, beliefs the falseness of which Paul is concerned his hearers should fully appreciate, but which he may have no reason to think they hold; though it remains possible that in some cases he did think, or at any rate fear, that they either inclined towards them, were not fully emancipated from them, or could fall back into them. As Ziesler says: 'The Romans as a church had some sort of relationship with the synagogue, so that in talking about the Jewish provenance of the Christian gospel Paul was talking at least partly about that relationship . . . The same goes for disagreements within the church about the relationship between Gentiles and Jews: Paul is talking about people who occupy space and time, not only about ideas' – but he does not think it prudent to say much more.[45] The spirit in which I suggest 2:1 may be read would see in it a kind of multi-purpose rhetoric related more to the scope of Paul's wider argument than the immediate concerns of his Roman addressees. His concern within the ambit of Romans 1–8 would be that of demonstrating God's infinite and unconditional love. Demolishing notions of privileged status in regard to righteousness would be diagnosed as Paul's primary motive for adopting the particular thematic slant that opens Romans 2.

By the end of the chapter this is a motive on which Paul has worked so hard that the relationship of righteousness to grace has got lost to view. Getting it back into view leads to a good deal of stress. With this the enthymematic factor figures again in less easily definable form and in contexts of highly complex tension.

2.4 The 'advantage' of the Jew in the context of universal sin. Affirmation and denial in 3:1–20. The proleptically enthymematic factor.

In Romans 2:28–9 Paul's argument leads him around to affirming that to be circumcised and bear the name of Jew means nothing if it does not relate to the inner state of the individual. On the strength of his inner state a man may be circumcised in his heart, and more truly a Jew than the man who is a Jew by race and bears the outward mark of circumcision, but whose inner state is such that he is not in any real sense a Jew at all. In 3:1 Paul anticipates the question this must prompt: τί οὖν τὸ περισσὸν τοῦ Ἰουδαίου ἢ τίς ἡ ὠφέλεια τῆς περιτομῆς; He replies firmly: πολὺ κατὰ πάντα τρόπον. But although manifold advantage is alleged, we hear only of one aspect, introduced by a 'firstly' never followed by a 'secondly'. What, in fact, 'advantage' ultimately adds up to, and to what extent it is deduced by Paul enthymematically, are matters to which I will attend in due course. First of all I must pursue the reasons for his question, not for his answer.

The question in 3:1 – once again in the manner of the diatribe – presents us with what is virtually a proposition set up to be contradicted: 'circumcision is of no value'. Moreover, the οὖν within it marks it as an inference. In fact it is the conclusion of an enthymeme – one of the kind frequently signalled by οὖν when it occurs in the opening sentence of a paragraph, one where the premises have to be supplied on the basis of material in the passages of argument that have gone before. Here that means those which have developed the non-equivalence of value with external factors. The importance of that which is hidden within has twice received specific mention (2:16 and 2:29). The syllogism behind the enthymeme can be formulated thus:

A   MAJOR PREMISE
   Value is not determined by externals.
B   MINOR PREMISE
   Circumcision as a physical fact and being an ethnic Jew are externals.
C   CONCLUSION
   Circumcision as a physical fact and being an ethnic Jew are of no value (or perhaps more precisely: constitute no index of value).

(The stylistic ploy of the invisible circumcision has to be forgotten.)[46]

The οὖν marks Paul's question in Romans 3:1 as the outcome of deduction, but it is deduction which – being posited expressly to be refuted – has the function not of proving the point Paul is wishing to make, but only of setting in relief what his point really is and how he affirms it. What, in fact, is here set in relief by the 'knock-down' technique turns out to be one of the thickest tangles of argument in all the Pauline writings. Yet it is clear that this tangle is itself in some way the outcome of the momentous nature of what he is here wanting to emphasise, and even more what he is preparing to proclaim. Having asked his question and answered it, Paul clarifies the 'first' of the many ways in which it is of advantage to be a Jew: God's λόγια have been entrusted to the Jews. Issues, the import and relevance of which are not obvious, then detain (distract?) Paul until, in 3:9, another τί οὖν;, followed by προεχόμεθα;, seems (if the latter is indeed interrogative) to constitute a reiteration of the question in 3:1. But this time the reply is an emphatically negative οὐ πάντως. So, what does this mean? Is Paul retracting his previous positive answer? Does οὐ πάντως admit of another understanding?[47] Is it, in effect, a different question he is asking with προεχόμεθα?[48] Are we to envisage a punctuation which leaves us with a statement instead of a question? Is our text in some way faulty?[49] Or was Paul only 'having us on' with his previous answer? Do we now see, that is to say, that the whole of the intervening paragraph was spoken in a tone of mockery? If it is indeed the review of preposterous options which it seems, it may well invite such a suspicion. An immense amount of thought has been expended on how Paul's apparent retraction of his earlier answer is to be explained, or else explained away.[50] I will assume that what we have in 3:9 is, in fact, a new answer to the same question as he asked in 3:1, an answer which appears to contradict it. For the moment it is this retraction, not the complicated outgrowth of his original answer, that I will pursue.

The reason Paul gives for his new answer in 3:9 is very closely linked to the arguments from which the conclusion parried in 3:1 might have seemed to follow (and is now allowed to). Indeed it is linked very closely with the whole drift of his argument in chapter 2: God rewards man according to what he does, not according to whether he is a Jew or a Gentile. The advantages which the Jew believes to be exclusively his can be lost; the Gentile can be a recipient of fruits the Jew misses – it depends on the goodness of his actions and on what he is inwardly. In chapter 2 Paul was describing what *can* happen. (I will not enter into controversy as to whether 'can' satisfies the implications of 2:12–16.)[51] In chapter 3 he is concerned with what *does* happen. The actions of both Jew and Gentile are in fact such that neither category deserves anything but condemnation. This is illustrated by a catena of OT quotations occupying 3:10–18 which certainly, following as they do on 3:9, appear as evidence no less for the sinfulness of the Gentiles than for that of the Jews. That this wrenches all the OT statements from their original social context in no way violates Paul's principles of OT allusion; however, his concern here is not with whether all Gentiles are sinful, but with the unthinkability of even a Jew not being the author of actions that must preclude his being judged righteous by God.[52] Thus, whatever advantages reside in being custodians of God's λόγια, righteousness is not one of them. Whatever the potential of God's word for the Jews, it does not enable them to perform in the way it demands of them. Therefore its role must be another, and Paul indicates forthwith in 3:19 what it is: it is (by virtue of the law which it embodies) to convict the Jew of his unrighteousness. But if thus, like all, he is condemned to fall into sin, then to be made conscious of his guilt, and the punishment which awaits him, looks like the very reverse of an advantage. Hence the οὐ πάντως. But is that all?

Romans 3:20 contributes two further members to the period begun in 3:19. Both contain markers casting them in an explanatory role (διότι and γάρ), and both relate to the way the knowledge of the law which God's word bestows on him enables the Jew to see the extent of the sin from which he cannot escape.[53] But the οἴδαμεν δέ with which Paul resumes his discourse in 3:19, after the spate of OT quotations, seems to mark the contents of that verse as being of a kind for which further argumentative support is not needed.[54] We are not led, therefore, to expect that any additional arguments he may see fit to add will constitute anything but recapitulation and supplementation. Verse 3:20a in fact consists in part of an OT quote such as Paul frequently employs to give additional weight to his arguments. For this reason some would see his διότι as virtually equivalent to a καθὼς γέγραπται, avoided perhaps because he has supplemented the original text: the words ἐξ ἔργων νόμου are not present in his apparent source, LXX Psalm 142:2.[55] They pick up the expression he has used in 2:15. He is about to use it again in 3:28, and if at this point his meaning is seen as involving the notion that ἔργα νόμου are not, and can never be, a means to salvation, then 3:20a broaches matters that go far beyond anything Paul has said so far. Maybe it does, for it is the occasion for the third appearance of the verb that is to play such a major role subsequently: δικαιοῦσθαι. The first time Paul had used it (in 2:13), the scope of its meaning was 'to be judged righteous' – 'to be judged righteous on the strength of having performed righteous actions'. Here it could mean simply 'no one will be judged righteous by God because no one has performed a righteous action (or, at least, no one has avoided unrighteous action)', thereby giving to the whole phrase the sense: 'no Jew is judged righteous through performance of the works of the law because, owing to the general corruption of human nature, no Jew is capable of adhering faithfully to what the law prescribes'.[56] It could, on the other hand, open on to a whole new dimension of the nature of righteousness, indicating that where man is adjudged righteous in God's sight it is not because of correct law-observance but for reasons which transcend that altogether.[57] If it is not construed as prefiguring such matters, then it just clarifies the reasons for the content of Paul's οἴδαμεν in more succinct terms than those of 3:10–18.[58] The clause which then follows, signposted by γάρ as offering further explanation, could be understood thus:

> *Since it is the effect/function of the law to show us how sinful we are, we can see there is no way in which, through obedience to it, we can attain to the status of being righteous.*[59]

It would, however, also be possible to see the γάρ of v. 20b as connecting up with 3:19 rather than 3:20a, i.e. 'All mouths are stopped and all are convicted because the law reveals to them their guilt.' Whatever may be the right construal the fact is that, thanks to v. 20b, the emphasis at the end of the period is left firmly resting on the awareness factor, in a way that seems to tie purpose to disadvantage in an inseparable union. Nevertheless they stand angrily matched, so that one might wonder whether Paul is not seeing the purpose as allied to a disadvantage which is in truth an advantage in disguise. And unless he is, what can he have been saying in 3:2–8? That it is a mockery to call being a Jew an advantage in any but a theoretical sense? Much depends on what νόμος implies, and to what precise sense of it λόγια in 3:2 relates. I take each in turn.

Most scholars today accept without too many reservations that the researches of E. P. Sanders and others have shown the 'general type of religion prevalent in Palestine before the destruction of the

Temple' not to have been a religion of works.[60] And the question now is, as Räisänen puts it, 'whether it is Paul himself or merely his latter-day interpreters who should be blamed for this distortion of Judaism'.[61] Räisänen himself 'cannot avoid the strong impression that Paul does give his readers a distorted picture of Judaism' maintaining 'that within it salvation is by works'.[62] Sanders did not, however, see Paul as arguing against Judaism as a legalistic religion: 'It is the Gentile question and the exclusivism of Paul's soteriology which dethrone the law, not a misunderstanding of it.'[63] Dunn, meanwhile, has developed the view that what Paul was arguing against was the Jews' view of law-observance as the mark of their privileged Covenant status. It was not the inefficacy of law as a principle that Paul was contesting so much as the law misunderstood as a 'boundary-marker' establishing Jewish identity, evidenced especially in the boundary-marking rituals of circumcision, sabbath keeping and food restrictions.[64] A counterpart of thus narrowing down Paul's devaluation of law-obedience is an upgrading of whatever he can be found to be saying or implying in favour of works. We cannot, Watson insists, smooth over the fact that 'belief in judgement by works is an integral part of Paul's theology'.[65] We have come a long way from Bultmann, according to whom the will to obtain salvation by obeying the law was the capital sin. Bultmann, says Watson, was 'wrong to define faith as "the radical renunciation of achievement"'.[66] Paul sees it as thoroughly active, once one has ceased to define it by a misinterpretation of the term 'works'. The Jews were wrong in relying on works in a narrow sense as a demonstration of their membership of the people to whom God has promised salvation; the Christian must, by his works, demonstrate in a comprehensive sense that he is a member of the community which has been saved by trust in Christ. There is now a fair consensus of opinion that something like this best approximates to Paul's attitude. Whether or not interpretation is thus on a surer path than it was with Bultmann,[67] it is clear that I need to take some account of how present-day theory affects any analysis of Paul's reasoning I may propose; and often major changes of critical perspective are the power needed to create movement in some major jam that exegesis has built up. Romans 3:2–8 is a 'black-spot' of the kind where interpreters have little hope of doing more than fret unless reached by the repercussions of a major shift of critical position (and a remarkable number converge upon it).[68]

In Deuteronomy 33:9 and Psalm 119:158 *shamru imratekha* and *imratkha lo shamaru* figure respectively as LXX ἐφύλαξεν τὰ λόγια σου and τὰ λόγια σου οὐκ ἐφυλάξαντο. These and other similar parallels associate λόγια more or less explicitly with that aspect of God's word which is a call to obedience. The etymological affinity of λόγιον with λόγος, moreover, sets up a direct (if not precise) association with τοὺς δέκα λόγους in Exodus 34:28 and Deuteronomy 10:4, of a kind which, of course, the Hebrew text does not set up with the etymologically unconnected *aseret hadvarim*. That λόγια could take the place of λόγοι where commandments are concerned is attested by the Philonic title Περὶ τῶν δέκα λογίων. The instance of λόγια in Romans 3:2 is a *hapax legomenon* in Paul. No parallel helps us to assess its referential scope. With 'no holds barred' the possible extent of this has even been conjectured to include the gospel itself (see Doeve's article of 1953).[69] Discussion has, however, regularly turned on the likelihood of a restrictive intention on the part of Paul. And this tends to result in the proposal of a choice between 'prophets' and 'promises'. Conversely, however, it is widely acknowledged as a fair probability that λόγια is no more than a substitute for νόμος, either in the sense of the Torah (with or without special reference to the body of legal material which it contains), or the Torah taken to cover the whole of the Tanach. That we have a specific reference to the 'promises' is a highly favoured hypothesis, and it has been so since the time of the Fathers.[70] The word itself easily admits of all these applications.

It makes a real difference to the argument whether or not Paul is intending any distinction of reference between the λόγια of 3:2 and the νόμος in 3:19 and 20. If no distinction is intended, then λόγια will have the connotations of sin disclosure it has in 3:20. In which case the 'advantage' of 3:1 must be understood in terms which cover that. If, on the other hand, 'the promises' are the special referent of λόγια in 3:2, then the sense is one which precludes exact parity of reference with νόμος in 3:19 and 20. However, even if the sin-disclosure factor is absent, the referential domain 'whatever-is-a-badge-of-Judaism' is potentially relevant in both cases. This potential is the background which enables Watson, while taking God's covenant promises to Israel as the semantic essence of λόγια in 3:2, to explain the apparent oddities of the ensuing argumentative exchanges as the outcome of two different understandings of what the promises comport.[71] The opponent Paul is addressing is arguing from a view which sees Covenant to be 'an advantage *as regards salvation*'. Paul is arguing its advantage on another basis. But what that basis is, he baffles his interlocutor by not disclosing. Arguing Covenant as an-advantage-as-regards-salvation leads to the insoluble problem that the universality of sin seems to prove that the Covenant has broken down, and with it the faithfulness of God. Paul knows – but at this stage keeps it to himself – that God's faithfulness is not compromised, even though, seen as a guarantee of salvation, the Covenant does not work. The undisclosed reason for this is that God's faithfulness is fulfilled not in its being a warranty of salvation for those who affirm their identity as Israel, but in its having opened up salvation for all who identify themselves with Christ. The enthymematic factor, therefore, here furnishes the very substance of the dramatic structure which bears Paul's argument.

Through applying the distinction between God's Covenant misunderstood as a marker setting the boundaries of his salvific purpose and God's Covenant seen as a promise limited only by man's response to Christ, Watson has opened up the proleptically enthymematic character of Romans 3:2–8; and as a result he has done something radical to loosen the jam of increasing intractability into which a basically unquestioned rigidity of the Interpreter's Highway Code had led its users. He analyses 3:2–8 in terms of a proleptic dependence on the fact that God's covenant-faithfulness is fulfilled in Christ. Its dependence is on 'the fact that' rather than 'the way that'. We could instead make more of the latter, and argue that the queer puzzle which the implied argument of Paul represents (until the open introduction of the Christ factor solves it) should be seen in terms of a tension set up by two rival lines of syllogistic reasoning. Let us call them α and β. The first combines two interlocking syllogisms. For their presentation, see p. 58.

Of the rival patterns, β is loser, because the (nowhere explicitly expressed) major premise consists in a proposition that makes little sense, against a background where neither Jew nor Gentile can avoid condemnation as unrighteous. Such an analysis involves taking λόγια as equivalent to (though perhaps it is sufficient to say 'inclusive of') νόμος in the sense of prescriptive law not just in the sense of Covenant equalling 'promises'. The emphasis I have in mind differs from Watson's: he does not, in fact, incorporate the contents of 3:19–20 into his proleptic interpretation of the debate touched off by the conclusion in 3:1.[73] What I am envisaging rests on our doing precisely this, for it affects what specifically we see the prolepsis as appealing to for advance credit.

We need an answer to the question why awareness of sin should

Pattern of syllogistic argument α

A   MAJOR PREMISE TO MAIN CONCLUSION (E)
The only source of advantage with God is not to be judged unrighteous.

B   MAJOR PREMISE TO INTERMEDIATE CONCLU-
SION (D)
No man is capable of avoiding actions which will entail his being judged unrighteous.

C   MINOR PREMISE TO INTERMEDIATE CONCLU-
SION (D)
A Jew is a man.[72]

D   INTERMEDIATE   CONCLUSION   (based   on
premises B and C) AND MINOR PREMISE TO MAIN CONCLUSION (E)
No Jew can avoid actions which will entail his being judged unrighteous.

E   MAIN CONCLUSION (having A and D as its
premises)
No Jew has any advantage with God.

Pattern of syllogistic argument β

A   MAJOR PREMISE
It is an advantage to be aware of one's own guilt.

B   MINOR PREMISE
Through his knowledge of God's law the Jew is aware of his guilt as the Gentile is not.

C   CONCLUSION
Through his knowledge of God's law the Jew has an advantage over the Gentile.

be an asset to one who has no means of escape from it. The contents of 3:21–6 provide it. They reveal that on account of Christ and the shedding of his blood, men are δικαιούμενοι in God's eyes at no cost to themselves (δωρεάν) other than faith.[74] A Jew has no advantage over the Gentile in the matter of salvation. Yet we have here the explanation of Paul's different answer in 3:1. It is the Jews to whom full knowledge of their sin is given through the law. The generosity of God's free gift is thus fully to be appreciated only by them. That is their advantage. We are thus able to revise the patterns of syllogistic argument α and β as α1 and β1. The former contracts and the latter expands. Prolepsis bites.

Pattern of syllogistic argument α1

A   MAJOR PREMISE
Faith in Christ is the only source of advantage with God.
B   MINOR PREMISE
Faith is not the prerogative of the Jew.
C   CONCLUSION
The Jew has no advantage with God denied to the Gentiles.

Pattern of syllogistic argument β1

A   It is an advantage to be aware of the greatness of God's generosity.
B   Through Christ God ascribes righteousness to man as a gift. (Through Christ man is not adjudged unrighteous because of actions for which he would otherwise be so judged.)
C   Unless a man is aware of his guilt he cannot appreciate the gift of righteousness.
D   Only a man aware of his guilt can appreciate God's gift in Christ.
E   The knowledge of God's law makes the Jew aware of his guilt as the Gentile is not.
F   A Jew can appreciate the generosity of God as a Gentile cannot.
G   The Jew has an advantage.

I have refrained this time from giving titles to the propositions because of the dual identity that arises where the syllogisms interlock. The bracketings alongside pattern β1 show clearly where this occurs. The first syllogism comprises propositions A (as major premise), F (as minor) and G (as conclusion). The second syllogism comprises propositions B (as major premise), C (as minor) and D (as conclusion). The third syllogism comprises propositions D (as major premise), E (as minor) and F (as conclusion). Proposition D, therefore, is both the conclusion of one of the two internal syllogisms and the major premise of the other. The conclusion of the latter, proposition F, links the outcome of the two internal syllogisms to the over-arching syllogism by 'doubling' as its minor premise.

If, however, the train of thought traced in *α1* and *β1*, embracing in advance the content of 3:21–6, provides an explanation of Paul's seemingly yes/no response to the question of Jewish 'advantage' (by anticipating the bearing of that content on the sin-disclosure aspect of the law, which had been the topic of his last comment in 3:20), it has to be admitted that nothing in the *immediate* follow-up reflects the $\beta 1$ side of the balance. Yet, after the kerygmatic and non-argumentative character of 3:21–6, an argumentative tone is at once vigorously resumed in 3:27ff and the pattern of Paul's affirmation soon renews the need for explanatory integration. The enthymematic factor is present in more than one way, and in fact in both a more and a less regular way than before.

2.5 'Boasting' decried; the law upheld in the context of boundary-effacing faith. Romans 4 as key to 3:27–31.

It is in the nature of enthymematic argument that it creates puzzles. There is every indication that Paul was well aware that his argument in Romans 3 was creating puzzles. Yet we would be hard put to say whether he was allowing this to happen intentionally or not. It may be that in trying to get a difficult point over he tacks like a yachtsman confronted with a wind against which only a zig-zagging course can make headway. He speaks as one very definite about what he wants to say, but we may feel unsure whether even he himself had a clear idea of how the pieces in the jigsaw fitted together. Dunn, describing 3:1–8, says:

> Paul at first perseveres with the diatribe style . . . but the debate becomes increasingly with himself. The questions are no longer merely rhetorical devices to help forward his own exposition, but hard questions with existential bite for his own faith . . . Although he is not ready to tackle these questions, the momentum of the diatribe and his own integrity force him to bring them into the open at once. But since he cannot provide a proper response to them at this stage the dialogue loses momentum and direction.[75]

Dunn does not see the need to trace the product of Paul's resumption of the diatribe style in 3:27 to quite such complex motivational dynamics, but he sees it as illustrative of the high degree of intentionality in the chapter's switches of tone.[76] In the climate thus portrayed by Dunn it would not be surprising if direct connections between the argumentative drift of one section of the chapter and another should seem to be rather wanting than forthcoming. Be that as it may, if in 3:21–6 it seems possible to find reasons why the law gives the Jews an advantage, when we reach 3:27 Paul's most pressing concern seems to be to reaffirm the strict limits within which their advantage is confined. For the question and answer with which he immediately follows his great exposition of Christ's role in salvation point to those elements in that exposition that endorse most strongly the negativity of his conclusion in 3:9. Negation there invested the question of how the Jew benefits from his identity. Now, in 3:27, negation strikes at the issue of the Jew being proud of it: ποῦ οὖν ἡ καύχησις; ἐξεκλείσθη.

The concept of καύχησις has been much discussed. It is clearly associated with περισσόν, ὠφέλεια and προέχειν. It seems likely that no more is involved than a transition from the formula 'the Jew enjoys no advantage' to the formula 'the Jew can boast of no advantage'.[77] The advantage precluded is 'advantage with God'. The advantage is always an advantage with respect to those who are not Jews. So I will take Paul's conclusion to be: 'The Jew can boast of no advantage with God that the Gentile does not share.' The grounds alleged involve renewed allusion in 3:28–30 to faith, law and justification. The meaning of these concepts is subject to so much interpretative variation that many different expansions of the premises would be necessary to accommodate it. However, Paul's conclusion is, in fact, based on an argument the logic of which functions independently of the areas of major controversy and uncertainty. It is simply the syllogism that I have already been led to envisage as *a1*; but the introduction of the 'boasting' factor has led to its becoming much more explicit, and I now incorporate that factor into the conclusion.

MAJOR PREMISE: Faith in Christ is the only source of advantage with God.
MINOR PREMISE: Faith is not a prerogative of the Jew.
CONCLUSION: The Jew can boast of (pride himself in) no advantage with God which the Gentile does not have.

Let me elaborate a little on the way in which the most thorny matters of controversy all lie outside the scope of Paul's proof. For example:

(a) whether justification involves more than faith *alone* (and where the works of the law do or do not impinge on its operation);

or (b) whether χωρίς could mean 'outside' in the sense of 'in addition to', not 'to the exclusion of';

or (c) whether πίστις refers only to faith from the human angle.

All are meanings which crucially affect our understanding of the message or teaching of the passage, but not our understanding of the logical basis for Paul's main conclusion.[78] We do not need to know what faith is, we do not need to know that the content of the 'advantage' is justification, or what the latter is or implies. We do not need to know anything about the law and what advantage it can or cannot yield. If the only source of advantage with God is faith, then it is clear that the Jew can have no superior source of advantage. The universality of sin was the negative reason why the Jew had no advantage over the Gentile. The universality of the field of operation of faith is the positive reason.

Nevertheless, although the content of 'advantage', the meaning of justification, the role of law, the scope and source of faith, are logically outclassed by Paul's positive reason for excluding Israel's pride, they *are* issues which affect the place of his argument here in the framework of his argument in general. In particular, they radically affect how his argument here stands in relation to the tensions of his argument in 3:1–20.

If we take Paul to be saying that faith is the *only* source of advantage with God; if we take him to be saying that even the most perfect fulfilment of every aspect of God's prescriptive law is of no avail as a basis for justification; if we see faith in terms of human response, then the confirmation which is here given to 3:9 as against 3:1 makes the contrast between those verses resurface as an issue.

If we favour, in any degree or manner, the options presented in (a), (b) and (c) above, then the contrast will be to some degree less acute, and the question will certainly arise as to whether it merits the concern I have been giving to it.[79] The question does not, however, remain one regarding what Paul has said earlier (and has now passed beyond); it arises anew out of what he is about to say.

Verses 27 and 28 stand tightly related to the verses into which they lead, 29 and 30. Then, the relation of 31 to them precipitates a pattern of discursive development such that the chapter ends with a structure closely parallel to the one with which it began. The pattern runs thus:

> *A body of argument appears to tend in a certain direction.*
> *Should we draw what appears to be the obvious conclusion?*
> *Quite the contrary.*

In 3:1 the envisaged conclusion was the uselessness of circumcision as mere outward compliance with the law. In 3:31 the envisaged conclusion is the abrogation of the law which appears to follow if salvation is by faith: νόμον οὖν καταργοῦμεν διὰ τῆς πίστεως; μὴ γένοιτο· ἀλλὰ νόμον ἱστάνομεν. The reasons for Paul's vehement 'on the contrary, I uphold the law' are certainly not explicit in the context. And we are again sent looking for the logical foundation behind apparent contradiction. In which direction is it to be sought?

Ziesler points to Rhyne's observation (in *Faith Establishes the Law*) that μὴ γένοιτο after a rhetorical question 'regularly introduces a topic for immediate discussion and never concludes a matter', and states with some confidence: 'Romans 4 is the clarification of 3:31.'[80] Unfortunately 4:1, where difficulty in explaining the syntax is combined with early signs of divergence in the textual tradition, provides no clear indication of the spirit in which Paul suddenly turns here to Abraham.[81] Eventually he comes up with a very clear reason for having done so. Summing up in 4:18–22 to the effect that Scripture says of Abraham that he was accounted righteous because he believed (in the truth of what God said to him), Paul adds the final observation in 4:23–5:

> *This was written so that we might know that we would be accounted righteous through our faith in the God who raised Jesus from the dead, since it was to that end that Jesus was handed over for our sins and was raised again.*

This final stress on faith as the key factor has been reached by an argument – not without tortuosities – that has returned repeatedly to the light in which what was said to Abraham (and *when* it was said to him) places the law, and more particularly the custodians of the law (οἱ ἐκ νόμου), making faith the sole criterion of inheritance, and the uncircumcised as much the heirs of Abraham as the Jews. Thus the discourse regarding Abraham continues the argument concerning the privileged position claimed by the Jews and reaffirms the levelling effect of the dependence of righteousness on faith. It is notable for the extremely negative light in which it places both law and works, anticipating the references later in Romans to the law as a source, not just an index, of sin, and virtually specifying that if

God had allowed righteous acts to save man from judgement the all-important operation of his grace would have been eliminated. None of this seems very much like an explanation of how Paul is in effect upholding the law. Indeed, it seems to aggravate the problem, driving the interpreter to construe Paul as saying (and I quote Ziesler's account of this mode of construal), 'if one really wants to do God's will in general, then where one must start is with justification by faith. In the long run, far from militating against the doing of God's will, it on the contrary enables it to be done.'[82] And so the law is vindicated – in the long run.

So long as the attitude towards Abraham in first-century Judaism was understood as seeing in him an example of righteousness through obedience to God's commands, it was difficult to read Romans 4 as anything other than a digression to dispose of an anticipated objection to Paul's general doctrine of salvation without works (and hence not as designed to explain why Paul can claim to uphold the law).[83] If, however, Paul is seen as attributing to Judaism 'not only an emphasis on "works", but also an emphasis on God's covenant-faithfulness' (as Watson stresses, and indeed most scholars would now insist), then what he is correcting in the Jewish view of Abraham at least *includes* a misunderstanding of the implications of that faithfulness (i.e. that it applies only to Israel, the descendants of Abraham being the exclusive beneficiaries of God's covenant). In which case he is not pointing to Abraham to dispose of an objection to the doctrine of faith without works, but because, trust not works being the basis on which righteousness is accounted to man, the law seals a promise of *universal* application and one for the fulfilment of which it *prepares the way*, but which, by the terms of the promise itself, it cannot effectuate. However, if this means seeing the law – to use Ziesler's terms again – in its 'predictive' not its 'regulative' aspect, it does not mean we have to take νόμος in 3:31 in the sense of the overall message of the Pentateuch rather than the law given to Moses. For the case of Abraham establishes grace as the principle of salvation, and it is the law in its condemnatory capacity – as the measure of the wrath which man's sin deserves – that most brings out the extent of the generosity which is engaged when God's faithfulness is vindicated in the fulfilment of his promise in the death and resurrection of Christ.

If it is in this way that we see 3:31 as receiving explanation in chapter 4, then the explanation is that yielded by the relation which

I would see as having already been implicitly established in the course of chapter 3 between the law as sin-disclosure and the appreciation of the magnitude of God's gift. The paradox between Paul's upholding of the law and its being no ground for boasting would rest on the same basis as the paradoxes of 3:1–20. How the Jew both has, and does not have, an advantage in fact comes out more clearly through the introduction of the 'boasting' factor. Two implied syllogisms can be set alongside each other. One revives the $\beta 1$ (the positive, 'yes-the-Jew-has-an-advantage') pattern of argument which my earlier analysis had led me to envisage, but which 3:27 seemed to have pushed out of the picture. It now finally resurfaces via 3:31 and the light shed on that verse by the Abraham discourse. (I give it in condensed form.) The other brings us back to the conclusion affirmed in 3:27, corresponding to the 'no-advantage' results of my $\alpha 1$ pattern of argument, but the premises are different, and the minor is identical with its opposite number:

MAJOR PREMISE:	To have full awareness of one's guilt is an advantage. (The full measure of God's grace becomes clear.)	To have full awareness of one's guilt is the opposite of an occasion for boasting.
MINOR PREMISE:	A Jew can appreciate the full extent of his guilt as a Gentile cannot.	A Jew can appreciate the full extent of his guilt as a Gentile cannot.
CONCLUSION:	The Jew has an advantage over the Gentile.	The Jew has no occasion to boast (quite the reverse).

We are thus left with two conclusions which easily conflate when their content is expanded in the light of the whole discourse, thus:

> *There is true advantage in the full awareness of his sin which the law gives to the Jew, but it is an advantage which decisively and dramatically excludes that his having been entrusted with it can be an occasion for boasting.*[84]

2.6   Beyond the enthymematic. Some methodological considerations.

Analysing the relation of 3:31 to 3:27 thus brings the enthymematic implications generated by the zig-zagging of the argument in Romans 3 into something like harmony. In doing so, however, there has been some elongation of the path which can properly be considered to be that of enthymematic analysis. For it is clear that limits have to be recognised to the range of 'enthymematic' implication as such. A borderline has to be drawn between the task of integrating what appear to be patterns of partly elliptical syllogistic reasoning in a text, and the more general one, that confronts us in almost any argumentative discourse, of reconstructing those areas of an author's argument that are not spelt out fully and leave room for conjecture. The explanation of Paul's upholding of the law may have strayed over that borderline, particularly insofar as appeal to chapter 4 is involved. Whether 3:31 comes within the ambit of the enthymeme is a moot point. I have argued that its logical foundation can be represented in terms of syllogistic propositions very nearly explicit quite close at hand in the text; and yet their identification has involved a span of reconnaissance extending as far as 4:25. However, it may be felt that this very fact shows up a serious risk of falsification which inheres in enthymematic analysis pursued in too narrow a sense. It is rare that an adequate account of the factors implicit in any particular unit of Paul's reasoning can be given unless reconnaissance is extended to cover very wide spans of his argument. I have chosen to consider the enthymeme in Romans 1–8 because these chapters provide something like a unitary argumentative span. But if, as many critics now feel, the argument of 1–8 is falsified unless 9–11 are reckoned part of the same unit, questions arise which I have not considered.[85] Some have implications for the way I have construed Paul's logic. For example, is it expressly to clarify the relation between ethnic Israel and the new Israel of those who believe in Christ that Paul concerns himself with the issues of law, justification and faith in the chapters I have been considering? Does he, in fact, reason about the source of the gospel's power in 1:16–17 primarily to show how its roots in faith make it available equally to Jew and Gentile? If so, I should have taken his *demonstrandum* to involve unique stress on the *extent* of the gospel's efficacy – which would place the role of faith in his deductive logic on a different footing from that which I gave to it. Again, is the express aim of the debate regarding the Jew's advantage/dis-advantage to clarify how the *true* and real priority of ethnic Israel in God's plan is *not* being impugned (simply her conception of it), and to display how that priority is not confined to the pre-history of multi-ethnic salvation, but remains a permanent reality? If so, to analyse Paul's argument in terms of an advantage to Israel associated with the preparatory or educative function of the law is clearly inadequate. But in these matters, and in others, I shall have to be content merely to note what I have not taken into account.

Enthymematic analysis, though it is by definition a probing below the surface of argumentative discourse, is likewise, by definition, a probing that does not go beyond a certain depth. How much value it can claim to have is an uncertainty to which the investigative parameters of this scrutiny will have to be acknowledged as being subordinate. I will try to maintain a heuristic openness of assumption as I proceed, noting where hazards of methodological short-sightedness seem particularly to warrant concern. For the moment I shall consider it sufficient if the cursory look at Romans 1–4 which I have here been taking has served to show how widely the form, scope and importance of the enthymeme can vary, and thus has prepared the ground for confronting the situations we shall meet in Romans 5–8, and of which I shall attempt a more penetrating analysis. However, it should be already clear that the more directly Paul's discourse relates to the significance he recognises in the Cross and Resurrection of Christ the more it leads him (a) into complexities of terminology and of inter-relationship between terms that leave the status of his argumentation very difficult to assess, and (b) into argumentative tangles where adoption of the cut-and-thrust style of the diatribe reflects something more than a mere show of directional uncertainty for didactic purposes. It is on the character and status of logical argument in Paul that I expect this study to shed light. That the precise drift of Paul's discourse is often so difficult to determine says something concerning both of these, but of course our ignorance of the external circumstances of the letter makes matters worse, and many problems fade (as Watson, Minear and others show) when a particular context is envisaged. I shall try to avoid the risk of not allowing sufficiently for such possibilities – a risk inherent in all discourse-oriented analyses even when much less narrowly focussed than mine.

3

WAYS IN WHICH ENTHYMEMES ARISE IN ROMANS 5–7

3.1 The peace of the justified in 5:1 as logically consequential. Uncertainties of enthymematic implication.

The extreme familiarity of the opening statement of Romans 5 may well tend to blunt the enthymematic edge which is a feature of it, and cannot be ignored, at least as long as it is construed in such a way that from the premise consisting of the three-word nucleus δικαιωθέντες . . . ἐκ πίστεως Paul is seen to be drawing as a logical inference the conclusion: εἰρήνην ἔχομεν πρὸς τὸν θεὸν διὰ τοῦ κυρίου ἡμῶν Ἰησοῦ Χριστοῦ. It is on the relationship between the δικαιωθέντες of the premise and the εἰρήνην ἔχομεν of the conclusion that the functioning of the deduction depends (see diagram 1).[1] However, insofar as the ambit of δικαιωθέντες is that of judge and defendant, its plane is not naturally that of peace and enmity (see diagram 2). As Cranfield says: 'between a human judge and the person who appears before him there may be no really personal meeting at all, no personal hostility if the accused be found guilty, no establishment of friendship if the accused is acquitted'.[2] It is only because of the further considerations which the Pauline context introduces into the situation that the two planes are brought into parallel. The relevance of such considerations and their general character are indicated in the amplification of δικαιωθέντες by ἐκ πίστεως, and by the fact that the judge with whom we have peace is God and that we have this peace through the instrumentality of the Lord Jesus Christ (see diagram 3).[3]

In contrast to the situation prevailing between 'a human judge and the person who comes before him' there is 'between God and the sinner' – to continue in Cranfield's words – 'a personal relationship', for God 'does not confer the status of righteousness upon us without at the same time giving himself to us in friendship and establishing peace between himself and us'.[4] The terms in which

Diagram 1

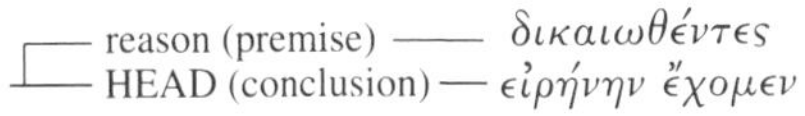

```
┌─ reason (premise) ──── δικαιωθέντες
└─ HEAD (conclusion) ── εἰρήνην ἔχομεν
```

Diagram 2

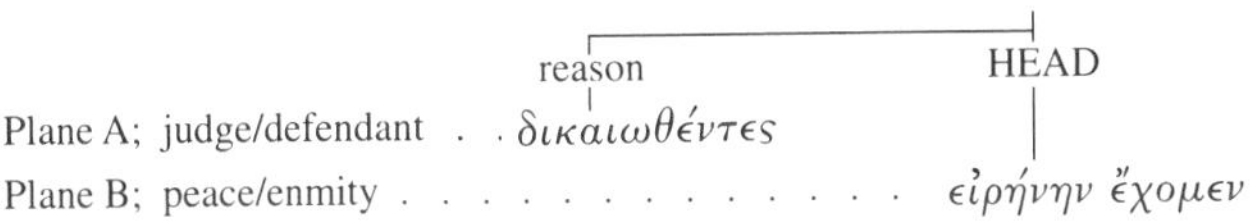

```
                         ┌─────────────┬──────────────┐
                       reason                        HEAD
Plane A; judge/defendant . . δικαιωθέντες              │
Plane B; peace/enmity . . . . . . . . . . . εἰρήνην ἔχομεν
```

Diagram 3

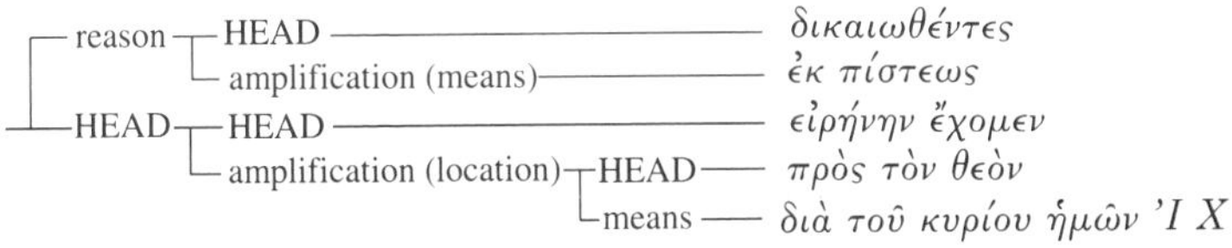

```
┌─ reason ┬─HEAD ───────────────────── δικαιωθέντες
│         └─ amplification (means)──────── ἐκ πίστεως
└─HEAD ┬─HEAD ───────────────────── εἰρήνην ἔχομεν
       └─ amplification (location)┬─HEAD── πρὸς τὸν θεὸν
                                  └─means ── διὰ τοῦ κυρίου ἡμῶν 'Ι Χ
```

Diagram 4

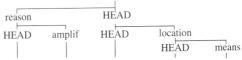

Plane of salvation . . δικαιωθέντες ἐκ πίστ εἰρήνην ἔχ πρὸς τὸν θ διὰ τοῦ κ ἡ

Paul formulates his inference in 5:1, therefore, depend for their logical cogency on contextual factors emphatically signalled as governing the way his terms are to be understood. The signalling, however, though emphatic, advertises implications to which it gives little precision. It conveys only that the notions of δικαίωσις and εἰρήνη admit of the logical relationship into which Paul brings them by virtue of their applicability to the scheme of human salvation effected by God through Christ and the operation of faith. They apply and function on the plane of salvation in such a way as to neutralize the discrepancy between the planes on which they naturally function (see diagram 4). But how precisely do they apply and function so as to come together on this plane? That remains the question. The simple answer is that since man's unrighteousness brings God's condemnation, the peace which should prevail between a loving God and the man he has created is made impossible. Through the work of Christ and the operation of faith, man's unrighteousness is so dealt with as to make peace no longer an impossibility. God's plan is one which involves both enmity being replaced by peace and the defendant not being condemned for unrighteousness by his judge.[5] But the fact is that the terms 'peace' and 'unrighteousness', and the manner in which unrighteousness is dealt with, leave scope for so many irresolvable uncertainties that to say what I have just said is far from providing a basis on which to measure the validity of Paul's logic. I will therefore attempt to single out and pursue at least some of the uncertainties that most affect how his logic may be seen to function. I will work from conclusion back to premise, from εἰρήνη to δικαίωσις.

With εἰρήνη the relevant area of uncertainty is relatively limited. The main question is: does Paul's conclusion refer merely to a removal of the enmity which prevailed between us and God on account of our unrighteousness, or also to the state of perceived and productive harmony that results from the removal of enmity? The dual tradition of Greek and Hebrew usage made a range of options available to him.[6] A branching diagram (5) provides a convenient way of presenting some idea of what it was. The basis of Paul's implementation of εἰρήνη in 5:1 is clearly the sequence of options

Diagram 5

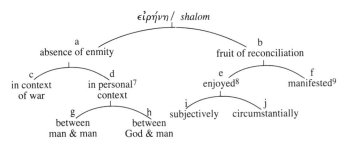

represented in diagram 5 by a, d and h. But this is made possible by virtue of the standard meanings of the Greek work, covered by a–c and a–d–g. It is generally considered that Paul is already looking forward to the reconciliation of which he is to talk in 5:10–11, and hence the application of εἰρήνη according to sequence b–e–j is no less in his mind than a–d–h. Whether the developments of meaning leading to i and f are also already envisaged by him is more questionable.[10] Hebrew precedent could have led him in this direction, though Dunn notes that von Rad finds only limited OT evidence of the development that leads to i.[11] Yet, though therefore cautious on that score, Dunn is very positive regarding sequence b–f: 'we can say that Paul has in view an actual relationship . . . whose outworking in life should be visible'.[12] Moreover, Dunn insists on the relevance of 5:10–11 where he discourages a sharp distinction between 'justification' and 'reconciliation'.[13] Ziesler, on the other hand, though acknowledging that 'peace' here 'may well include a subjective feeling of peace with God' (which would imply the process of semantic development b–e–i), sees the 'focus' as being 'on the objective reality which would give grounds for the feeling' (sequence b–e–j).[14] If we follow the path down which Dunn would lead us, and see justification and reconciliation as little more than alternative ways of viewing one and the same thing (which was the conclusion reached earlier by Barrett), then the inferential character of Paul's affirmation in Romans 5:1 may dissolve altogether.[15] Enjoying harmony with God becomes no more than the explication of what it means to be justified. But if, with Ziesler, we see justification as the reason we enjoy harmony with God (the point Cranfield was anxious not to allow Barrett's equation to obscure), then we do have an inference the validity and value of which invite examination.[16] Clearly it is impossible to separate how we interpret εἰρήνη from how we understand the fact of δικαίωσις. In the course of vv. 9–10 δικαίωσις and καταλλαγή are both equally declared to be the outcome of Christ's sacrifice, but rhetorical factors influence both the pattern[17] and the argument[18] of these verses. So I shall consider, within the range of meanings which δικαίωσις and εἰρήνη are capable of carrying, some of the consequences which different patterns of possible interplay entail for the validity of Paul's logic.

If, in inferring in 5:1 that we have peace with God, Paul was not intending to go (at this point in his argument) beyond the notion that we are now *in a position* to enjoy such peace, then it would be sufficient, for the purposes of logical validity, if the δικαίωσις referred to in his premise were seen to be something that removed whatever had been precluding our being at peace with God.[19] If it was our unrighteousness that had been precluding it, then it would suffice (for logical purposes) that δικαίωσις is a process which clears us of the incrimination of guilt. It would not be any concern of logic how the incrimination is disposed of nor what it involved nor what its removal entails. Paul's argument could be seen as implying a syllogism along the following lines:

A MAJOR PREMISE:
   Being held guilty of unrighteousness must preclude man
   from a harmonious relationship with God.
B MINOR PREMISE:
   We are no longer held guilty of unrighteousness.
C CONCLUSION:
   We are no longer precluded by unrighteousness from a
   harmonious relationship with God.

The elements made explicit by Paul are integrated by supplying his
implicit major premise. We would have before us a straightforward
example of an enthymeme of the first order. But if, as Ziesler says,
this is not the sum of what Paul here has in mind, but only where the
focus lies; if Paul is inferring from the fact of our δικαίωσις that we
not only enjoy the possibility of a harmonious relationship with
God but are already launched by the process of δικαίωσις itself into
the fertile enjoyment of that harmony, then the δικαίωσις must be
more than mere acquittal. Analytically, if δικαιοῦσθαι means
merely 'to be cleared of unrighteousness', then only the removal of
the impediment to peace with God can be inferred with certainty;
full experience of peace in terms of b e i j f may be a consequence
which in point of fact arises out of it, but it is a consequence outside
the ambit of what logic can claim as being entailed. And so long as
the righteousness which is ours through δικαίωσις is strictly a
matter of our standing before God, a standing with which we are
credited on the basis of Christ's merit alone, and not anything
within ourselves, then it can never provide a logical basis for
inferring that we actually enter into full fruition (b e i j f) of peace
(a d h). It will not make much difference whether the status with
which we are credited is seen in terms of unrighteousness overlooked, unrighteousness regarded as other than it is, or unrighteousness no longer to be reckoned as an impediment to salvation. None
of these interpretations eases the difficulty of deducing entry into
the enjoyment of peace from a δικαίωσις which consists exclusively
in the conferral of status.[20] If, on the other hand, δικαίωσις were
seen as involving a change in the sinner which is not merely a matter
of our status before God – if it is a process which entails an actual
change of disposition and behaviour in the one who undergoes it –
then it becomes logical to see it as also entailing more than the mere
possibility of peace between man and God, and as resulting necessarily in a state of perceived and productive harmony with God on

the part of man. It is still the official view of the Roman church, proclaimed by the Council of Trent and claiming the support of Chrysostom and Augustine, that where Paul speaks of present justification he speaks of God's work of making righteous by inner renewal, as well as of making righteous through remission of sin. Focussing on the special way remission of sin figures in Paul's thought, Bornkamm sees the tension as being between the forensic and the existential:

> Justification does not relate to actual sins committed in the past but to release from sin as a power which makes men its slaves. But even the term 'justification' does not as such render the fullness of salvation, of 'this grace in which we stand', however much it may be the basis of believers' 'state of being saved' (Rom 5:1f.). As a result, to describe present salvation in Christ, Paul often uses schemes of classification not directly stemming from his doctrine of justification. They are not properly forensic, but 'existential', terms. Such are sacramental statements like Romans 6 and Galatians 3:26ff., 'putting on' Christ (Gal 3:27; Rom 13:14), the 'body of Christ' and its members (1Cor 12:12ff.; Rom 12:4f.), and 'being' in Christ. These are so frequent and of such importance that some have regarded them as actually of the essence of Paul's gospel and theology. Nevertheless, they are not to be played off against his gospel of justification, or separated from it or ranked above it. Influential as these mystic-ontological concepts and expressions are, Paul hardly ever uses them unqualified by his doctrine of justification.[21]

This would leave us where we were with the logical problem, but concern not to let 'mystic-ontological concepts' obscure the principle of justification may now seem outdated, given the developments that more recent research on Paul's understanding of righteousness has brought into play. Where this is seen as Ziesler,[22] for example, sees it – as denoting 'activity within a relationship' which on God's side means it is never an attribute but always the way God acts and on man's that it is power (power in two senses, that 'under which' and 'by which' he lives) – we are able to escape from a syllogistic substructure which would not work (α) to one which does (β):

α   *Invalid syllogistic substructure*
Being held guilty of unrighteousness must preclude man
from a harmonious relationship with God.

We are no longer held guilty of unrighteousness.

We enter into the realisation and fruitful enjoyment of a
harmonious relationship with God.

For this to be valid, a further hidden proposition would have to be
conceded: 'Entry into the realisation and enjoyment of a harmonious relation with God must follow once the incrimination of guilt
has been revoked'; so that Hamilton's 'supreme canon of the syllogism' – recalled by Jevons, *Elementary Lessons in Logic*, pp. 289–90
– can clearly be seen to have been exceeded.[23] But disposal to
obedience ensures a harmonious relationship with God to those for
whom, as sinners – guilty of unrighteousness and disposed only to
disobedience – it was inaccessible. Hence:

β   *Valid syllogistic substructure*
Entry into a harmonious relationship with God follows
from man's being disposed to (and capable of) obedience.

Our guilt no longer held against us and free from subjection
to disobedience, we are disposed to (and capable of) obedience.[24]

We enter into the realisation and fruitful enjoyment of a
harmonious relationship with God.

'The question' – as Sanders sums up – 'is precisely whether or not
Paul has shifted the meaning beyond that of the law court.'[25]
   Paul's use of δικαιόω, δικαιοῦσθαι and δικαίωσις has to be seen
in relation to his use of δίκαιος and δικαιοσύνη, but the meaning he
attributes to the first three cognates does not by any means become
self-evident through their relation to the other two. The usage of the
LXX and the Hebrew terminology that it stood for, together with
Jewish interpretation of this terminology and its implementation in
rabbinical works came to invest the δικ- cognates we find in Paul
with a high degree of polysemic flexibility. How much of this
touched Paul it is impossible for us to determine. It was a flexibility
within which – as Sanders has pointed out – the mutations of *ẓdq*
encompassed notions of leniency in judgement as well as the

recognition of obedience, of a righteousness dependent on faithful adherence to the Covenant, not only on a preponderance of good deeds, let alone on the total avoidance of sinfulness.[26] When Paul refers to a process of δικαίωσις ἐκ πίστεως 'it is a standard debate', Sanders notes, 'as to whether "be made righteous" or "be justified" catches the meaning better'.[27] Many see fit to read considerable complexity into the first two instances of δικαιόω in Romans (2:13 and 3:4).[28] But neither instance is a clear case of δικαιόω implying any meaning beyond the straightforward acknowledgement of activity which is above blame. We do not need to understand its meaning as going beyond this even where it next occurs (in 3:20), and we first find it associated with the question of what benefit it is possible for man to derive from having been entrusted with God's law. (Paul need not here, in fact, be saying any more than that because no one actually fulfils the law, no one can be acknowledged righteous on the basis of law-obedience.) The next four appearances of δικαιόω follow each other in quick succession (3:24, 26, 28 and 30), and now the background against which it stands is in the process of changing dramatically. In 3:24 sinful men are referred to as δικαιούμενοι δωρεάν. The purpose of the action of God which makes them so is given as εἰς το εἶναι αὐτὸν δίκαιον καὶ δικαιοῦντα τὸν ἐκ πίστεως Ἰησοῦ, whence Paul affirms λογιζόμεθα . . . δικαιοῦσθαι πίστει ἄνθρωπον χωρὶς ἔργων νόμου, and expands on the matter by looking at it from God's angle again: ὁ θεὸς . . . δικαιώσει περιτομὴν ἐκ πίστεως καὶ ἀκροβυστίαν διὰ τῆς πίστεως. The divine action which in all these cases is described by δικαιόω is directed not at those who have fulfilled the law but at those who have not. It is directed at those who have faith in the Lord Jesus Christ. The phrase λογίζεσθαι εἰς δικαιοσύνην which Paul uses in 4:3 seems to hold the key, and to authorise us to gloss δικαιόω as he is understanding it by this stage in his argument as '*account/reckon* righteous', and – if we take into account the δικαιοῦντα τὸν ἀσεβῆ of v. 5 – as 'account/reckon righteous *those who are not*'. In whatever sense righteousness applies in 5:1, it marks an attribute not possessed by the δικαιωθέντες until through δικαίωσις it can be ascribed to them. How far it indicates a disposition to obedience may be debated. There is nothing at all to invite us to see in it any hint of the fruits of obedience. And the fact that ἐκ πίστεως is specified seems to confirm that concern with status here leaves little room even for disposition. Though it may be less easy to be sure that both disposition to and fruits of obedience are not in Paul's mind when he repeats δικαιωθέντες in 5:9, this does not warrant our assuming these to be what he has in mind already in v. 1. Crucial for Ziesler's interpretation of δικαίωσις as understood by Paul in Romans are vv. 5:12–21.[29] For *Syllogistic substructure β* to operate, what becomes more fully explicit in 5:12–21 has to be read back into 5:1. And this, admittedly, may be thoroughly appropriate, since, where such a fundamental element in Pauline thought as δικαίωσις is involved, even another appeal to prolepsis to account for any such reading back would hardly be called for. However, it may still be preferable to see 5:1 as containing an element of illogicality, albeit an illogicality which is on the way to being cleared up.

Is it, in fact, either necessary or appropriate to worry about vindicating Paul's logic in 5:1? Why not let him be seen as shifting his ground between premise and conclusion? It is in keeping with the eschatological context involved. 'Justification', according to Käsemann, 'opens the door to the eschatological present.'[30] This is a time in which the now and the not yet are constantly, fittingly and inevitably (not to say, impenetrably) interwoven. Shifting logic may actually be a faithful (necessary) way of conveying the situation, provided we are not led by flexibility of interpretation to discounting logic as a factor of importance here for Paul. Cranfield, at any rate, is very firm about this. His approach – the approach that provided me with the starting point for this discussion – largely bypasses the issue which led me to make my distinction between *Invalid syllogistic substructure α* and *Valid syllogistic substructure β*. The need to safeguard this argumentative perspective, moreover, leads him to be decisive in his rejection of an alternative reading of 5:1 which otherwise casts a shadow over exegesis: namely that which gives ἔχωμεν, and makes the main clause exhortative. Though it is usually discounted, the NEB opts for it. It would totally transform the enthymematic implications of the verse. But here I will set the limit to what I can reasonably try to take into account in the way of interpretational variation. The grounds on which Cranfield argues against it are: 'It would surely be strange for Paul, in such a carefully argued writing as this, to exhort his readers to enjoy or to guard a peace which he has not yet explicitly shown to be possessed by them.'[31] But is the possession of this peace 'explicitly shown' in justification? It is shown in the fact that 'justification involves reconciliation', and involves it 'because God is what he is'.[32] These are Cranfield's answers. But they are answers which do less to resolve than to intensify the complexity of the argumentative dynamic to which the variables in Paul's logic give rise.

3.2 The Christian's confident hope; two-sided enthymematic support for 5:5. (The uncertain role of 5:12–21).

In Romans 5:10 Paul says ἐχθροὶ ὄντες κατηλλάγημεν ... We were God's enemies. Now that we are reconciled, are we, therefore, God's friends? Was the enmity that prevailed between us and God a two-way process? Interpreters argue over how far enmity and reconciliation are reciprocal. Dunn notes a variety of opinions, himself siding with Cranfield's, namely that a two-sided enmity is what Paul had in mind.[33] And though it is beyond question that it is God alone who has effected reconciliation, nevertheless in 2Cor 5:20 (as Cranfield observes) men are called upon 'to be reconciled'; hence, according to Ziesler, 'we are reconciled to God, not he to us'.[34] But, this being so, can 'reconcile' be said, as by Käsemann, to refer not 'to an inner event but to the objective ending of enmity'?[35] Despite such differences, there is no doubt that, however strictly we may deem Paul, in the δικαιωθέντες of 5:1, to be concerned with the status that is the foundation of our salvation and not the response on our part which is its outworking, nevertheless from 5:2 onwards there is evidence that his thoughts start moving towards the latter. This movement may start already with τὴν προσαγωγὴν ἐσχήκαμεν εἰς τὴν χάριν ταύτην ἐν ᾗ ἑστήκαμεν (but it may not); it clearly has, however, when he says καυχώμεθα ἐπ' ἐλπίδι τῆς δόξης τοῦ θεοῦ.[36] For 'καυχάσθαι is a second mark of the state of salvation and is the response of faith to the dawning δόξα' (Käsemann).[37] This is not a case of doxological expansion, for the 'hope' with which the expansion winds up becomes in fact the theme of Paul's next unit of argument.[38] It is also becomes the occasion for an enthymeme.

It would not be like Paul to speak of hope which was hope without a rational foundation. And in fact he does not delay long in working round to why we should entertain what the RSV renders as 'our hope of sharing the glory of God'; 'our hope of the glory which God will bestow on us' might be a better rendering. Romans 8:17 speaks of our future sharing in the glory which will be Christ's. There the meaning is unequivocal. Here, however, there is some uncertainty as to whether the genitive is subjective or objective. A comparison with 3:23 seems to militate in favour of its being the latter, particularly if, as Dunn reckons, Paul is reverting in both cases to the 'Adam motif . . . the divine purpose in salvation being understood in terms of a restoration (and completion) of fallen humanity to the glory which all now fall short of'.[39] However, a comparison with 9:23 seems to indicate that we must see it in some sense as being both. Perhaps, in any case, it is an unnecessary distinction, if δόξα τοῦ θεοῦ is explained in Cranfield's compendious phrase as 'that illumination of man's whole being by the radiance of the divine glory which is man's true destiny'.[40] It is a hope in which we exult. It makes us exult also in suffering because we know that via patience and its character-developing properties suffering promotes hope. So says Paul in 5:2–4. Then in 5:5 he affirms that this hope will not let us down, and the reason that we can be sure of this is that through the Holy Spirit we experience in our hearts the outpouring of God's love. Paul's words are these:

> ἡ δὲ ἐλπὶς οὐ καταισχύνει, ὅτι ἡ ἀγάπη τοῦ θεοῦ ἐκκέχυ-
> ται ἐν ταῖς καρδίαις ἡμῶν διὰ πνεύματος ἁγίου τοῦ
> δοθέντος ἡμῖν.

The tenses involved are present and perfect. I have construed Paul as affirming that 'this hope will not let us down'. English translations usually stick to the present, leaving what is meant unclear. Dunn notes the difficulty and comments: 'Though the thought is of the final vindication of the hope for a complete salvation and favourable verdict in the final judgement, the verb should probably be read as a present rather than as a future (καταισχυνεῖ). Indeed the present effect of the hope may mark some distinction from the predominantly future-oriented passive use of the verb in the Jewish tradition, since it is rooted in an eschatological fulfilment already experienced.'[41] On this basis we can see Paul's statement as an enthymeme implying at least two interlocking syllogisms of which the second needs to be a polysyllogism.

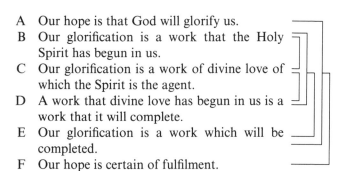

A   Our hope is that God will glorify us.
B   Our glorification is a work that the Holy Spirit has begun in us.
C   Our glorification is a work of divine love of which the Spirit is the agent.
D   A work that divine love has begun in us is a work that it will complete.
E   Our glorification is a work which will be completed.
F   Our hope is certain of fulfilment.

Proposition F is the conclusion of an over-arching syllogism the major premise of which is represented by proposition E and the minor by proposition A. It is thus as the major premise of the outer syllogism that the conclusion of the internal syllogism here doubles. In the internal syllogism, according to the standard pattern of polysyllogisms, the second premise (proposition C) stands as major premise in relation to the first (proposition B) and as minor in relation to the third (proposition D).[42] As usual in enthymematic argument, integration is largely a question of giving expression to implicit major premises.

It is an unquestioned assumption of Paul's reasoning that the work of the Holy Spirit has begun in those who are being addressed. What, in practice, the effects and proofs of this are is not focussed on till later, in Romans 8. It is not that to which the present discourse ostensibly leads. It turns instead to what seems like a supplementary basis for hope. At any rate, the γάρ of 5:6 appears to cast in that role the argument which now follows and which is: from what Christ has done already we can infer the much more that will be done for us hereafter.[43] It spells itself out thus:

> *If God's love for us was such that it led to Christ's dying for us when we were his enemies, it is sure to lead to our final salvation now that through Christ we are reconciled and exult in him. If so much has been done for us in our guilt, how much more we can expect now that we are reckoned not guilty and exult in our reconciliation with God.*

But behind this we can no longer discern the logic of the syllogism; it resembles that logic where rhetoric claims it has proof when all it really alleges as evidence are pointers, even if they are, as Dunn calls them, 'a sequence of rhetorically balanced affirmations which pulse and glow with the confidence of faith'.[44] And yet Paul may be being more rational than this. He truly sees in what God has done the absolute certainty that he will do more. Paul has structured his argument so that it depends on the fact that we are not the ones we were when God extended the hand of friendship to us, and his son came and died for us. It is what we are now, and what the effects of the Spirit working in us give proof of our being, that gives us the certainty that God will save and glorify us as an inevitable culmination of the work he has begun. What more than the certainty of salvation thus afforded can render our hope such as cannot possibly let us down? A further syllogism is in effect implied: a kind of gloss on the six-proposition syllogistic argument formulated earlier.

A   MAJOR PREMISE
    Assurance of salvation is an unassailable basis for hope.
B   MINOR PREMISE
    Our new Christ-given freedom from bondage to sin and the
    reconciliation in which we exult provide us with assurance
    of ultimate salvation.[45]
C   CONCLUSION
    We have an unassailable basis for hope.

At least this much is deductive logic. But though as such it is valid, it
is only as true as its premises are true, and the proposition that
constitutes its minor premise has only the argument I was just now
associating with rhetoric to support it. To the extent, however, that
Paul truly believes his data to prove his assertions, it might perhaps
be fairer to rate his reasoning as inductive rather than rhetorical.
And we may be confronted with the real dilemma: is the argumentation we have in 5:6–11 rhetoric dressed up as logic, or logic
dressed up as rhetoric? And it is possible to see in what follows a
continuation of the argument, not in the way it is most usually seen,
namely as drawing further conclusions from what has already been
said, but on the contrary as providing further grounds for the
conclusions that have already been made, notably regarding the
certainty of Christian hope. For in 5:12–21 we encounter expansion
on both what God did before we were where we are now and where
it will lead in the end. It expands on these so monumentally that the
section is often seen as the climax and peroration of a whole major
compositional unit of the epistle – reckoned by some (e.g. Bruce) as
starting from 3:21, by others (e.g. Dunn) as going right back as far
as 1:18.[46] Could it both fulfil a culminative function and still have its
motivation in adding weight to the argument for hope? I am not
sure.[47] I would merely point out that the two climaxes the passage is
shaped so as to work towards both bear directly on the salvation the
'assurance' of which provides the last suggested syllogism with its
middle term.

The first climax is that of 5:17b (πολλῷ μᾶλλον . . . ἐν ζωῇ
βασιλεύσουσιν . . .); the second is that of 5:21b (οὕτως . . . ἡ χάρις
βασιλεύσῃ . . . εἰς ζωὴν αἰώνιον . . .). The first refers to the victori-
ous life of those who receive the gift of righteousness. The second
refers to the eternal life which is the outcome where grace is victo-
rious through the righteousness of which it is the channel. The

passage therefore articulates itself as an elaborate double build-up to the affirmation of eternal life which is the essence of salvation. If it is related to 5:1–11 in the way I mention, the διὰ τοῦτο of 5:12 would constitute (in the phrase used by Leenhardt) 'a general indication that the author is entering on an explanation of what precedes'. To take the διὰ τοῦτο in this way is one of 'two possibilities of interpretation' envisaged by Barrett.[48] Cranfield sees it as 'not even remotely possible', Barrett as straining Paul's language.[49] Leenhardt is very much in a minority in preferring it.[50]

3.3 Sinning in the interests of grace. The 'knock-down' enthymeme of 6:1. The tangled basis of its confutation (6:2–11).

In the course of the double build-up of Romans 5:12–21, Paul notes two effects which derive from the relation of the law to sin. Firstly (5:13) the law makes it possible (as was not possible before it was given) to ascribe sin to man and to assess the extent of his guilt.[51] Secondly (5:20) the law accentuates man's sin and indeed causes it to abound.[52] That sin both becomes ascribable and increases through the agency of the law is not said here by Paul as if to discredit the law, for the build-up of 5:12–21 in its successive waves invests man's very sinfulness with a distinctly (disquietingly) positive character. For example, three times Paul extols the magnitude of God's act in Christ by relating it to the magnitude of the sin which it disposes of. He does this by means of three contrasts, the sum of which is that whereas through the sin of the one man, Adam, many sinned, fell under judgement and died, through the single act of righteous obedience of the one man, Christ, many receive the grace to become righteous in God's sight and live. From this it might well seem to follow that, if so many had not sinned, there would not have been an outpouring of grace of such magnitude, and God's act would not have been as great as it is. The greatness of God's reign of grace, and the eternal life which is integral to it, are the outcome of the extent to which sin has exercised a reign of death. The positive effects of sin seem thus to be brought out with deliberate emphasis, so that it does not seem at all illogical to syllogise thus:

A   MAJOR PREMISE
    Abundance of sin leads to abundance of grace.

B MINOR PREMISE
It must be good to follow a course that leads to abundance of grace.

C CONCLUSION
It must be good to sin.

And Paul in 6:1 envisages an enthymematic formulation that seems to imply precisely this pattern of reasoning: ἐπιμένωμεν τῇ ἁμαρτίᾳ ἵνα ἡ χάρις πλεονάσῃ. It is a 'knock-down' enthymeme, and Paul at once indignantly dismisses it. And he is right to do so, because the moment the implied syllogism is fully spelt out, its flawed logic is clearly apparent. It depends on the assumption that abundance of sin leads always and only to abundance of grace. But it is not on these grounds that Paul refutes it.

He may, of course, simply not have seen the logical fallacy clearly himself. But even if he had, its pursuit would have led to a flatness of discourse as alien to his mood as it would have been detrimental to his purpose. His tone and his technique at this point are once again those of the classical diatribe, the aim of which was to drive home its point by force of impact, and not via the niceties of logic.[53] Perhaps anyway it is what Paul is about to say (and introduces in v. 3 by the phrase 'Do you not know . . .?') that really concerns him, and the 'knock-down' enthymeme is only a device for leading into it and attracting attention. However, in that case, would he return – as he does in v. 15 – to the same deduction supported by a different argument (envisaged as before only to be at once knocked down)? It really seems more as if he were quoting arguments which were actually being voiced (and acted on). Or it may have been that opponents were attributing the argument to him, as he had noted in Romans 3:8.[54] In any event, the question here twice confronted by Paul reflects a major theoretical and practical problem: how should those who live the life of the Spirit view their position in regard to sin? Paul's approach between 6:1 and 6:15 is not one which makes for smooth logic. It is essentially a combination of an affirmation and an imperative. They may be summed up thus: the life of the Christian is not ruled by sin; so, Christians, do not sin! But the affirmative constituent is supplied by the extended passage of complex argument which occupies 6:2–11. Amid a plethora of inferences in which γάρ, οὖν and οὕτως take turns with one another to mark the intricacies of the labyrinth, and conditional clauses alternate with participial constructions of ambiguous status heading us now one way now another, or leaving us in doubt as to which way they would head us, two moments can be singled out as crucial: v. 2 'We are dead to sin'; and v. 6 'Our old man was crucified with Christ, so that the sinful body should be destroyed and we should no longer be slaves to sin.' Taking these to be the reasons to which Paul is pointing in order to cap all other reasons that might prompt anyone to treat 'let us sin' as a logical proposal, the underlying pattern of implicit syllogistic mechanisms that I think may be discerned behind his argument runs something like this. I propose a pair of inter-dependent syllogisms, aware of the many questions that, owing to the intricacies of Paul's discourse, they inevitably beg:

Syllogism 1

A MAJOR PREMISE
It is the hallmark of sin's dominion that it brings about man's death.

B MINOR PREMISE
Christ submitted to the death which sin exacts of man but rose again.

C CONCLUSION
Christ invalidated the principle on which sin's dominion depends for identity.

Syllogism 2

A MAJOR PREMISE
Christ, by dying the death concomitant upon sin and rising again, overthrew both sin and death.

B MINOR PREMISE
We, through baptism, share in the death and resurrection of Christ.

C CONCLUSION
We cease to be subject to either sin or death.

A pervasive source of difficulty in analysing Paul's arguments is the metaphorical factor in his statements. I have noted this before. But nowhere hitherto has it come up as it does here. The death of Christ on the cross was death in the most real and literal sense of the word. But sharing in this death through baptism can be real only in a very different sense. Yet the logic of Paul's conclusions does often seem to depend on what can be deduced from an identity of words, without real regard for varying levels of metaphor. How we should understand Paul as proving his point in the present passage is profoundly complicated by such problems.

The basis for the major premise of my Syllogism 1 is touched upon by Dunn when relating Paul's use of the phrase 'dying to sin' in 6:10 to his use of it in 6:2. 'What is in view in both cases is the effective power of sin over human life as demonstrated most emphatically in the death which none escape.'[55] Some warranty for the minor premise and conclusion of Syllogism 1 could similarly be found as Dunn goes on to refer specifically to Christ's dying to sin. 'It is because he shared the human condition to the full that his overcoming the death which all die can effectively break the despair and fear of death, and so already break its grip on human life.'[56] But both here and in connection with 6:7 it is Christ's conquest over death that Dunn emphasises. Though he admits that 'the degree to which Paul is dependent on or has adapted a particular proverbial formulation remains unclear', he is eager not to exclude the possible echo in 6:7 of the rabbinical: ' "when a man is dead he is freed from fulfilling the law" '.[57] And he avoids seeing Christ's 'dying to sin' in 6:10 as carrying implications of any uniquely christological expiatory efficacy. ('Death is the end of sin's dominion for man [everybody]; but only one man [Christ] has died a death which broke the final grip of death.')[58] It is only an occasional commentator such as Scroggs who sees in the ὁ γὰρ ἀποθανὼν δεδικαίωται ἀπὸ τῆς ἁμαρτίας a reference to Christ, who by his death brings justification.[59] On the strength of such a reading, of course, the conclusion to Syllogism 1 is found to be more fully explicit than it otherwise would be. Cranfield, however, goes so far as to recognise in ὁ ἀποθανών a precise allusion to the beneficiary of justification. It refers to 'the man, who has died with Christ in God's gracious decision with regard to him, that is, who has died that death in God's sight to which his baptism points back and of which it is the sign and seal'.[60] The verse is thus also rendered foundational for the minor premise in Syllogism 2, though only by dint of viewing as implicit in it the full doctrine of vicarious atonement Cranfield insists as being relevant to 6:10 (even though it is not the atonement aspect as such that Paul is concerned here to bring out but the finality of Christ's dying to sin and hence of the believer's dying to sin). 'What is actually meant here by "dying to sin" has to be understood from what Paul says elsewhere about the relation of Christ's death to sin . . . He died to sin, that is, he affected sin by his dying, in that, as the altogether sinless one who identified himself with sinful men, he bore for them the full penalty of their sins and so – in the pregnant sense in which the words are used in 8:3 – "condemned sin in the flesh".'[61] However, as Ziesler says in commenting on 6:3: 'Of course there has been only one relevant literal, physical death, that of Christ himself. The physical deaths of Christians are not of interest at this point.' Although 'belonging to Christ involves dying' it is 'not in the meantime a physical dying, but a dying to all that has controlled the old self and in particular to sin'.[62]

Ziesler's view of 'dying to sin' permits him to see 'Man's not being ruled by sin' as signifying that man is now free (as he was not before) to choose not to sin. On his reckoning the affirmative represented by 6:2–11 provides a foundation perfectly consistent with declaring intolerable the proposal ἐπιμένωμεν τῇ ἁμαρτίᾳ. In consequence he rejects the possibility that Paul could be meaning Christians are sinless. But there is a long tradition that that is precisely what Paul *is* saying – or at least that at the literal level this is what his words imply. Sanday and Headlam paraphrased Paul's claim in 6:2–4 as 'the baptized Christian cannot sin' (which of course does not exclude the possible necessity of interpreting it as in need of qualification and attenuation – indeed they gloss their reading with 'This at least is the ideal, whatever may be the reality').[63] Dunn admits that there is an ambiguity in Paul's affirmative, one thrust of which would seem to be saying 'that the sinful act is no longer possible'; but he appeals to the context (5:21) as support for what he sees as the more probable thrust, namely 'that what Paul had in mind is a death which puts the individual beyond the power of sin . . . unable . . . to live . . . under its authority'.[64] The more being dead to sin (no longer serving sin) is taken to entail the impossibility of sinful action, the more 6:1 partakes of the logical inconsistency of declaring the impossible intolerable. Let me attempt to display schematically (diagram 6) the pattern of Paul's discourse which differing critical interpretations thus invest with varying degrees of logical irrelevance. My display technique (compare earlier simpler examples *supra*, chapter 3.1) is a standard one (extensively illustrated in Cotterell and Turner, *Linguistics and Biblical Interpretation*, pp. 188–229). As I implement it here it involves listing in a central column the communication units (condensed and interpreted) relevant to Paul's argument.[65] Lined up with them on the left are labels determining the pattern of their relationships to one another. 'HEAD' indicates a CU to which other CUs stand in a support relationship. The support CUs are labelled descriptively, e.g.

Diagram 6

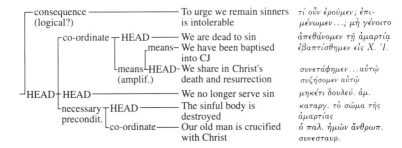

'consequence', 'means', etc. The extreme right-hand column indicates the sections of Greek text to which I would appeal as foundation for my English formulations. It will be seen not only that my
analysis involves some reordering of the elements, but also that the
relations which my labels identify as obtaining between the CUs
do not correspond to the grammatical relationships which are
instated by the surface structure of Paul's syntax.[66]

The Christian's dying to/being no longer a slave to sin is logically
relevant so long as it spells merely his freedom to choose not to sin.
With every other interpretation canvassed the logic is, in varying
degrees, uneasy.[67] The illogicality which thus lurks in 6:2–11 is
brought out into the open when in 6:12 Paul switches from affirmative to imperative.

3.4   Christian eschewal of sin; prescribing what is affirmed. Enthymematic construal of logical anomaly in 6:12. Its sequel.

It is not logical to encourage the sinless to be good. If the οὖν with
which Paul links 6:12 to what has gone before signals things said
earlier as the basis of the admonition it contains, it may have to be
accounted a non-sequitur. And if we should find we are obliged to
acknowledge it as such we should be simultaneously obliged to see
Paul as doggedly attached to it, for, having said in v. 12, μὴ οὖν
βασιλευέτω ἡ ἁμαρτία ἐν τῷ θνητῷ ὑμῶν σώματι he then in v. 14
reverts to saying ἁμαρτία . . . ὑμῶν οὐ κυριεύσει. Diagram 7 maps
how this non-sequitur would bring out the potential for illogicality
charted by my previous display.

According to the implications which are read into 'dying to/being

Diagram 7

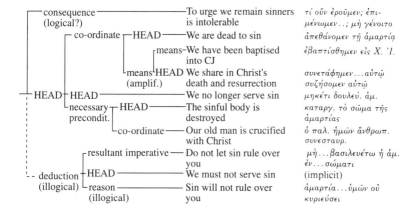

no longer a slave to sin', this pattern of argument can be seen as involving a relatively insignificant 'anomaly' (Ziesler's term) or a fundamentally and profoundly meaningful 'paradox' (Bultmann's term).[68] 'That those who have died to sin still need to be told not to let it continue reigning over them' is how Ziesler spells out the anomaly, and he continues:

> The Christian may have died with Christ to sin, and so no longer be under sin's dominion, but Paul obviously does not expect immediate sinlessness. What is crucial, however, is that there is now the possibility of defeating sin. It is no longer futile to encourage people not to be governed by sin; it is not futile, but it is necessary. This is a measure of the degree to which a victory won in principle still has to be worked out and made specific in practice. 'Become what you can now become' (Käsemann, p. 173).[69]

The reference is to Käsemann's revision of the formula 'Become what you are' implemented by Bultmann. Käsemann recognises the advance represented by Bultmann's assertion that in Paul 'the imperative of moral demand does not merely presuppose the indicative which speaks of God's gift; it paradoxically coincides with the indicative to the extent that it calls for obedience as verification of the gift'.[70] (The contingency is such that it 'makes one responsible, without basing salvation on this responsibility'.)[71] However, according to Käsemann, the imperative 'is integrated into the indicative and does not stand paradoxically alongside it'.[72] It is not that 'Christ's lordship is not contested' or that there is not an 'ever necessary summons to its grace and its service', but salvation is not to be made 'autonomous over against him who brings it'; resistance to the power and victory of sin depends 'on Christ remaining Kyrios over us as the one who imparted himself to us in baptism'. Nevertheless, 'verse 11 . . . solemnly sums up a first train of thought . . . according to which Christians are set free from sin with a definitiveness which death alone can achieve. This is a thoroughly dogmatic statement to which the label "ethical and hortatory" . . . fails to do justice.'[73] The difference between 6:1–11 and 6:12–14 needs to be related to the righteousness of God, which, though hitherto 'predominantly described as gift', is in fact 'the eschatological manifestation of its Giver, so that, like sin, it has the character of a power that determines existence'.[74] And sin being not 'a moral phenomenon' but a 'power' (as Käsemann insists is the Pauline understanding, p. 175), the imperative is essentially an imperative to produce verification. Romans 6:12–14 is dominated by imperatives because it deals with the outcome of the message of freedom from the power of sin (which is the focus in 6:1–11) 'in its practical verification' ('in ihrer praktischen Bewährung' – neither 'verification' nor 'confirmation' conveys quite the sense).

Even so, commentators do not find it easy to reconcile 6:12 and 6:14a. Conzelmann's assertion that 6:14a means that for Christians it is impossible to sin is judged by Dunn to be a 'dangerous mis-statement of Paul's teaching'.[75] Ziesler, whose view of such matters is even more decisive than Dunn's, does not in fact see in the verse any special difficulty: it means simply that Christians are not under sin's power. 'Escape is now possible, though *not a foregone conclusion*' (my italics).[76] Dunn, like Käsemann, has recourse to stressing the futurity of what the verse affirms: 'the resurrection reality which is no longer exposed to threat', as Käsemann says; 'a promise of what will certainly be for believers when they fully and finally share in Christ's resurrection', as Dunn says, adding that it is also 'a promise already being enacted by grace and righteousness' albeit in the form of 'the possibility of grace to live now as one will live with Christ in the future'.[77] Cranfield confronts the possible illogicality of the verse very seriously.[78] He has previously taken exception to the interpretation of the whole passage by Sanday and Headlam in terms of the essential sinlessness of the baptised person (though they read more tension between the ideal and the reality into Paul's argument than Cranfield's references would suggest).[79] Here he resolves the question against the background to 'affirmative' versus 'imperative'. Paul was under no illusion about himself and other Christians. 'Though sin will still have a hold upon them until they die (in the natural sense), they will henceforth, as subjects of Christ over whom he has decisively reasserted his authority, be free to fight against sin's usurped power, and to demonstrate their true allegiance. So understood the sentence makes good sense as support (γάρ) for the imperatives of vv. 12 and 13.'[80] As I understand Cranfield's analysis here, he would be reading those imperatives as enthymemes the syllogistic implications behind which would depend on an imagined major premise in which the concept of allegiance comes under special scrutiny:

A MAJOR PREMISE
Allegiance to a lord to whom one owes liberation from bondage to another involves an active, not merely a passive, use of one's freedom.
B MINOR PREMISE
The freedom Christ gives to his followers is freedom to resist the lordship of sin from which he has liberated them.
C CONCLUSION
Christians must actively resist sin.

The result is not so very different from that which follows from Käsemann's discussion of the passage in terms of the balance between gift and task which 'integrates' imperative and indicative. 'Gift and task coincide in the fact that both designate standing under Christ's lordship, which only inadequately, namely, from the truncated anthropological view, can be brought under the idealistic formula: "Become what you are" (Furnish, *Ethics*, 225ff.). The point is that the lordship of the exalted one be declared in the following of the crucified one.'[81] Hence the key factor 'Bewährung', 'showing to be true'. So Paul's logic (stemming from his *ontologically* based anthropology) is: 'you enjoy freedom from sin's power: *SO*, show it to be so'. The syllogistic implications I would see Käsemann as thus reading into Paul's imperatives would be

A MAJOR PREMISE
One's being under a particular lordship means following the way of one's lord.

B   MINOR PREMISE
    The way of Christ is the way of sacrificial self-denial.
C   CONCLUSION
    Those whom Christ has liberated and brought under his
    lordship must follow the way of sacrificial self-denial.

With Cranfield it is the concept of *allegiance manifested* that generates the imperative; with Käsemann it is the principle of *lordship
attested*. By invoking the principle of lordship, namely that he is
one's lord to whom one's behaviour demonstrates one's allegiance,
both Käsemann and Cranfield integrate affirmative and imperative.
It is a method which almost reverses the direction of the can/must
inference.

> *As a Christian you cannot sin because allegiance towards him
> who has become your lord makes it a contradiction in terms.
> Sin will not reign in your life, because your changed alle-
> giance has terminated the possibility of your letting it do so.*

(The 'affirmative' defines what has been made logically [?] impossible by the moral 'imperative'.)
    At any rate the argumentative cogency thus established enables
6:12 to link 6:3–11 with the 'knock-down' enthymeme in a way
which, if it were a non-sequitur, it could not do. My CU displays
have shown how the air of a non-sequitur attaching to it leaves the
overall argument of 6:1–14 unfocussed. With 'affirmative' and
'imperative' duly integrated, it would admit of reinterpretation as in
diagram 8. But if in this way we may have got 6:2–14 construed as an
effective refutation of 6:1, a similar 'knock-down' enthymeme
involving the same unacceptable conclusion is about to spring up. (I
am taking the ἁμαρτήσωμεν of 6:15 as essentially equivalent to the
ἐπιμένωμεν τῇ ἁμαρτίᾳ of 6:1.)[82] It is as if the tracing of 'must not
sin' to 'cannot be ruled by sin' actually leads Paul back to the risk
from which the argument he has been demolishing arose, and
revives it. And this happens because in 6:14b he is led back to the

Diagram 8

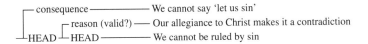

subject of grace: ἁμαρτία γὰρ ὑμῶν οὐ κυριεύσει· οὐ γάρ ἐστε ὑπὸ νόμον ἀλλὰ ὑπὸ χάριν. It is as if, in closing his argument by saying:

> *Obedience figures as an inseparable consequence of Christ's gracious gift in becoming your lord and has nothing to do with the imposition of law-observance,*

Paul sees a direction in which this might lead and forestalls it by at once adding:

> *If any should think that grace means we can do whatever we want, and that further support is given for the principle 'let us sin', in fact the very opposite is the case. We will want only whatever conforms to the will of Christ, our lord.*

With Paul's thought interpreted in this way, the whole course of the rest of the chapter is accounted for with remarkable (perhaps suspiciously untroubled) ease.

It is the mention of grace that appears to lead Paul's mind towards the renewed protest of 6:15. But precisely what false reasoning does the ἁμαρτήσωμεν ὅτι οὐκ ἐσμὲν ὑπὸ νόμον ἀλλὰ ὑπὸ χάριν envisage as having come into play?

     (a) that sin causes grace to abound?

or (b) that, since grace ensures forgiveness, and indeed a right-eousness not of the law, if we sin and break it we shall be vindicating our freedom from its harmful constraints?

or (c) that, being under grace, we incur no harm by sinning, and might as well sin, since we do so freely?

Paul's protest is against any encouragement to sin which sees its charter in our being 'under grace' not 'under law'. Our freedom from the constraint of the law, rather than the scope it offers for multiplying grace, is now to the fore. Argument (a) is overshadowed by (b) or (c).[83] A syllogistic structure is apparent behind both of these. I have almost spelt it out in formulating the questions. But whatever the logic that Paul was envisaging as integrating the 'knock-down' enthymeme represented by Romans 6:15, and whatever its validity or non-validity, Paul does not pursue it. As in 6:1, he avoids all attempt to overthrow the enthymeme logically, and in 6:16 he proceeds with another 'do you not know?' as in 6:3, resorting again, as from 6:1 on, to arguments that provide *a priori* reasons for ruling out a logical foundation for inciting sin. But this time his arguments are much less involved. Their logic is clear, and a syllogistic element is unusually evident. The reasoning depends on the solidity of the oppositions on which it is based. It presupposes that sin and righteousness are alternatives exclusive of all other possibilities, and it presupposes the same of slavery and freedom.[84] On these assumptions it syllogises thus:

A   MAJOR PREMISE
    Freedom in respect of either regime goes with submission to its alternative.
B   MINOR PREMISE
    You are freed from sin.
C   CONCLUSION
    You are slaves to righteousness.

Given the assumptions the syllogism is valid. The enthymematic factor lies almost entirely in the assumptions, for the propositions of the syllogism are fully explicit in 6:16–22. What view we take of the assumptions will depend on how we perceive the figurative dimension.

The inadequacy of the slavery motive as imagery seems to be signalled by Paul himself with his ἀνθρώπινον λέγω. Dunn refers to it as a 'strained', 'forced' metaphor.[85] Ziesler is very specific about the limits of its aptness, as indeed is Wilckens, who nevertheless sees it as a precise definition of how the relationship alternatively to sin and to righteousness is perceived from the human angle.[86] Barth, in fact, though seeing as necessarily inadequate anything we 'dare' to say about 'grace', had insisted that it is 'in the strictest sense of the word' that both sin and grace are defined here as slavery.[87] And Käsemann says, 'grace establishes corporal obedience so radically that comparison with slavery is justifiable'.[88] Behind such discussion lie important differences over the extent to which Paul is speaking figuratively; F. Watson thinks insufficient allowance for the metaphorical sense in which Paul speaks of slavery has encouraged Käsemann to get the whole concept of righteousness in Romans 6 out of perspective.[89] But insofar as Paul's aim is to demonstrate how unthinkable it is for the Christian to say 'let us serve unrighteousness', it is thoroughly sound from the point of view of logic to relate his position to that of the slave whose condition by definition places any alternative service out of the question. It is surely worth noting that what Paul (assuming it is Paul) implies in the letter to Philemon regarding Onesimus illustrates precisely the presumption on which his logic here depends. 'Let us sin' is an option as totally outside those open to the Christian as a change of master is for the slave. But is it all just metaphor? The question again arises whether that which is presented as logical argument merely uses logic as a disguise for something else.

It is interesting that, in the closing verses of Romans 6, Paul turns to consolidating his argument by an appeal to the proofs grace offers to his hearers of its rule over them in the form of the tangible fruits of sanctity. This perhaps confirms what so much of the argument in the chapter seems to be tortuously hinting at, namely that the model of reasoning that ultimately governs it is the maxim that grace which does not produce good fruit, and inhibit sin, is not grace.

3.5 The spirituality of the law upheld in refutation of the bipartite enthymematic 'Aunt Sally' of 7:7a and 7:13a.

The rhetorical 'Aunt Sally' is not a device that Paul is ready to set aside at this point in Romans; and chapter 7 is built around two, or rather one which involves two propositions: 'the law is sin' (7:7), and 'the good has been the death of me' (7:13). Each is presented in interrogative form and is promptly quashed by a μὴ γένοιτο. The argument which introduces the first is notable rather for being unenthymematic than otherwise, but in that which leads forward to and envelops the second, enthymematic factors play a notable role. The overall pattern of discourse we have before us is shown in diagram 9 (Roman numerals distinguish the segments into which it falls). The question Paul asks in segment II, τί οὖν ἐροῦμεν; ὁ νόμος ἁμαρτία; is one that he has led up to by a piece of analogy that must surely count as one of his strangest (segment I). Commentators seek to mitigate its strangeness in a variety of ways. That it is essentially a parable the point of which lies in a single correspondence is the most persuasive.[90] This being so, to pursue its appropriateness outside the area of that single correspondence is to miss the point. But in view of the nature of my present analysis, that is precisely what I shall do, exploring where it leads us if we try to follow through the logic of Paul's analogy in all its details.

The analogy is that of the woman the death of whose first husband leaves her free to marry a second. When it is applied to us,

Diagram 9

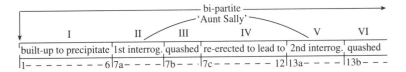

the first husband corresponds to the law, to which via the body of Christ (the sacrifice of Christ) we have died (although for the analogy to fit it should be the law that has become dead for us), leaving us free to take another husband, Christ, from which union fruit (offspring?) will accrue to God, not (as fruit accrued formerly) to sin, when in the flesh the law aroused sinful bodily passions (i.e. – presumably – within the bond of the marital union in which the law was our husband). Now we are released from the law, being dead to that which had held us captive (i.e. the 'husband' law who has no claim over us since we have died, although according to the analogy it should be he, the law, whose death has released us), so that we serve Christ (presumably as wife serves husband) not on the old terms of the law (as codified in writing) but on the new terms of the spirit (which by contrast – do we infer? – cannot be codified in writing).

If the law aroused sinful passions in us when we were married to it, the conclusion that the law is sin does indeed seem to follow by virtue of a deduction about as immediate and as unenthymematic as an inferential deduction can be.[91] But it is a false deduction (segment III). Sin is not to be seen as something to which the law gave rise as a result of anything which is part of its nature, but something which – being an independent inimical force – perverted it to its own ends, making it an instrument of death and not what it should have been, an instrument of life (segment IV). Hübner sets out the argument very clearly: 'Because the *nomos* is misused by *hamartia* as its operational base, no guilt can be attached to it. Rather it was, in its basic imperative, concerned with life: ἡ ἐντολὴ ἡ εἰς ζωήν. It is *hamartia* that was guilty of the perversion of the εἰς ζωήν into an εἰς θάνατον (7:10).'[92] He accepts the view that 7:8b–11 allude to Genesis 3, though he sees that it raises difficulties.[93] And many question it (e.g. Michel, Fitzmyer, Moo). Dunn, conversely, sees the passage as 'a consistent allusion to Adam and Gen 2–3', and points out:

> Both the emphasis on the role of the commandment . . . and the ἀπέκτεινεν are likewise derived from the Genesis account. God had attached the warning of death to the commandment. . . . The serpent/sin in using the command-ment to provoke disobedience to that command thus used it to bring the warning into operation and effect. Paul clearly wishes to press the paradox: it was the command of God which sin has used to bring death into its dominant role on the stage of human life (5:12).[94]

Hübner – with more thought for the difficulties he sees in the parallel – explains: 'Paul "reports" how sin (the Serpent) deviously used an "anti-promise" against the paradisal command which promised life and thus *at that time* misused the command of God as an operational base for its loathsome activity. In this way however Paul at the same time has *already in mind* how man through hearing the Law experiences confrontation with the sin that dwells within him.'[95]

Throughout Paul's argument there has been an uncomfortable inconsistency between death seen as the agent of release to new life (the unusual role in which Paul likes to cast it) and death as the destroyer of life (its conventional role). From figuring more as the former in the earlier part of this discourse, it here returns to figuring as the latter. Of ἀπέθανον in 7:10 Cranfield comments: 'It need scarcely be said that the death referred to here is, of course, some-thing entirely different from the good death of 6:2, 7, 8; 7:4'.[96] Dunn thinks Cranfield unwise to make so sharp a distinction: 'the death of Christ and with Christ (6:2–11; 7:6) is one outworking of that same sentence of death (Gen 2:16–17); to die one's own death is another (6:16, 21, 23; 7:5).'[97] But only death seen as a bad thing can generate the second focal proposition of the 'Aunt Sally' (segment v), for it does so by dint of the very clearly implied syllogism:

A MAJOR PREMISE
The law is good.
B MINOR PREMISE
The law was the cause of my death.
C CONCLUSION
The good was the cause of my death.

And to the enthymematic interrogative of segment v, τὸ οὖν

ἀγαθὸν ἐμοὶ ἐγένετο θάνατος; the response (segment VI) is also (ultimately) enthymematic. For it is very complex. This time Paul explains why his proposition cannot stand, not by recourse to arguments that exclude it *a priori* as in chapter 6, but by addressing its contents directly, even if initially he proceeds a little obliquely. He follows the μὴ γένοιτο with which he strikes down his enthymeme, with a 'but', as if he were saying: 'Not at all. On the contrary . . .', and perhaps he implies: 'The answer might seem to be "yes". BUT, because of x, y and z, it is not.' The mystery of how an apparently watertight syllogism is invalid lies in the purpose for which the death wrought by the law occurs. Sin has to be made to stand out for what it is. And it is to this all-important, indispensable end that the law not only shows sin up for what it is, but also acts as a stimulus for sin and hence becomes an instrument of death. As Ziesler puts it: 'The function of Law is to make sin perceptible and actual, not merely potential and implicit . . . On the one hand this is good, as it enables symptoms to appear and thus the underlying and hitherto undetected malaise to be dealt with. At the same time it is bad, because in the process sin palpably increases.'[98] But even though it brings death through the accentuation of sin, on the 'hand' that it is 'good and holy', it is also 'spiritual'. The γάρ which in v. 14 introduces Paul's enunciation of this further point seems best understood as casting it and what follows in the role rather of supplementation than explanation of what he has just said in v. 13; indeed it helps to link it with what he has already said in v. 12. But what follows is, in fact, a long and remarkable piece of argument, the place of which in the general picture offers scope for widely differing views. I think that the particular nature of my concern allows me to ignore the major sources of controversy, namely whether Paul is speaking here of himself or hypothetically, of the believer before or after conversion.

What I have to consider is how οἴδαμεν γὰρ ὅτι ὁ νόμος πνευματικός ἐστιν fits into his earlier argument. Is it an explication of things already said, or is it an essentially new point? I think it is the former. It seems to be something like the desire to establish such a perspective that leads Barrett to take the step of beginning his rendering of 7:14 with an extra clause: '*There is no question of the goodness of the law* (this clause, which is not in the Greek, is to be understood as the necessary antecedent of the "for" (γάρ) that follows), *for we know that it is spiritual*.'[99] It is our knowledge of the spirituality of the law, nevertheless, which now *becomes* the main point, and with that the main reason why we can say the law is good – even though it causes sin and death. And the basis for its 'spirituality' is best sought in a line of reasoning that draws very much on what is to come. First of all, the long sequence of observations that occupy vv. 14–25 – however we take them – unquestionably serves to show how only one thing unlocks the trap in which the law imprisons us, and that is Christ and our awareness of what he has done for us. It is that alone which wrests the law from the grip of the sin within us, making the death it inflicts on us a death which is a release from death into life. It is that alone which brings the goodness of the law to light. Secondly, the next chapter concentrates on the life of the Spirit which follows upon the believer's death-that-has-become-a-means-to-life, and the spirituality which is the essence of that life reflects back on the law which, through the believer's acceptance of Christ, became instrumental in generating it. The law is thus all part of the process by which God's spirit operates on its way to the fulfilment of its work in those who put their faith in Christ. What Paul says here integrates the upholding of the law which in 3:31 he insisted was his purpose. He has nowhere upheld it more than he does now in affirming it to be spiritual. The foundation of his thought, in 7:14 as in 3:31, can be seen as syllogistic.

A   MAJOR PREMISE
God's gift in Christ occasions the outpouring of the Spirit and makes possible the believer's life in the Spirit, which is the fulfilment of the Spirit's work in us.

B   MINOR PREMISE
The law, in being perverted by and accentuating our sin, and in bringing upon us the death due to it, also measures it and so reveals to us the extent of God's gift to us in Christ, placing that gift within the grasp of faith.

C   CONCLUSION
The law is essential to the realisation of the work of the Spirit.

The conclusion, however, should not be taken to mean that the law is a pre-condition of the work of the Spirit, but rather that it is a tool forged and preserved by the Spirit for the furtherance of its purposes. The law is spiritual (despite its being manipulated by sin) because it promotes the work of the Spirit, and because its ability to do this (and make essential capital out of sin's manipulative effrontery) results from its being itself a product of the Spirit, designed for a spiritual purpose.

I have attempted to condense into one syllogism what really needs breaking down into several. But I must set some limit to the degree to which I go into each matter that arises. Further analysis might, instead, be opportune here, if only because I think it would show that however much one worries at Paul's argument in this section of Romans there will always be something left unresolved, his reasons savouring of devious ingenuity and mystification. Nevertheless in Romans 7 – much more, I would say, than in Romans 6 – there is a sense that Paul is battling with contradictions he cannot resolve, and that, rather than *playing* with logic, as he sometimes seems to do, he is frantically trying to find in logic some way to ease or eliminate his problems.[100] All the same, logically, Romans 7 seems to function as a digression prompted by the 'let us sin/not sin' debate of Romans 6. We cannot say 'let us sin' – but we did indeed need to know sin (as through the law we come to know it) before we could know Christ as our saviour.

3.6   Linking the role and status of the enthymeme to how and when it arises within the ambit of Romans 5–7.

In the course of Romans 5–7 enthymematic argument has been seen to arise in contexts where it is associated with three features of special note:

(a)   contexts where metaphor is a factor for which due allowance has to be made in any attempt at logical analysis;

(b)   contexts where other argumentation is involved that may have to be seen as governed primarily by the dynamics of persuasion and effective communication, and not those of deductive logic;

(c)   contexts where the eschatological factor generates ambiguities which, though problematical from the logical point of view, are essential and unavoidable.

I will recall the principal cases of enthymematic argument being associated with each of these three features.

> *Contexts of type (a)*
> The most conspicuous instances are those of the Christian being a slave to righteousness, and of his being dead to sin. The possibility, however, has also to be considered that the entire topic of justification may constitute another.

Contexts of type (b)

It is Paul's elaboration of the grounds the Christian has for absolute confidence in his hope that provides the main instance of such a context. At the same time it must be noted that every 'knock-down' enthymeme, by virtue of its nature, establishes its context as being essentially of this type.

Contexts of type (c)

The theme which does most to bring into play the feature distinctive to (c) is the Christian's need to eschew the sin to which he is already dead. Nevertheless no aspect of Paul's thought is immune to the ambiguities generated by the eschatological factor; this is evidenced here by the relevance it obviously has for the peace of the justified.

Where enthymematic argument arises in contexts of type (a), or of type (b), the effect is to place in doubt whether the logical factor is being treated as of serious consequence, and not merely as a dress in which Paul chooses to present ideas which are essentially a-logical in their foundation.

Two issues in particular illustrate the kind of question that would precipitate such marginalisation of Paul's enthymematic logic in Romans 5–7.

1. *The confidence of Christian hope*
   If the Christian can be sure his hope will not let him down, is Paul really saying that this is because logic demonstrates that it cannot, rather than rhetorically presenting as certainty what the signs point to too impressively to be mere probability?

2. *Christian eschewal of sin*
   If it is unthinkable that the Christian should commit the sin which he still has to be enjoined to eschew, is Paul really saying that it is because he operates under the terms by which a slave is related to his lord, when, in fact, the real reason is that he is caught up in a time of tension between what is and what is to be?

Example 2, however, at the same time as illustrating the kind of questioning that marginalises the enthymematic, also introduces the feature on which context (c) depends, and which can do most to counter such marginalisation. It does so for the following reason.

To the extent that this or any of the contexts in which enthymematic argument arises are associated with the eschatological dimension, that dimension results not in arguments being passed off as logical which are not, but in propositions which do not appear wholly logical being the only appropriate argumentative mode. As a result Pauline argumentation displays a tendency, on the one hand, to seem to shift its ground as it proceeds, and, on the other, to become caught up in paradox.

A clear illustration of the former is the uneasy logic of the peace of the justified. The spirituality of sin-promoting law illustrates the latter, harking back to the zig-zagging arguments of Romans 3 and the paradox of Jewish conviction under, in spite of privileged custodianship of, God's commandments.

> 1. *The peace of the justified*
>   Man's being accounted righteous is an accomplished fact. It is a fact man's awareness of which, in terms of a perceived and productive harmony with God, has yet to mature. The illogicality (reflecting the ambiguities of the eschatological context) of deducing what-is-not-yet-accomplished from what-is prompts Paul to draw a conclusion whose ambit is experiential ('peace') from a premise whose ambit is forensic ('acquittal').
>
> 2. *The spirituality of sin-provoking law*
>   In the end time the law, as an instrument of the Spirit, annuls the law as an instrument hi-jacked by sin; the tension, however, between the 'already' and the 'not-yet' makes contradiction the only mode in which what needs to be said of it can be said, with inevitable loss of logical coherence.

Whether this loss is real or apparent becomes something of an ontological conundrum, the abstruse nature of which, however, resolves itself (for the practical purposes of Pauline criticism) into a simple but radical interrogative:

> Is the argumentative mode an appropriate mode for the material with which Paul is dealing? Why is Paul so attached to the argumentative mode, and to appealing to deductive logic, when its relevance is so questionable?

The rhetorical and epistolary practice of the time points to a major and formatively crucial motivational agency: of that there is no doubt. But I have explained in my opening chapter why I see it as desirable and expedient to locate the problem in a wider semiological perspective. In line, however, with the intention I expressed on p. 32 *supra*, I am postponing further discussion at that level until I have extended analysis to cover Romans 8. There the issues highlighted by the ways in which enthymemes arise in Romans 5–7 come to something of a head.

4

HOW ENTHYMEMATIC ARGUMENT STANDS IN ROMANS 8

4.1 The Christian's reprieve and the two 'laws'. The case for seeing 8:1 as an inference enthymematically drawn from 8:2. Different ways of unpacking ἄρα, and their bearing on the issue.

Romans 8 opens with a statement which is at once supported by a reason signposted as such by the usual γάρ. The resulting two-member unit is itself signposted as consequent on what has gone before by the less usual ἄρα (very unusual in being paired here not with οὖν but with νῦν). These facts in themselves are insufficient to warrant the expectation that the dependence in either direction is of a kind that involves the principle of deductive logic. If I say 'the pavements are not dry yet for it has only just stopped raining' I am probably just *naming* the cause of the situation. If I say 'the pavements cannot be dry yet as it has only just stopped raining', I am applying the principle of deductive logic. Paul here may be doing either of these things. And, given the nature of his theme, it is not easy to be sure which is involved.

In the case of the dependence signalled by γάρ, assessment will obviously begin from a consideration of the two members which the particle serves to link as they stand before us in the text. In the case of the dependence signalled by ἄρα, the question that at once arises is: what area of text is relevant? I believe the two cases here to be closely inter-related, but let us start from the former where the area of text to be focussed on is not in any doubt.[1]

> οὐδὲν ἄρα νῦν κατάκριμα τοῖς ἐν Χριστῷ Ἰησοῦ. ὁ γὰρ νόμος τοῦ πνεύματος τῆς ζωῆς ἐν Χριστῷ Ἰησοῦ ἠλευθέρωσέν σε ἀπὸ τοῦ νόμου τῆς ἁμαρτίας καὶ τοῦ θανάτου.

The textual witnesses disagree over the pronoun which follows ἠλευθέρωσεν. Alongside the generally accepted σέ are to be found also μέ and ἡμᾶς.[2] What is really needed – to match the form in which Paul phrases the consequential implications – is αὐτούς. For the σέ, μέ or ἡμᾶς to make strict logical sense a further premise has to be seen as implicit, which will specify that the referent of σέ, μέ or ἡμᾶς is among those 'in Christ Jesus' whose condemnation is affirmed to have been waived. This is, of course, a logical nicety, which it is entirely natural to over-ride. It prompts me, however, to implement the code letter 'r' as a designation for the comprehensive referent who for Paul is at one and the same time 'you', 'them' ('me' or 'us'). It will make for strictness of analysis as well as expedition as we now proceed to the more significant inferential complexities which confront us in the passage, notably: are we dealing here with a case of deductive inference?

It may look on the surface as if we are. Romans 8:1 presents itself as a conclusion drawn from the premise contained in 8:2.[3] The premise speaks of two laws: that 'of the spirit of life in Jesus Christ' (let us call this Law A); that 'of sin and death' (let us call it Law B).[4] The proposition is that Law A liberates 'r' from Law B. A key factor in the argument is incorporated in 8:1: the liberation of 'r' under Law A from the jurisdiction of Law B is contingent on 'r' being 'in Christ'. Three categories of 'r' are thus posited: 'an "r" under Law A', 'an "r" under Law B', and 'an "r" who is in Christ'. These then constitute the three terms of a syllogism which articulates itself thus:

A MAJOR PREMISE
   Any 'r' who is under Law A is an 'r' exempt from condemnation under Law B.
B MINOR PREMISE
   Any 'r' who is in Christ is an 'r' under Law A.
C CONCLUSION
   Any 'r' who is in Christ is an 'r' exempt from condemnation under Law B.

Compare this, however, with an example – from today's world – which must give us pause.

A tourist newly arrived from abroad has committed a parking offence. He is told by the magistrate: 'You will not be fined on this occasion because we have a policy in this country of not punishing foreign visitors for first parking offences.'

Do the magistrate's words constitute an instance of deductive inference? There is clearly a syllogistic pattern of reasoning behind what he says.

A MAJOR PREMISE
Foreign visitors are not punished for the first parking offence.
B MINOR PREMISE
The accused belongs to the category envisaged in the major premise.
C CONCLUSION
The accused should be let off his fine.

And yet surely the magistrate is merely explaining the cause of the defendant's acquittal. If mediate deductive inference can be said to be involved at all, it is of the special kind on which all legal judgements are based. A principle of law constitutes the major premise. The minor premise establishes the relevance of the principle to the case in point. What judgement this entails then constitutes the conclusion. Are not the limits within which deductive inference applies in this forensic context going to apply also on the forensic plane where Paul places himself by his choice of language? That the 'r' who is in Christ benefits from the exemption which Law A guarantees from condemnation under Law B may do no more than explain why 'r' is not condemned. ('The pavements are not dry yet, for it has only just stopped raining.') Or is Paul not merely explaining that, for the reasons he gives, 'r' is not condemned, but arguing – on the strength of these reasons – that condemnation is impossible? ('The pavements cannot be dry yet, as it has only just stopped raining.')

The magistrate says: 'You will not be fined because of our special policy concerning foreign visitors.' Paul says: 'You will not be condemned because you come under a law that exempts you from condemnation.' The magistrate does not have to persuade the foreign visitor that he has been acquitted, or that the grounds for acquittal are good ones. Paul speaks as if that were the position of 'r' – much of the time. He tends to treat the evidence that the believer has of his acquittal as if it were as solid as that which the accused in our illustration has in the fact that he receives no bill for his fine. It is, however, clear that Paul does appreciate that it is a solidity of which his hearer still has, if not to be convinced, at least constantly reminded. And in 8:1ff. Paul is focussing on the reasons why 'r' need not doubt that he is no longer condemned under Law B. If he is in Christ he comes under Law A. And Law A is the law of the Spirit, and it is in living under the law of the Spirit that he has complete solidity of proof that his bill is not being served on him. The premise in 8:2 does not provide merely the reason why the statement in 8:1 is true, but also something of an argumentative basis from which it follows as an inferential deduction. But since 'spirit', 'life', 'sin' and 'death' – partly owing to ambiguities of syntax, partly to inherent semantic flexibility – function more as cryptic indicators than explicit pointers, much is left implicit, and the deductively inferential dimension they are responsible for is enthymematic as well.

In rendering the phrases νόμος τοῦ πνεύματος τῆς ζωῆς ἐν Χριστῷ Ἰησοῦ and νόμος τῆς ἁμαρτίας καὶ τοῦ θανάτου I settled just now (following the RSV) for 'the law of the spirit of life in Christ Jesus' and 'the law of sin and death'. If such renderings can really be said to make any sense at all, they make a sense which reflects only one of a perplexing variety of different ways the Greek can be construed. I refer to the construal whereby 'law' is seen here as carrying the sense of 'principle': Law B = the principle whereby sin brings death; Law A = the principle whereby the Spirit, through Christ, brings life. Sanday and Headlam liken the usage to that of νόμος in 7:23: 'It is no longer a "code" but an authority producing regulated action such as would be produced by a code.'[5] Dodd, rather than 'authority', speaks of a 'principle or system'. 'As "sin's law" (the sinful principle or system) brought death, so the "law of the spirit brings life".' 'It is not,' Dodd affirms categorically, 'the Mosaic Law that is in view.'[6] But it is particularly difficult to sustain that Law B is not the Mosaic Law. 'Paul has already linked the law, that is, the Torah, too closely with sin and death to allow readily of any other conclusion (5:12–14, 20; 7:5, 9–11, 13, 23–4).' This is Dunn's attitude,[7] and it leads him to the observation that 'It would throw the thought into some confusion to understand the first νόμος differently.'[8] He feels there are good grounds for supposing the explanation to be along these lines: 'Paul is able to think of the law in two different ways: the law caught in the nexus of sin and death, where it is met only by σάρξ, is the law as γράμμα, caught in the old epoch, abused and destructive . . .; but the law rightly understood, and responded to ἐν πνεύματι οὐ γράμματι is pleasing to God (2:29). The two-fold law of v. 2 therefore simply restates the two-sidedness of the law expounded in 7:7–25.'[9] Two passages from Hübner take account of further important factors:

> The expression 'law of the spirit' most likely refers back to 7:14: 'the law is spiritual, πνευματικός'. In 7:14, however, it is clearly the Torah which is meant. . . . The point that the Torah is by nature pneumatic is however made within the context of a discussion of its death-'effect' (7:13).[10]

> 8:2 can . . . be understood as follows: those *for whom* the *nomos* is the law of the spirit, i.e. those who exist in the spirit which is the giver of life . . . are, when they look at the Law, freed from the perverted Law, that is from the compulsion to misuse the Law as the 'Law of works' under the dominion of *hamartia* and thus from the fate of being abandoned to death.[11]

If such arguments deserve credence – and a considerable controversy has now arisen as to whether they do or not – the extent to which they involve reading 8:2 in the light of the preceding chapter is very striking, and they would seem to be uncovering very effectively, and with considerable precision as to verse and phrase, what areas of Paul's text are envisaged by the ἄρα of 8:1.[12]

I prefer first to take the question of how precisely 'sin' and 'death' are involved in Law B so as to make it a law under which man stands condemned. Then, secondly, we will consider how 'Spirit' and 'life' are involved in the liberating power which Law A exercises wherever 'r' is in Christ.

So long as νόμος τῆς ἁμαρτίας καὶ τοῦ θανάτου is taken as the 'principle' that the punishment for sin is death, no more basic constituents are inherent than the elementary pair seen in diagram 10. But once 'law' here is identified with Torah, 'law' and 'sin' acquire an intimacy of connection which leads to a wholly new set of problems. From a 'law' the terms of which are that 'sin leads to death', we pass to a law which leads to death because it is a law 'of sin'. This raises at least three thorny issues. Is it a law 'of sin' because under it 'r' stands no chance of being other than convicted? Is it a law 'of sin' because it actually makes 'r' sin to an extent and in ways he would not have done in its absence? Is it 'of sin' in being a tool of sin, hi-jacked by sin and deflected from its intended purpose? Much less than an unqualified 'yes' to all three would suffice to ensure such a law was 'of death' in that it was 'of sin'. But a 'yes' to

Diagram 10

```
 ┌─ cause ──────── 1. 'r' sins
─┤
 └─ HEAD ──────── 2. 'r' dies
```

Diagram 11

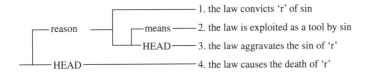

```
                        ┌────────────── 1. the law convicts 'r' of sin
 ┌─ reason ──┤   ┌─ means ──── 2. the law is exploited as a tool by sin
 │           └── HEAD ──── 3. the law aggravates the sin of 'r'
─┤
 └─ HEAD ──────────────── 4. the law causes the death of 'r'
```

one does not exclude a 'yes' to any of the others, and in the case of a 'yes' to all three, the pattern of underlying affirmations is complex (see diagram 11). It is not necessary that 1 and 3 should both apply. 2 does not have to be the means by which 3 becomes effective. However, if of all the anticipations of Romans 8:2 that appear latent in Romans 7 only that in 7:5 were in fact posited, then the implications of ὁ νόμος τῆς ἁμαρτίας καὶ τοῦ θανάτου would already be such as to involve the whole complement of statements. An indication that they may well all be involved is perhaps provided by the fact that Paul at once turns explicitly in 8:3 to the impotence the law owes to its having been hi-jacked by σάρξ as a way of leading into his exposition of how through Christ this impotence has been dealt with. The enrichments conferred by the anticipations of 8:2 in 7 upon the liberation concept (via notions of 'exemption', in 7:6, or 'rescue', in 7:24–5) fit the idea of 'r' as a victim of both craft and pressure.[13] These are points we may need to have in mind in proceeding now to consideration of how 'spirit' and 'life' figure in the power of deliverance which Law A stands for and is distinguished by.

As against the 'principle' that 'r' dies because of sin, Law A would seem to affirm the 'principle' that 'r' lives because of the Spirit, the two notions involved being shown in diagram 12. But unlike the principle 'sin brings death', 'the Spirit brings life' is a derived principle, dependent on the principle that what brings liberation from sin and consequent death brings life. It comes complete with that as its content (diagram 13). A law the terms of which are that 'the Spirit brings life' is of necessity the law 'of' that Spirit, in the sense of the law being the law which is activated by it. ὁ νόμος τοῦ πνεύματος τῆς ζωῆς does not confront us with a choice of break-

Diagram 12

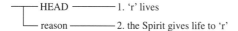

```
┬─ HEAD ──────── 1. 'r' lives
└─ reason ─────── 2. the Spirit gives life to 'r'
```

Diagram 13

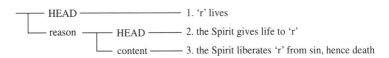

```
┬─ HEAD ──────────────── 1. 'r' lives
└─ reason ──┬─ HEAD ─────── 2. the Spirit gives life to 'r'
            └─ content ────── 3. the Spirit liberates 'r' from sin, hence death
```

Diagram 14

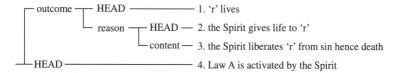

```
┌─ outcome ─┬─ HEAD ──────── 1. 'r' lives
│           └─ reason ─┬─ HEAD ── 2. the Spirit gives life to 'r'
│                      └─ content── 3. the Spirit liberates 'r' from sin hence death
└─ HEAD ──────────────── 4. Law A is activated by the Spirit
```

down options, and is accounted for without difficulty in terms of those statements already listed (diagram 14). Difficulty arises with the ἐν Χριστῷ Ἰησοῦ which follow the ζωῆς. Here we are indeed confronted with conflicting explications – at least the following four, and each excludes the others. The first three come of taking the phrase with 'life of the Spirit', the fourth with 'liberates'.

A   The life the Spirit gives is a life in Christ.
B   The life of the Spirit is given to those who are in Christ.
C   The gift of life in the Spirit originates in Christ.
D   The liberation the Spirit actuates is actuated in Christ.

The chosen explication has then to be slotted into its proper niche in diagram 14. *A–C* would thus all figure as attaching themselves to member 2: *A* as amplification of 'life'; *B* as amplification of 'gives'; *C* as amplification of the whole proposition. *D* attaches itself to member 3 as amplification of 'liberates'. They do not interfere with the functioning of the other members, and they do not affect the issue of whether Law A is 'Torah' or not. That this is in fact how Paul is understanding it we may hesitate to query in view of the anticipations in 7:6 and 7:14, though neither can be said to remove all room for uncertainty. But the significance of these, along with all the anticipations we have been considering, is affected by the whole debate on whether Romans 7 is the right place to be looking for light on the implications of the Law A/Law B dichotomy of Romans 8:2.

Can we, in fact, be pursuing a right approach to Paul's argument if we find ourselves elucidating the material signposted as explanatory of 8:1 by the γάρ of 8:2 via recourse to material of which 8:1 seems itself to be signposted as the outcome by its own ἄρα νῦν?[14] Perhaps ἄρα νῦν is intended to steer our thoughts back to a much wider area of Paul's discourse, and to point to it not so much as a basis for 8:1 and the conclusion contained in it as for 8:1 + 8:2 – for the drawing, that is, of the conclusion in 8:1 from the premise of 8:2 (a basis not for the conclusion but for the drawing of the conclusion).[15] The ἄρα νῦν would then add up to this: 'so you can see now why I say that because of the xyz of 8:2, the abc of 8:1 can be confidently affirmed'. It is necessary to posit some assumptions about the overall drift of Paul's argument to see how this might work out. Let us posit it to be as follows. The gospel is a message for all mankind, a message of hope endorsed by the present experience enjoyed by those who receive it of the Spirit working in their lives. The argument of Romans 1–4 is oriented primarily towards the proposition that the gospel is for all. Romans 5–8 probe the foundation of the believer's hope in his experience of the Spirit. However, at first, the argument for hope draws its strength from the believer's being accorded gratis the status of righteousness before God, and the apparent devaluation of the law and of ethical discipline that this may seem to entail occasions the pattern taken by the discussion in both Romans 6 and Romans 7. But hints have been dropped of what the long-term focus of the argument will be, and that is where it in fact centres with the opening of Romans 8. It could be nothing less than this whole expansive sweep of discourse that ἄρα νῦν should be seen as encompassing.[16] I cannot discuss how far it is correct to posit Paul's overall argument thus. Above all I cannot enter into the differences which arise according to whether Romans 1–8 are or are not seen as apprehensible without including Romans 9–11. It is a perspective, however, that sets in relief a singularity which (independent of all speculation) marks the opening of Romans 8. In presenting man's situation in terms of two νόμοι set over against each other as they are in 8:2, Paul makes an arresting use of the term νόμος, and it is one that invites reasoned thought. He then leaves this dual application completely without any explicit follow-up.

Those who would understand both νόμοι as Torah do so by seeing Laws A and B in the sense of '"the Law" *as* A' and '"the Law" *as* B'.[17] What Paul intended, however, is not only not made clearer by what follows, it is confused by a shift of emphasis to the new life in the Spirit, which, through the work of Christ, becomes possible for 'r', and the way the law figures in it. If, in this new life, the just demands of the law, met in their penal aspect by Christ on behalf of 'r', now no longer irretrievably hi-jacked by sin, become demands which in their prescriptive aspect can be met by 'r', are we thus confronted with ' "the Law" as B' having become ' "the Law" as A'? It is possible.[18] Dunn, however, thinks it best to see Paul as having found that his duplication of the law had got him into difficulties:

> The impression that Paul has caught himself in contra-diction is hard to shake off . . . It is the exhilarating sense of being liberated which marks out v. 2 so clearly . . . The 'Spirit', drawn back into the argument here, he clearly experienced as a power whose transforming effects marked his own ministry in no uncertain manner . . . in some distinction from the law . . . How then could he link the law with the Spirit and describe it as that very same liberating power?[19]

The way the contrast drawn so dramatically in 8:2 between the two laws is lost to view in favour of that between the life of the Spirit and the life of the flesh suggests strongly that he saw that he could not. If so, it would demonstrate very clearly that Paul was using the two-law dichotomy as an argumentative ploy rather than as a statement of explanatory fact. The evolution of the passage reveals the explanatory affirmation of 8:2 for what it is: an argument appealing to the hearer to recognise (a) that his own experience testifies to the truth of what is being said, and (b) that this all-decisive experience is nothing if not a pattern of behaviour. It could be summed up thus:

> The life 'r' lives in the Spirit, and in which he experiences and displays his capacity to overcome sin, shows him to have victory over death.

A second syllogism behind Paul's argument would be needed in integration of the one I drafted to begin with, which had 'r' being under Law A as its middle term and the 'r' who is in Christ as the subject of its conclusion. That failed, however, to show the role in the argument performed by the interplay of the factors 'life', 'death', 'sin' and 'Spirit'. The factors that really constitute the operative elements in the argument require that we envisage a further syllogism in which 'sin' is the middle term and the 'r' who lives in the Spirit is the subject of the conclusion.

A   MAJOR PREMISE
    The 'r' who enjoys freedom from the power of sin enjoys exemption from condemnation to death.
B   MINOR PREMISE
    The 'r' who lives in the Spirit enjoys freedom from the power of sin.
C   CONCLUSION
    The 'r' who lives in the Spirit enjoys exemption from condemnation to death.[20]

Paul's move away from two laws to two modes of life suggests that his concern in talking of two laws was not just to explain the basis of the freedom from condemnation enjoyed by the 'r' who is in Christ, but to draw the attention of every such 'r' to the proof of this fact that he has in his experience of the Spirit. This not only invests Paul's initial reasoning in 8:1–2 with the character of deductive inference, but does so at the cost of accounting it highly dependent on unstated implications regarding the key factors in the logic. For this reason I see it as presenting the characteristics of enthymematic argument. The resultant feeling of being on unstable ground which the interpreter is left with does not, however, seem to work against the impact of Paul's discourse, but rather to enhance the surge of his thinking whereby a logic utilising terms and concepts from his earlier discourse is swept aside by his concern with the logic of the life of the Spirit. Through the way he continues from 8:3 onwards, this is emphatically established as the subject he wishes the reader to focus upon.

4.2   Mortality, spirituality and filial inheritance. 8:9–17 and the regrounding of the argumentative dynamic through the enthymematic implications of Christian sonship.

Between 8:3 and 8:17 the word πνεῦμα occurs sixteen times. Its referent, however, is neither consistently clear nor constant, and the section is not without its logical complexities.

Verse 8:10 presents us with a conditional proposition in which a double outcome is affirmed to be attendant on the fulfilment of the

Diagram 15

εἰ δὲ Χριστὸς ἐν ὑμῖν $\left\{\begin{array}{l}\text{(Outcome 1) } τὸ ~ μὲν ~ σῶμα ~ νεκρὸν ~ διὰ ~ ἁμαρτίαν \\ \text{(Outcome 2) } τὸ ~ δὲ ~ πνεῦμα ~ ζωὴ ~ διὰ ~ δικαιοσύνην\end{array}\right.$

condition (see diagram 15). The condition on which either outcome depends is that Christ should be in you. Each outcome, however, adds further information concerning the agencies involved in bringing it about. Having rendered Outcome 1 as 'your bodies are dead because of sin', the RSV – by going on to render Outcome 2 as 'your spirits are alive because of righteousness' – implies the following syllogistic substructure:

A   MAJOR PREMISE
   The spirits of those in whom the righteous demands of the law meet with fulfilment are alive.
B   MINOR PREMISE
   The presence of Christ in you makes you individuals in whom the righteous demands of the law are fulfilled.
C   CONCLUSION
   Your spirits are alive.

English usage, however, in the matter of the possessive adjective and of number has forced the Greek wording out of its original ambiguity, and the result is open to question from various angles. It is widely felt that πνεῦμα in 8:10 should be understood as 'the Holy Spirit'.[21]

The principle that our life according to the Spirit is one with our being in Christ, and consists in the fulfilment in us of the just demands of the law which his coming has made effective, is the core of the doctrine appealed to by Paul in all he says from 8:1 as far as 8:8.[22] In 8:9 we encounter something of a switch from talk of our being in Christ to talk of Christ being in us, and of our being in the Spirit entailing the Spirit being in us.

If 'The Spirit gives life to you' is taken as the import of Outcome 2, the pattern of reasoning becomes as in diagram 16. The problem is further compounded by the absence of finite verbs in the Greek; hence the scrupulous translate Paul's formulation of Outcome 2 as 'Because of righteousness the Spirit is life' (Ziesler: 'life-giving'), which affects the clarity of the reasoning – emphasis falling on the life-giving power of the Spirit, the implications for the

Diagram 16

Condition	Outcome

Condition

Outcome

Christ is in you

{
1. through sin your bodies are dead

2. through righteousness the Spirit gives you life

one who is in and indwelt by Christ being left implicit. The possibility is thus not excluded that the Spirit gives life to the body which otherwise, because of sin, would be dead. Dunn, in fact, makes a point of clarifying that it is the body of sin, not that indwelt by the Spirit, whose mortality is irretrievable.[23] And thus, in the matter of Outcome 1 as well as 2 the RSV translation would have to be reckoned misconceived, for it is not only the fate of the body of sin that is relevant for those who are indwelt by the Spirit: more relevant looms the fate of the body to which the Spirit has power to give life. Dunn does not like the interpretation that sees the allusion here as being to the deadness *to* sin of those who are in Christ (who have died with him in baptism) – which is probably the most widely favoured option today, and indeed the one favoured by Ziesler, albeit without confidence, since he believes concern for rhetorical symmetry may have led Paul here into virtual unintelligibility.[24]

Within the scope of such uncertainties lie both complexity of syllogistic implication and its elimination.[25] A clear and straightforward syllogistic foundation is perceptible, on the other hand, behind the interpretation which is now generally discredited altogether. 'What is most unlikely,' says Ziesler (for example), 'is that here . . . Paul is talking about two parts of the human being, one of which (body) is dead because it is sinful, and the other of which (spirit) is alive because it is righteous.'[26] If he were, the syllogism implied would be:

A MAJOR PREMISE
The life of your body is a life of sin.
B MINOR PREMISE
The presence of Christ in you puts an end to the life of sin.
C CONCLUSION
Christ being in you, your body (the bodily part of you) is effectively dead.

This would be to take the σῶμα of 8:10 as the equivalent of σάρξ in 8:3–9. We may indeed have to accept that this is not to understand Paul here correctly.[27] In fact, if we did so understand him here, then 8:11 would seem decidedly inopportune with its references to life being restored to the mortal body.[28] However, it is then strange to see σῶμα seeming to be equated with σάρξ a moment later, in 8:13,[29] where it provides the very logic on which Paul bases the next stage of his argument, or rather would be seen to base it according to a plausible construal of 8:13 and what follows it, the construal which identifies the pattern of development thus:

The logical basis
The deeds of the body kill (σάρξ is a killer). By killing the deeds of the body, you kill the killer, and so live (your life is made secure).

The next stage
Your life in the Spirit depends on your killing the killer. You can kill your killer because you are led by the Spirit. You can do it because of a quite particular ingredient in the life of the Spirit. You can do it because, living in the Spirit and being led by it, you share as brothers of Christ in his inheritance.

In such reasoning could be said to reside the connection between 8:13b and 8:14 to which the γάρ of 8:14 has the office of pointing: εἰ δὲ πνεύματι τὰς πράξεις τοῦ σώματος θανατοῦτε, ζήσεσθε. ὅσοι γὰρ πνεύματι θεοῦ ἄγονται, οὗτοι υἱοὶ θεοῦ εἰσιν. If its object is not identified along these lines it will figure as a rather loose link serving merely as a sign that Paul is moving on to the next topic: divine sonship as the central factor in life according to the Spirit. Which it is Michel sees as an open question. The enigma resides in 8:14. Picking up his particular translation of that verse,[30] Michel articulates the analytical alternative: (a) is Paul's emphasis merely on the renunciation of the flesh as significant evidence of our being Spirit-propelled ('ein wichtiges Zeichen des "Getriebenwerdens durch den Geist"'), or (b) is his point not rather that our new obedience, being no less than God's spirit in operation, is part of the gift of sonship?[31] The second option sees in Paul's argument a sudden dramatic taking-off, involving enthymematic implications which it is not extravagant to see as amounting to the following:

A MAJOR PREMISE
Co-heirs of Christ share in his victory.

B   MINOR PREMISE
As sons of God you are co-heirs with Christ.
C   CONCLUSION
You share in Christ's victory (and this is what you have
evidence of in your power to kill the deeds of the body).

The supplied major premise constitutes a huge implicit component
that draws on the credit of much that Paul has yet to say. However,
it also depends on three arguments which he makes explicit at once.
The spirit which is in you is one of sonship. Where there is sonship
there is expectation of inheritance. Where the sonship is sonship of
God, the inheritance of which there is expectation is that of Christ.[32]

It is not extravagant to see inheritance on these terms as implying
inheritance of the fruits of Christ's victory. Indeed it is impossible to
see it as implying less. It is not extravagant, however, to go even
further. Our being sons of God, our being co-heirs of Christ in his
victory, are all fruits of the fact that God in his love for us is ready to
bestow upon us 'all things'. This involves seeing Paul's argument as
immediately stretching out from 8:14 right the way forward to 8:32.

From the masterful surge of Paul's thought drawing all argument
towards a total absorption with the work of the Spirit in us, we are
now confronted with a kind of re-grounding of cogency due to a
great widening out of Paul's conceptual horizon, the direction of
which will not be fully apprehensible until with 8:28 he begins to
home in on the final direction his argument is going to take. Let me
use two branching diagrams to illustrate this expansion of horizon
whereby sonship can be counted a reason why he who lives in the
Spirit can kill the deeds of the body (see diagrams 17 and 18). These
two diagrams display the range of what man's openness to the
gospel means for him in sequences of unfolding units of content.
Each diagram starts from what is the basis of all that is said in
Romans 8: the Spirit as the agent of God's love in the life of the
man who, through openness to the gospel, enters into fruition of the
benefits of Christ's sacrifice. What this means in terms of how the
beneficiary is to see himself is presented in diagram 17, unit a. This
diagram then displays, as units b, c, d and e, that present effect of
God's love which is man's becoming as a son who shares in Christ's
inheritance. Thus far it corresponds to what is made explicit in
8:15–17. Units f, g, h, i and j then cover what entry into that
inheritance means for him.[33] Units f and h correspond to factors
made explicit; g, i and j represent that which led me earlier, as my

Diagram 17

Diagram 18

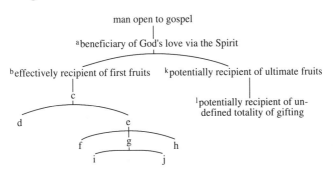

first observation concerning the syllogism drafted, to speak of a
'huge implicit component'. It is the victory aspect of Christ's work,
on which the syllogism depends for its major premise. The entry into
play of this factor – if we opt for the inferential construal of γάρ in
8:15 – brings about the first stage in the expansion of horizon which
diagrams 17–18 are designed to illustrate. Diagram 18 illustrates the
second stage. It restates all contained in diagram 17 and adds to it.
The units of content involving sonship and entry into the inheritance of Christ and his victory I here indicate merely by their code
letters. In the perspective of this second stage of horizon expansion
they lose their determining role in the argument to become factors
indicative of what really plays the determining role: that abundance
of God's love which is his readiness to give us all things. Units k and

I, therefore, display the 'great widening out of Paul's horizon' – as I have put it – and the content this will entail when we reach 8:32. The inheritance we share with Christ is not really understood until it is understood in these terms. And when it *is* understood in these terms, the detail of argumentative substance which is itemized in diagram 17 ceases to count as it did at the stage in the argument there represented. This is what diagram 18 is designed to bring out.

What in fact *is* thus brought out is of such sublime importance that it leaves the sonship factor fulfilling a role which entails something like role reversal:

> *It is not because you are his sons that God loves and empowers you. It is because God loves you that you are as sons to him. It is not because the Spirit makes you sons that you can kill the killer 'body'. It is because God in his love for you has endowed you via the Spirit with power to kill the forces that threaten to make you slaves. You are thus enabled instead to become as sons to him.*

If this seems an interpretation difficult to square with the way our sonship figures in Galatians (where several propositions match exactly with those found here), let me appeal to Cranfield's insistence on what differentiates the two passages, and on the undesirability of interpreting what Paul says here in the light of what he says there.[35] Cranfield is in fact led to see sonship as above all the image of our expectation of sharing in the glory of God's own life.[36] His conclusions thus provide endorsement for the perspective I have been illustrating. So I will sum up by offering the following assessment of how it affects the efficacy of Paul's discourse at this point.

It is as if Paul builds an argument on an image (that of sonship) which, in the compulsion that drives him to penetrate deeper into the real causes of what his image is introduced to explain, leads to its function being superseded even as he is still making use of it. His direction is not predictable.[37] The feeling is of greater thoughts being imminent which will make those just entertained seem makeshift by comparison. What these greater thoughts are is being strongly hinted at, however, and the talk of 'sharing in God's glory' cannot but precipitate a redimensioning of lesser notions, one in which hope is reaffirmed as the hall-mark of the life of the spirit, in line with 5:2–5, where both were already explicitly related to God's love.[38]

4.3   From sonship and invincibility to totality of gifting. The enthymemes of 8:31–2: their finality and its redimensioning.

The argument which will ultimately count as the fundamental guarantee of the hope the gospel proclaims, that of the embrace of God's love which enfolds us, has to be seen against the backdrop of a present which is not an experience of the Spirit working in us untroubled by the conditions of our earthly life, either external or internal. We enter into the inheritance of God's son via sufferings comparable to his.[39] The power of the Spirit displayed in this aspect of our experience is manifested in our patience when confronted with adversity, our capacity to withstand the onslaught of evil forces, to persevere in spite of weakness and not to be overcome by incidental failure. This is a part of our inheritance as sons. I return to diagram 18 and augment it by units of content which cover this (see diagram 19). However, the notion that hope is the channel via which the Spirit gives us strength has led Paul to emphasise anew its centrality in our experience of salvation, not now to pursue its certainty, but rather the fact that hope, however certain, is always expectation and not possession.[40] And having come round with yet another γάρ to affirming in 8:24 τῇ γὰρ ἐλπίδι ἐσώθημεν, he comments: ἐλπὶς δὲ βλεπομένη οὐκ ἔστιν ἐλπίς.[41] And that it is in our waiting as such that we learn our invincibility as God's loved ones paves the way for an enthymeme that leads him right to the core of his present argument: εἰ ὁ θεὸς ὑπὲρ ἡμῶν τίς καθ' ἡμῶν.

Verse 8:31 is one of two instances in Romans 1–8 where the rhetorical question τί οὖν ἐροῦμεν is not engaged for the purposes of setting up an Aunt Sally. The 'no one' which the 'truly reverent defiance' of the ensuing interrogative demands as its answer is the reverse of a demolitory μὴ γένοιτο, constituting instead emphatic endorsement of the affirmation disguised under the rhetoric.[42] The interrogative 'Who can be against us?' which oratory has here brought forth stands simply for 'no one can prevail against us'. Moreover, the condition 'if God be for us', whence the interrogative stems, stands in relation to it as the minor premise of an implied syllogism the unstated major premise of which would be 'no one can prevail against God'. The whole unit of discourse offers a classic instance of the enthymematic factor serving oratory not argumentation.[43] But this does not account for any but the most superficial level of the involvement of the enthymematic factor at this argumentative juncture. The background to what is being thus

Diagram 19

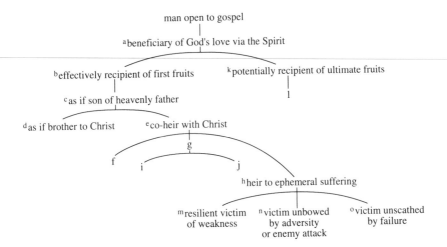

rhetorically projected is where the substance lies, and if the point is made with a defiance which is 'truly reverent' it is because of the sublimity of the argumentative foundation with which the co-text extensively undergirds it.[44]

As is axiomatic where the τί οὖν ἐροῦμεν formula is involved, there is referral back to the abc in view of which we ask 'shall we say xyz?'[45] But since here the answer duly returned is positive in substance, what matters is not so much how abc come to prompt the question as how they authorise the endorsement of xyz, and how they relate to (anticipate or interact with) any subsequent arguments by which the endorsement is further affected. It is a relationship the pattern of which in the present instance is susceptible to a variety of possible construals. It will be well if we take note of three.

1. What the οὖν points towards authorises our saying that God is for us, and makes this a certainty from which we now can draw the conclusion that nothing can threaten us.

2. The conclusion that nothing can threaten us is already clearly to be inferred along with the premise that God is for us from what the οὖν points to, and is not a new step in the argument.

3. The τί οὖν ἐροῦμεν is here a serious question despite its rhetorical pedigree. It really is asking whether, in view of what the οὖν points to, we can indeed affirm that God

being for us nothing can threaten us, or whether there is more to be said.

Whichever is the case a further reason is at once given: another affirmation disguised as a question. 'He who did not spare his son for our sake can deny us nothing.' Whether this new argument will figure as amplificatory or as argumentatively determinative is bound up with which of the above options we have settled for. All these issues will, of course, be radically affected by what precisely we see the οὖν of the τί οὖν ἐροῦμεν as looking back to.[46]

Here, at least, there is no difficulty in connecting it with what has immediately preceded it. Indeed, once the referent of the οὕς in 8:30 is taken as inclusive of the ἡμῶν of 8:31, then the sequence of God's acts which 8:30 presents as following unfailingly upon the initial act of our election gives us so comprehensive a reason for saying 'God is for us' as virtually to preclude supplementation. The fact that this sequence is itself an elaboration of the affirmation in 8:29, that God transforms those whom he has chosen into the likeness of Christ, means that the whole unit which comprises 8:28–30 assumes that air of definitive statement beyond which no more can be said which is about to establish itself as the hall-mark of the increasingly defiant reverence pervading the remainder of Romans 8.[47] However, it needs to be noted that 8:28–30 impinge at a point in the chapter where some antidote is needed to the concentration on the difficulties of our present position that has characterised the foregoing section since 8:18, and the attention that section has given to the negative dimension of hope.[48] So that the τί οὖν ἐροῦμεν of 8:31 includes the idea 'does what I have been saying about election, sanctification and glorification suffice to counterbalance what I was previously saying about the extent to which suffering and as yet unfulfilled expectation must characterise our present situation?'. There is a sense in which verses 8:29–30 are being quite specifically pointed to as grounds for saying that God is for us, whilst at the same time 'nothing can threaten us' is being said with quite specific reference to such threats as the unfulfilled dimension of our hope may well lead us to fear. Because of the abc of 8:29–30 we can certainly say 'God is for us'; and in the precision with which the verses explicate in just what way God's being for us articulates itself lies the power of abc as an argument for our invincibility in the face of present difficulties. So it is premise and conclusion together, rather than premise alone, that point to 8:28–30 as their justification.[49] That is to say option 2 above is to be favoured over option 1.

It is in the uncertainty over which option is to be understood as constituting the basis of Paul's argument that the enthymematic factor can here be said to reside. If the interpretation I have just been suggesting is correct, the 'therefore' in the proposition 'we can therefore say "God being for us none can prevail against us"' can be seen as grounded in the following syllogistic pattern of reasoning:

A MAJOR PREMISE
No enemy is to be feared by those to whom God has shown his favour by calling them to ultimate glory.

B MINOR PREMISE
God has shown his favour to us by calling us to ultimate glory.

C CONCLUSION
No enemy (and so neither weakness nor suffering) is to be feared by us.

But this does not dispose of option 3.

The substance of what Paul is asking in 8:31 may be this. 'Do you still wonder, in spite of the abc of 8:29–30, whether we can say that nothing can threaten us? You shouldn't, but if you do, then consider this.' And with that he introduces a totally new argument. 'If God gave his son for us it is clear that he will deny us nothing.'[50] Much more than the insignificance of our present misfortunes is thus guaranteed, so that the point is clearly carried. But occurring in such a way that a great deal more than that issue alone comes into view, its resolution has rather the effect of making it seem more natural and correct to see 8:32 not so much as capping at a stroke all prior argument behind 8:31, as laying the basis for a quite new line of reasoning. From argument founded on the unpacking of the substance of God's favour towards his elect, attention shifts to the meaning and principle behind it. But these lead us away from its function as guarantee and source of assurance to its absolute value as an object of superlative and disinterested wonder.

I have used the phrase 'deny us nothing' to render τὰ πάντα ἡμῖν χαρίσεται in order to delay having to face the difficulty of what is meant by πάντα and by χαρίσεται. If χαρίσεται means 'bestow', then is the πάντα covered by the actions of God listed in 8:29–30? Or is it something the totality of which Paul has yet to do all he can to convey?[51] The question also arises whether χαρίσεται should be understood as 'forgive'.[52] It is certainly notable that it leads on immediately to the question of whether the elect of God are accused.

This also makes one think that the talk of God being 'for us' might not be devoid of regard for the fact that he has good reason to be 'against us' as sinners. Clearly among the gifts God is here envisaged as bestowing upon us is forgiveness.[53] However, that the content of the 'all' that God will bestow on us is more than forgiveness and that it needs to be expressed in terms that go beyond all earlier ones (by dint of supplementation or amplification, or by being of a breadth which includes but transcends them) is amply clear in the build-up of rhetorical questions which now dominates the pattern of Paul's argument.[54] Occupying the span of text from 8:33–5, these culminate, via an exemplary spelling-out in 8:37 of the positive counterpart of the negative answer each anticipates, in the grand statement of conviction of 8:38. This, invested by its γάρ with the air of a premise to which 8:37 relates as conclusion, in effect just sets the seal upon the certainties implicitly enumerated in the questions comprising the build-up.

4.4 Security in the love of God. Paul's assurance (8:38) and its foundation in enthymeme and truism.

We see once again the flexibility of γάρ, ranging as it does from being no more than a meaningless link word, through being a marker of explanatory accessories, to being a bearer of hidden inferences and a witness to hidden argument. In Romans 8:38 it performs the office of introducing the loftiest of all Paul's pronouncements. Coupled with the πέπεισμαι that initiates the pronouncement, it has the effect of making Paul seem to say, 'if I am able to speak as I have done, this stems from the firmness of my conviction that nothing in the universe or beyond it can ever detach us from God's love for us'. It is in the total certainty of his unalienable love that we finally perceive the fullness of God's gift; but by the time Paul gives it this final emphasis it is already clear. Indeed, the διὰ τοῦ ἀγαπήσαντος already integrated into the plain speaking of 8:37 renders the sequel essentially epexegetical.[55] And its basis has been laid in the material to which that plain speaking relates, notably the chain of rhetorical questions in 8:33–5, which develop the train of thought out of which they arise (and which in 8:31 had first set the interrogative pattern in motion).

The form each takes is that of envisaging some risk the exclusion of which is so certain as to make denial superfluous if not improper. In 8:33–4 the reference is to the risk of our being accused and

condemned. It can be seen to relate thus to the position reached by
the argument at that stage. Our election by God to glory excludes
the possibility of our being accused and successfully condemned by
anyone. God does not accuse us because it is he who is responsible
for the justification via which his elect are glorified. Nor can condemnation of us possibly emanate from Christ, who, having died
and been raised for our sake, pleads on our behalf at God's right
hand. Verse 8:35 refers to the possibility of those responsible for
inflicting hardships or persecutions on us cutting us off from
Christ's love. But it is his love through which we overcome hardship
or persecution. It enables us to meet them in the knowledge that
glory awaits us beyond.[56] Whether this is in fact Paul's reasoning
here is not entirely clear.[57] If it is, then reiteration of the argument
behind 8:31 can still be seen as the essence of his approach, with 8:32
as the inferential deduction that certifies glory to be indeed our
destiny. That, in any case, is the deduction to which Paul's 'conviction' of 8:38 has to be traced back. But his 'conviction' gives a
content to the 'all', which – developed and essentially clarified in the
course of 8:33–7 – is uniquely foregrounded as Paul rhapsodises in
8:38–9 on the object of his persuasion. The affirmation of the
conviction is – for good measure – accompanied by further references to factors that might seem to, but in fact are powerless to,
interfere with it. It is a list designed primarily so that every possible
source of interference is excluded in terms of absolute comprehen-
siveness.

In argument of this kind it may seem that we are confronted with
quite the opposite of the enthymematic. Far from leaving arguments
unstated, Paul seems to be at pains to make sure that every possible
argument should be made absolutely explicit. But multiple reasons
tend to obscure the ultimate ground of conviction; they often betray
looseness of argument, and by no means exclude its being elliptical.
We need to analyse with care what Paul is doing here. To rally all
the material of possible relevance to his conviction a lengthy CU
display is called for (see diagram 20). In CU 2 the wording I have
given in brackets clings closer to the text of 8:29, but I judge that in
view of the reference to 'God's chosen' in 8:33 my first wording
involves no unjustified interpretational bias. CUs 14, 19 and 20 are
'*arrowed* in' to a HEAD or other support CU, because they relate to
a particular concept not the CU as a whole, and that concept is duly
named. (For this device see Barnwell, *Introduction to Semantics and
Translation*, p. 216.)

Diagram 20

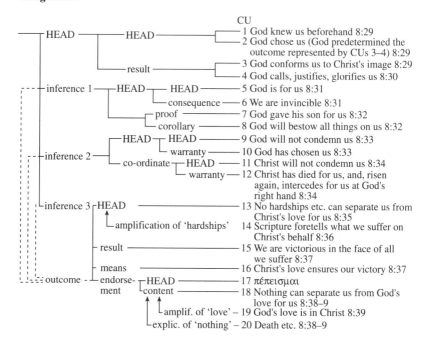

The multiplicity of Paul's reasons is reflected in a multiplicity of critical perspectives on the part of commentators. Most see Paul's conviction as having experience as well as reason as its foundation. Dunn is an example. 'The conviction of course is based primarily on God's love in Christ (vv. 35, 39) as displayed especially on the cross (v. 32) and subsequent triumph (v. 34; cf. particularly 14:9; 1 Cor 15:25–7; Col 2:15); and not simply as a matter of rational persuasion, but also as something experienced (5:5).'[58] Presumably Dunn intends 'experience' here to cover not only that of Paul but that of his hearers too. Leenhardt was concerned to stress this aspect. Referring back to what he has just been saying about 8:37 and Paul's victory over his sufferings which is not 'passive resistance' but 'a participation in the power of the love of God', he continues: 'This evocation of the tribulations of the apostle lends to the πέπεισμαι, "I am sure", the force of a personal witness even though the vision of the writer here embraces horizons which far surpass the bounds of personal experience.'[59] For Dodd it is neither argument from reason nor argument from personal experience – it is not argument at all – that really matters either to Paul or to us in this passage. Having extolled 'the strong and coherent, though complicated, thread of argument, from Rom. 1:17 to 8:39', he reflects: 'How far the Romans followed the argument is a question to which one would like to know the answer . . . No doubt to them, as to us, the epistle became really thrilling when argument passed into prophecy, and with its "I am certain" challenged, not logical discussion, but spiritual assent.'[60] Käsemann sees the essence of Paul's argument to be that the 'certainty' of which he speaks is not *his* certainty but a certainty independent of all opinion. 'πέπεισμαι γάρ does not merely mean the apostle's own persuasion . . . but manifests complete certainty.'[61] This was how Pelagius (quoted by Cranfield) construed Paul's words.[62] How Paul sees the role of Christ in bringing about our certainty is also accounted for by commentators in ways that involve differences of emphasis. For Barrett, for example, what Paul sees as important is that it is through Christ that we acquire our certainty; for Bruce, that it is to Christ that we owe the fact that such certainty is possible. The statement that nothing can separate us from the love of God 'which is in Christ Jesus' is glossed by Barrett with 'of course not; for Christ Jesus is – the Lord . . . God is *for us*; and it is in Christ Jesus that we know him and trust him'.[63] There is something of a contrast between Barrett's 'In Christ Jesus . . . we know God' and our experience of the father as something which Christ has won for us which Bruce's construal of Paul's words brings out: 'Nothing . . . can sever the children of God from their Father's love, secured to them in Christ.'[64]

There is inevitably, in all these perspectives, a reflection of the differences in the overall understanding of Paul's theology that characterises each commentator. It is these differences that govern which areas of Paul's argumentative apparatus each tends to privilege, whether it is to see CUs 13–16 (in diagram 20) as working alongside CUs 5–8 as Dunn and Leenhardt do, and to give substantial attention to Paul's appeals to deduction and experience, or whether it is to see these as effectively overruled by the categorically affirmative character of CUs 1–4, with only such recourse to deduction as is involved in CUs 9–12, as Käsemann and Dodd do. Either way Paul's is a certainty that points to more than logic or personal experience as its basis. What that more may be it is not my province here to consider. If we say that it is the product of the gift of faith, then we touch the limit of what can be said about it. In considering whether it has a logical component we avoid looking beyond where finite reason takes either him or us. There is a place for doing both. And if Paul's is indeed an 'I am certain' which says 'the content of my certainty would still stand even if some power should convince *me* otherwise',[65] then it surely has more to do with the certainty of prophecy than logic. If we discuss the nature and extent of its logical component, it is right that we should have always in mind – as Moule sought to ensure we should – that the certainty we are talking about is of a kind which men die for rather than disown.[66] And it is not without this in mind that I say, of the battery of reasons Paul adduces, that we need to note particularly where it is lacking in logical weight.

CUs 9–12 illustrate one way in which this lack of logical weight shows itself. It is wholly reasonable that as one step in demonstrating the certainty of God's love for us Paul should dispose of all doubt that God or Christ might condemn us. But how does he do it? To say that the one who justifies us cannot also be the one who condemns us is to say that he who forgives us does not call us to account, which is a truism. Similarly truistic is to say that he who has rescued us from condemnation cannot be the one to condemn us. From our present angle CUs 1–4 look rather the same. What causal connections are here perceived by Paul? God glorifies us by transforming us into Christ's image because he has decided to do so. So the sum of what Paul draws from these two CU groups is that nothing can separate us from God's love because God has decided that nothing should. Where something did, in fact, separate us from it, his prior decision meant that it could not continue to do so, hence he did what was necessary to neutralise ongoing interference. Is Paul in fact saying more than that inasmuch as σεσωσμένοι we are surely σωζόμενοι? He rallies facts which merely reciprocate endorsement. And if they are facts which, in unpacking the totality of divine gifting that Paul's conviction embraces, afford direct grounds more than sufficient to account for his certainty, they do not, as they stand, account ultimately for their own determinative finality – unless it be in their taking for granted factors Paul leaves unexpressed, but might well be expecting us to supply on the strength of an over-arching conceptual build-up. In fact, taking into account the emphasis on the Spirit as guarantee of the fulfilment of our hope (linking, more like a fly-over than an arch, 5:3–10 with 8:15–24) we could see the following syllogism as here implicit:

A   MAJOR PREMISE
Those whom God has chosen to love experience the out-
pourings of his Spirit.
B   MINOR PREMISE
We experience the outpouring of God's Spirit.
C   CONCLUSION
We are the chosen objects of God's love.

This being the background which Paul can presume upon, there
would be no need for him to do more than set in relief by means of
truism or tautology the facts to which his conviction here appeals
but which stand unverified. Another syllogism is in fact readily
inferred which fully integrates the logical basis of his reasoning:

A   MAJOR PREMISE
To be certain of glory is to be certain that nothing can come
between us and God.
B   MINOR PREMISE
From our experience of the Spirit we can argue certain hope
of glory.
C   CONCLUSION
We can be certain nothing can come between us and God.

That it is along these lines that Paul is thinking, and expecting his
hearers to think, may seem to find confirmation in CUs 13–16,
which carry internally an argumentative weight absent in 1–4, 9–12.
By 'internally' I mean by virtue of factors we need not seek elsewhere, appeal being directly made to proof that we are securely
enfolded in God's love: the victory we experience in the face of
hardship and danger. Here too it is put before us as a fact that we
owe this victory to the support we receive through Christ's love. But
this victory in its turn is practical evidence of the support we receive
and can be used to verify that love. Tautology is eluded. However,
in highlighting foundations of the practical experiential kind for
Paul's conviction, are we not falsifying what I have represented as
the grand sweep of Paul's discourse: the shift away from *proving
God's love by arguing from experience* towards *proving our election
(and all its related consequences) by arguing from God's love*? And it
is in fact a theoretical argument focussed sharply upon the latter
that generates in CUs 5–8 a basis for Paul's conviction which not so

much accounts for as offers a clear motive for all that we may perceive as tautological expansion.

Nowhere else is Paul's conviction so cohesively justified as it is here by being grounded in the totality of gifting attested as God's design for us by the supreme gift of his son. Logic builds on the christological revelation integral to Paul's conversion experience to yield a theoretical argument which sharply distinguishes itself from, even as it plunges beneath and underpins, any experiential arguments enthymematically latent in CUs 1–4 and 9–12 or unenthymematically itemised in 13–16. Part of the logic is left implicit, so the mode of expression is technically that of the enthymeme; but there is no uncertainty over what is being implied, though it is not so inherent in what is made explicit as to render insignificant the enthymematic factor. The enthymeme is of the most usual kind, in which it is the major premise that has to be supplied; i.e. it is of the first order.

A MAJOR PREMISE
   To give a son is a sign of supreme love.
B MINOR PREMISE
   God gave his son for us.
C CONCLUSION
   God has shown his love for us to be supreme.

It might perhaps be said that it partakes also to some extent of the third order in that 'God will grant us all things' stands in relation to the conclusion as I have formulated it more as a corollary than as an equivalent. In addition, for the conviction of 8:38 to follow from it the further assumption is involved that the love in question being God's – if it is supreme in extent, it is supreme in its operational efficacy – nothing can come between it and its object.

However effective his argument here, we have to reckon that Paul, who so often seems to play with argument or dally with dubious argument, has at this point in Romans – where in effect he has an incontrovertible argument – moved into an area where argument is no longer of primary concern to him. Dodd sees him as having moved into the realm of prophecy. But that turns out ultimately not to mean his argument is no longer rational; it is a case of his concern having shifted from what the good news of the gospel means for us to wonderment at the sublime reality that makes it that good news. It is as if the argument of divine self-sacrifice turns the mind away from argument. Whether in giving his son God was seen by Paul as giving *himself* we cannot know; it hardly seems likely that he could consciously hold the view. Cranfield sees the import of 8:39 as precise and definitive at least to the extent of conveying the message: 'the love of Christ is not truly known until it is recognised as being the love of the eternal God himself, and it is only in Jesus Christ that the love of God is fully manifest as what it really is'.[67]

4.5 Range and limits of the implications of Romans 8 for the role of the enthymeme in Paul's discourse.

Looking back over Romans 8 as a whole, we see Paul often stretching logic and shifting his ground: sometimes infelicitously, even waywardly, but often not so at all, but rather in a straining of logical reasoning which is dynamic and effective. However, the position to which he has moved by the end of the chapter places it all in a new perspective. Everything is elevated to a plane of wider horizons, of loftier thought and greater intensity of feeling. Nor is the result that logic ceases to play a role. Perhaps it is to this moment in Paul's discourse that we should look for the paradigm of his attitude towards the place of logic in his proclamation of the gospel. Or perhaps, however powerful, this moment should not be taken as paradigmatic because in fact it is not typical.

Now that I have reached the end of the section of Paul's letter that I proposed my enquiry should cover, the general principles to which I hoped such an enquiry would provide a guide may perhaps find, in the issue raised by the concluding section of Romans 8, an angle from which they can profitably be addressed.

I was prompted at the end of the last chapter to ask whether the argumentative approach is really an appropriate mode for the material with which Paul is dealing, and why he was so attached to argument involving logical deduction when the relevance of logic to matters that necessarily defy human comprehension is so questionable. During Romans 8 we see the certainty that our condemnation as sinners is waived being (1) traced to our experience of the power of the Spirit, (2) regrounded in our position as God's adopted children (destined to share as heirs in the glory of Christ), finally (3) ascribed to the fact that to the chosen objects of his love God gives all things. The logic at each stage stretches forward, so that what begins as talk of two 'laws' soon gives place to the notion of empowering, which in its turn is superseded by the theme of inheritance, itself in due course quite overshadowed by the concept of self-sacrificial love. The result is that reasoning dissolves into affirmation, and affirmation into adoration. Our certainty of acquittal is not something to be demonstrated by pointing to proofs of God's love, but something in the celebration and rehearsal of which we extol that love. What had appeared to be the role of argument (i.e. the persuasion of the reader/hearer to a certain viewpoint) is marginalised and redimensioned. It is in the very act of accounting for his own persuasion that Paul effectively brings about this redimensioning.

How does this then leave us with regard to other questions which my earlier analyses have raised? There is an obvious link, a kind of justification and explanation, of everything that has given the impression that Paul is not entirely serious about his logic: that he uses it as a means of giving drama, colour and emphasis to what is essentially affirmation.[68] His seemingly slippery use of terms like 'law', 'death' or 'body'[69] may have more to do with limited concern for logic than unscrupulousness of persuasive technique. But logical argument counts for more in Paul than would thus be allowed for, witness

(1) the tangled nature of much of it, and the extent to which he permits argumentative intricacy to compromise the clarity of his statements,[70]

(2) the air of one arguing in earnest that is by no means infrequently conveyed, of one arguing as much for his own sake as for any other reason.[71]

Whatever the fate of argument in Romans 8, it was the appearance of the risen Christ to Paul that had made the affirmation and exaltation we find there possible. It was through his encounter with the risen Christ that Paul saw that it was the immortal firstborn of God whose blood had flowed at the Crucifixion. The gospel of Paul had its roots in his having been the beneficiary of that particular category of sign-productive event which is 'Recognition', a case of it in which the meaning of historical events took shape before him through the agency of inferential deduction. From an imprint made on the continuum of historical time he deduced the meaning of time itself. He grasped the fact that 'the saving event of the death and resurrection of Christ forms the centre from which the beginning and end of history may then be seen' (Käsemann).[72] But I have noted (in Chapter 1) how 'Recognition' becomes its own tyrant. The significant object itself limits the play of the very reason on which, to acquire significance, it depends.[73] Paul is caught where the vehicle itself of the great depth of meaning he recognised in the Cross becomes generative of major dilemmas.[74]

When Paul's argument seems otiose, an impediment rather than an advantage to communication, it may be that it is indeed such. The peculiarity of semiological situation in which Paul finds himself leads him to pursue argument into areas where craters open up before him and to go further cannot benefit him or his reader. But whilst this can and does happen, nevertheless, just as we have seen various *less* radical reasons for gratuitous argumentation in his discourse, so we need to take account of certain *more* radical reasons: not reasons for gratuitous argumentation, but reasons why argumentation is not necessarily otiose because local hazards blow holes in the ensign of logical exactitude. A subtler appreciation is needed both of *signification as a process* and of *logic as a method* if this contingency is to be taken adequately into account. My opening chapter aimed at providing a starting point for the kind of appreciation I refer to. My closing chapter will now pursue it, and thus prepare the way for a final consideration of what conclusions are to be drawn from this study. The first two sections of the chapter take note of (and make some attempt to analyse) *those aspects of signification the value of which is not easily measured in terms of cognitive yield.* Section 3 investigates *the error of assuming that concepts which are inexact cannot be valid channels of logical deduction* (and so of necessity preclude methodical assessment). The question of *what benefit accrues to the reader of Paul* through the argumentational procedures we have been observing in Romans 1–8 has then a new basis on which, in sections 4 and 5, I can address it, demonstrating – as I presume to hope – the substantial promise of the directions in which my basic analysis of Paul's semiological situation has caused my enquiry to develop.

5

KNOWING WHAT TUNE PAUL IS PLAYING

5.1 Coding and clarity in Guiraud and Prieto. Paul's own view of communication, and the problem it highlights.

In my opening discussion I took Eco as my mentor in semiological theory and relegated any references to other theoreticians to the notes. Consideration of the theories of other semiologists and of the relation of semiological theory to other kindred disciplines such as communication theory and linguistics (as well as psychology, anthropology and aesthetics) occupies a great deal of space in his writings. It is possible, in consequence, to trace back to earlier research the vast majority of his basic ideas, though their relation to it is almost always complex, and it is rare for him to adopt an idea without in some way remodelling or redeploying it.[1] In due course this chapter will lead me around to Eco again, but in the earlier part of it I shall bring into play some theories which (though reflected in his) display a particular relevance to Paul in their original form, or at some stage in their development prior to their assimilation by Eco, like the analytical refinements of the coding factor in semiosis for which I turn to the two linguists Pierre Guiraud and Luis Prieto.[2] This is my first step in that 'subtler appreciation of significance' which I have said we need to pursue (*supra*, p. 131).

Guiraud stresses the way coding assumes opposing forms according to whether intellect or feeling is in the ascendant (the former being promotive of order, the latter of disorder), and according to how many or how few are the elements offered for decoding by a given message (the temperature of the message being measured as 'hot' where they are many, 'cool' where they are few). At one extreme are scientific codes which aim at neutralising such variables as stylistic modes and connotative meanings, with a view to achieving precision. At the other are aesthetic codes which have quite the opposite aim: to bring to life and develop these variables, with no view to achieving precision and unperturbed by the imprecision they foster.[3] Coding, as it ranges between them, depends on agreement among the users of the sign, which may be more or less conscious, more or less extensive and precise, in parallel with the character of the sign involved, which may be monosemic or polysemic, explicit or cryptic, denotative or connotative, natural or artificial, motivated or arbitrary.[4] Two factors which Guiraud calls 'attention' and 'communion' (and his terms decode better when read as French, rather than as the English homographs the translators of his work content themselves with) play contrasting roles. 'Communion' goes with feeling; 'attention' with thought. The more there is of the one, the less there is of the other. In 'communion' the corporate dimension of coding is to the fore; in 'attention' the degree of intellectual concentration involved. The level of cognition is high where the level of 'attention' is high; where the level of 'communion' is high, that of cognition is low.[5]

I would single out three features of Guiraud's account as being of particular relevance to our present purposes:

(a) the importance his profile of the code gives to the differing moods in which the messages that signs convey are received;

(b) the effect which the level of the group factor has on how codes are differentiated by him;

(c) the weight he gives to other values than precision and a high cognitive yield in defining the role of the code.

For the moment let me focus on the relevance of (a) and (b) for imparities in semiosis of which Paul reveals explicit analytical awareness. Different types of sign will promote different types of response. The same sign will promote different responses in different people. Of Paul's regard for both eventualities we have notable evidence in his discourse on the relative merits of 'tongues' and prophecy in 1Cor 14, and in his characterisation of the gospel in terms of the 'wisdom/folly' alternative of 1Cor 1–2. Both illustrations point the moral that where the audience is not right for the sign, or the sign not right for the audience, semiosis will misfire. Reader response and the reception factor are necessarily of peculiar concern to all the NT writers. In none, however, is this more obvious, in none is it more integral to (or more explicit an aspect of) the discourse than it is in Paul. It goes without saying that he does not think (as some modern upholders of the importance of the reception factor do) that the identity of the message in a piece of communication is in any sense determined by what it means for those at the receiving end.[6] For him it is rather *their* identity than that of the message which is determined by their response. To subject him to the criteria of present-day reception or reader response theory would be to turn *his* ideas on the subject upside down.[7] Nevertheless what status his argumentation enjoys in the encounter of the arguer with the addressee is not fixed or foreseeable, nor such as to render unequivocal whether the identity of the message or that of the recipient is the one which undergoes definition; for there is an inescapable truth in the dictum, enunciated by Hobbes in *Leviathan*, that he who uses arguments in order to persuade makes the one to whom he speaks 'judge' of the force of his inferences.[8] But I have brought in Paul's statements concerning communication precisely because they highlight a special problem to which his use of argument gives rise.

It is true that they do not relate to the same situation as that of his letters. In 1Cor 1–2 Paul is talking about the impact of the gospel on those who hear it preached for the first time. In 1Cor 14 Paul's position itself is not clear, since we do not really understand how he can be saying that 'tongues' are a sign for unbelievers in view of the other statements he makes along with this one (and no commentary succeeds in providing a satisfactory explanation).[9] Paul's main concern, however, is clearly with the question of how 'tongues' do or do not serve believers, and therefore the addressees he has most in mind are of the same category as those he is speaking to in his letters.[10] At the same time 'tongues' are an idiosyncratic verbal phenomenon with no possible place in epistolography, and a place in public discourse only in the context of meetings; nevertheless, 1Cor 14:6 authorises us to use what Paul is about to say as a quarry from which to extract the principles he saw as governing the language which is the appropriate vehicle for revelation, knowledge, prophecy or teaching; and of these types of discourse (whatever uncertainty surrounds their precise nature in this context, and in spite of the fact that Paul is here thinking of their role at meetings) all are such that at least echoes of them reach his letters, even the argumentative sections of them. But whether this state of affairs does or does not seem to justify cautious application of Paul's own criteria of communication to his use of argument I shall not probe further, since it is not the *application* of these criteria but the problem they highlight that I am pursuing – to which end I turn to Prieto.

His work illuminates with particular clarity the different ways in which semiosis comes to misfire.[11] According to his analysis the codes governing semiosis involve two universes of discourse, that of the 'indicator' and that of the 'indicated'.[12] Every emission, every reception of a particular sign operates with these two 'universes'. The universe of discourse of the 'indicator' is the universe from which a given sign is drawn; the universe of discourse of the 'indicated' is the universe to which a given sign refers. In the first Prieto locates what he calls the 'Sematic' field, in the second the 'Noetic' ('sematic' not 'semantic' to show he is talking about sign repertoire[13] as against potential message yield[14].) In any given case of a sign being used, successful communication depends on a match-up in both fields uniting emitter and receptor.[15] Suppose I have just put a pen in my pocket when someone says, 'Give me that pen.' I understand him to mean the one I have put in my pocket. He, however, has noticed me stretching towards another pen lying on the table between us, and he was referring to that one. I decode correctly what the indicator 'pen' is employed to indicate as far as the sematic field is concerned, but not the noetic. It is possible for misunderstanding to arise from the occurrence of mismatching in either field or both.[16] The contrast is very like that between denotational and referential fields.

Paul was well aware that there would not be a satisfactory match where a great many of those who heard his preaching of the gospel were concerned. He envisaged his hearers as falling into two categories, σωζόμενοι and ἀπολλύμενοι. With the former there would be an accurate matching of the universes of discourse and the gospel would be received as σοφία and δύναμις θεοῦ. With the latter there would be a mismatching of the universes of discourse and the gospel would be dismissed as μωρία. The disposition of the hearer on which the accurate matching depends is the work of the Holy Spirit. The letters of Paul are directed towards those to whom the Holy Spirit has granted the power of relating sematic and noetic fields in such a way that the meaning of the Crucifixion is recognised as Paul recognises it. However, although the correct understanding of Paul's words is thus in a certain sense placed outside his power to promote, verbal discourse is nevertheless viewed by him as the fundamental channel of communication. It is through the power of words to convey meaning that the Spirit accomplishes its work. Words which do not speak with clarity do not foster it. This comes out strikingly when in the references to 'speaking in tongues' in

1Cor 14, he refers (v. 9) to the primacy of the εὔσημος λόγος: διὰ τῆς γλώσσης ἐὰν μὴ εὔσημον λόγον δῶτε, πῶς γνωσθήσεται τὸ λαλούμενον; ἔσεσθε γὰρ εἰς ἀέρα λαλοῦντες.[17] In 1Cor 14:7–8 two parallels, drawn (as he points out) from the world of sound made by inanimate objects, albeit musical instruments, have illustrated the importance of clarity of meaning. It is remarkable that Paul thinks of musical sound in connection with meaning at all. The parallels figure as rhetorical questions:

> τὰ ἄψυχα φωνὴν διδόντα, εἴτε αὐλὸς εἴτε κιθάρα, ἐὰν διαστολὴν τοῖς φθόγγοις μὴ δῷ, πῶς γνωσθήσεται τὸ αὐλούμενον ἢ τὸ κιθαριζόμενον; . . . ἐὰν ἄδηλον σάλπιγξ φωνὴν δῷ, τίς παρασκευάσεται εἰς πόλεμον;

Each parallel envisages the eventuality of clarity being wanting: as a lack, in the first parallel, of the property διαστολή, and, in the second, of the quality to which ἄδηλος disallows pertinence. Three instruments figure in bilateral comparison, flute and lyre as against trumpet. The consequences of clarity are seen on the one hand as recognition/understanding of what is being played, on the other as recognition/understanding of the call to battle.

Paul's setting of verbal signification against the background of non-verbal signification falls remarkably in line with the principles of semiology. The semantic scope of γινώσκω, moreover, allows for a reading that would find him envisaging semiosis as recognition.[18] Translators, however, seem to deem it expedient to settle for formulae featuring 'know', which enable them to match 'know what (tune) is being played' in v. 7 with 'know what is being said' in v. 9. And indeed the analogies with flute, lyre and trumpet may, in reality, be little more than stylistic decoration. Nevertheless, affinities with modern views of signification present themselves in this Pauline pericope which extend to other factors as well. In two cases the affinity is really quite remarkably subtle and precise, and is such as will – I think – bring effectively into focus the issue towards the discernment of which this section is aimed. In one case the affinity is with Saussure, in the other with Peirce.

For Saussure language comes into play by virtue of a single factor, 'différence'. The sounds to which Paul's φθόγγοι in 14:7 refer comprise various elements but, as they are *musical* sounds, a vital constituent must be pitch, and that is clearly the one that Paul has mainly in mind in the first of the two parallels. The only basis on which a distinction of pitch can rest is that a given note is that particular note and not any other. It is 'a relationship *in absentia*, i.e.

between the element in question, which is there, and other elements, which are not'. I borrow words from the description in Lepschy's *Survey of Structural Linguistics* of the relation between one sign and another as understood by Saussure, the so-called 'paradigmatic' relationship that contrasts with and is the complement of the 'syntagmatic'.[19]

Central to the theories of Peirce was his notoriously elusive concept of the 'interpretant', which is very far from being the equivalent of the interpreter, and certainly not the interpreter as receptor or beneficiary of the communication of which the sign is the vehicle, nor as the emitter of the sign anticipating the way in which it will be interpreted; nor is it even equivalent to the two of these taken together. It is more the factor by virtue of which the interpreter (in either of the above senses) interprets – i.e. is *able* to interpret.[20] Morris, in the 1940s, viewing the problem from the angle of behaviourism, set about attempting 'to carry out resolutely the insight of Charles Peirce that a sign gives rise to an interpretant, and that an interpretant is in the last analysis "a modification of a person's tendencies toward action"'.[21] The fulfilment of this aim led him to locate the interpretant in the 'disposition to respond' which the receipt of the sign sets up in the receptor. He saw this disposition as operating according to five main modes. It is the fourth of these that entails 'disposition' in the most obvious sense: the disposition to act in a particular way; it is the ambit of the prescriptive sign, such as 'Go away!'[22] In relation to a good many kinds of language this understanding of 'interpretant' via 'disposition' tends to force qualities upon the material that may not really seem to be there to any but a committed behaviourist. However, it is particularly appropriate to biblical language, where the relation of discourse to disposition is always a matter of major relevance, and never more overtly so than in the writings of Paul. This is, of course, primarily the case in a pervasive and fundamental way. It is very precisely and specifically so in the trumpet illustration of 1Cor 14:8.[23]

I do not wish to labour the import of these coincidences between Paul and modern semiological theory; they point, however, to a two-sidedness in sign-functional effectiveness which is of particular relevance in Paul. The factors that characterise the two sides of this divide are *articulacy* and *impact*. The way the coincidences discussed relate to this two-sidedness may be charted as in diagram 21.

There is a direct parallel between this two-sided effectiveness and the antinomies of Guiraud. Codes, he claims, major *either* on 'intellectual concentration' accompanied by a high level of cog-

Diagram 21

parallel involving	(A) *lyre/flute*	(B) *trumpet*
giving rise to affinity with	Saussure	Peirce/Morris
in the matter of	'différences'	'disposition'
thus highlighting the aspect of signification which is	articulation	impact

nition, *or* on 'corporate feeling' accompanied by a low level of cognition. As signs function only by virtue of the operation of codes, the more a code is of the former type, the more aspect (A) of sign-functional power will tend to eclipse aspect (B), and vice versa.[24] But just as both (A) and (B) are desirable types of function in the sign, so codes of either type promote sign-functional value in complementary ways. When Guiraud says that one type of code involves a higher level of 'cognition' than another he is by no means intending to affirm its superiority. He considers those kinds of coding which depend on shared feeling to be no less important in the enhancement of awareness that they promote than is intellectual concentration in its promotion of 'cognition'.[25] (I return thus to feature (c) of those I singled out earlier in Guiraud's analysis only to leave it until now without follow-up.)

The correct matching of the noetic and sematic fields on which Prieto sees successful communication to rest is dependent on the codes which preside over the emission and reception of a given sign. For Paul, effective gospel communication is always the outcome of the Holy Spirit, who works (as far as our apprehension of its message is concerned) through such channels. If we relate this to the attitude of Guiraud, then just as the articulacy of high 'cognitive' levels of coding is fundamental to the work of the Spirit, so is the intensity of low cognitive impact.

The relation of either to Paul's use of argument is then the problem with which we are faced, because it is not at all obvious by which of the two kinds of coding it is governed. Whether Paul lives up to the 'clarity' of the εὔσημος λόγος he extols, and in what ways he may or may not be judged to do so, is a question the answer to which is inseparable from how we resolve this problem.

5.2 Clarity and the enthymeme in Romans 1–8. How should the coding be characterised? Aesthetic and other approaches.

My study of Paul's use of the enthymeme in Romans 1–8 does not seem to have done much to vindicate the coherence of his argumentation. Indeed, precision and clarity of thought have emerged from it as being compromised in quite a remarkable variety of different ways. His arguments, for example, follow a zig-zag course in the matter of Jewish 'advantage' (*supra*, chapter 2.4). He prescribes eschewal of the sin which he affirms (in a Christian) to be out of the question (*supra*, 3.4). How his reasoning should be construed where faith and righteousness are concerned, or law, or peace, or death, is never unequivocally clear. Where, as in the matter of God's self-giving love, his logic is clear and unchallengeable, argumentation is in the process of being overtaken by rhapsodic affirmation (*supra*, 4.3). In attempting to clarify, and perhaps explain, such irregularities and uncertainties, I noted the part played by metaphorical or rhetorical factors on the one hand, and by the ambiguity inherent in the eschatological context on the other (*supra*, 3.6). And I asked: on balance, does the overall picture of Paul's argumentational practice in Romans 1–8 do more to vindicate it as an advantage to communication or convict it as an impediment (*supra*, 4.5)? This is clearly the issue on which the data of Romans 1–8 call for a decision. As such it typifies the issue raised by much of the argumentation elsewhere in Paul. The present study is based on the theory that such a judgement can be satisfactorily tackled only against a background of semiological theory. It is clear that intellectual habit rooted in the cultural influences of his time has some responsibility for the dislocated and disparate character of Paul's arguments, but in my opening chapter I suggested that we can trace it to something deeper, and by taking into account the exact position in which the message he was communicating placed him in relation to the fundamental principles governing human communication, locate its origin in personal alacrity of mind.

But if seeing it thus, as the result of an individuality rather than a conventionality of intellect, makes it something to be 'welcomed, even excited by' (as I said *supra*, p. 28), are the problems to which the idiosyncrasies of Pauline discourse give rise necessarily 'alleviated' (as I suggested *supra*, p. 10)? If Paul's intellect was ardent in its search for clarity of understanding, clarity of reasoning was not where it habitually led him. In section 1 of the present chapter I have been broadening the semiological background as originally outlined in Chapter 1 so as to make it a more adequate match for the complexity of our problem. This broadening of the background has the immediate effect of putting before us an important and radical option. May not the very tangles of Paul's argumentation lay claim to a 'clarity' construable in terms of 'impact', no less valid than that to which orderly argument would appeal on the strength of its 'articulacy'? May we not, in other words, be led towards that end of the antithetical coding span envisaged by Guiraud, which he characterises as aesthetic – the end where such variables as connotative meanings are brought to life and developed, rather than neutralised, as they are at the scientific end, in the interests of precision? It will be my contention that we are not necessarily led in this direction, and I will proceed *infra* section 3 to outline in what direction I feel we may more profitably proceed. But before doing that, I think it will be well to take stock of the direction from which we shall be turning away, for it takes us into a mysterious department of the significatory process, one the possible relevance of which can by no means be disregarded. Here I turn to Eco again as guide.

I believe one of Eco's major contributions, both in relation to his own output and to the thinking of this century, to be his ideas on aesthetics. They come widely spread over his publications and are marked by a certain inconstancy of emphasis (though this impression may well be due to my incapacity to grasp the full subtlety of his thought and the exact import of his terminology).[26] Accordingly, he seems now in fact no longer to use a formula which articulated the key concept in his earlier discussion of the subject in his 1968 *La struttura assente*. Relating his considerations to the question asked by Jakobson, 'What makes a verbal message a work of art?', he there sees the aesthetic principle as entering into operation when normal codes governing the transmission and reception of the message are suddenly placed in jeopardy by the appearance of a fresh factor, and this factor is 'the global isomorphism of the aesthetic idiolect'.[27] In order to elucidate this, let me start from the 'idiolect'.

'Idiolect' is not a term in any way exclusive to the language of aesthetics. The idiolect of a given unit of discourse is that wherein its idiom differs from the idiom of any other unit of discourse. The term can be used in many ways and of many aspects of discourse, but it is particularly useful as a description of that which distinguishes the voice of a given writer from that of any other writer. This is obviously a conspicuous factor in the NT. There is a Pauline, a Johannine and a Lucan idiolect, so marked that confident assumptions are regularly made on the basis of what are construed to be unquestionable variations of idiolect. The imperfect recreation of the idiolect is one of the most common grounds for alleging pseudepigraphy. In the case of Paul, within the span of material where variations of idiolect are generally reckoned compatible with singleness of authorship, differences of idiolect are recognisable between one epistle and another, and within epistles between original and inherited (credal, hymnic, parenetic) material. The term is one which obviously comprises features for which the words 'style' or 'language' are commonly considered sufficient, but it would have advantages over them if only in the fact that it covers both and focusses on the 'distinctiveness' factor. Its usefulness in the context of aesthetics arises from its capacity to designate a unique individuality of idiom.

The process of individualisation of which the 'idiolect' is the product becomes the dominant and distinctive peculiarity of aesthetic units, for, in aesthetic communication, all the elements of which a message is made up cease to be of primary importance for whatever communicative value they may otherwise possess and derive meaning from the purely formal relationship they establish with one another, so that the totality of the factors that determine signification becomes subservient to a single criterion of meaning: the formal, relationships of a purely formal nature being possible only by reference to such a totality. This reduction of all relationships to the level of form, and the necessity of reference to such a global context for formal relations to be established, constitute the 'global isomorphism' of aesthetic sign-productivity.[28] Thought along such lines owes a special debt to Mukařovský, a member of the Prague school of the 1930s whose work received only limited international attention until the 1960s and 1970s.[29] The global dimension in aesthetics is especially clearly enunciated by him. Aesthetically viewed, 'the utterance "means" not that reality which comprises its immediate theme but the set of all realities, the universe as a whole, or – more precisely – the entire experience of the author, or better, of the perceiver'.[30] Compare Jakobson: 'Poeticalness is . . . a total re-evaluation of the discourse and of all its components whatever.'[31] Since the role of each constituent of the totality changes with each new aesthetic unit involved, no single element in the unit will be making to the significance of the whole a contribution identical with any previous sign-productive function it has performed. The peculiar impact exerted by semiosis, in which the aesthetic principle has the ascendancy, is due to the manner in which each sign-productive element is rendered new and unfamiliar by virtue of its assumption into the ambit of the aesthetic.[32] It is an 'invention', the result of 'a semiotic mode of production in which something is mapped from something else which was not defined and analyzed before the act of mapping took place', as Eco later put it when (in *A Theory of Semiotics*) he set out his panorama of the four main modes of sign production: Recognition, Ostension, Replica and Invention.[33] We are confronted with the 'idiolect' in what is perhaps its most extreme form, certainly at its most untranslatable.

It is not, however, necessarily that kind of discourse which is most conscious of an aesthetic dimension that is most aesthetically effective. The role played by the kind of impact peculiar to the aesthetic mode, and even the transference of a piece of communication from meaningfulness at a non-aesthetic level to meaningfulness at an aesthetic level, is not by any means always the result of conscious choice on the part of a communicator.[34] In fact the kind of aesthetic value which I am envisaging we might be led to see in Pauline argumentation has nothing to do with any self-consciously artistic principles of the kind it is even remotely possible Paul himself might have been motivated by.[35] It is a value most likely to come into play where the energy with which Paul is arguing is at its most intense, and this may well be where confusion abounds.[36] Mukařovský maintained that 'the greater the bundle of extra-aesthetic values an artistic artifact attracts and the more dynamic it renders their interplay, the greater the independent value of the artifact will be'.[37] It is a value by the nature of which the communicativity of Paul's argumentation would be proportional not to the degree of lucidity or validity it succeeds in achieving, but to the energy with which it pursues these goals. The more dynamic the interplay of ideas the greater the communicativity. But the message is a message the import of which is no more and no less than its impact: its medium is the untranslatable idiolect of isomorphic semiosis.

If such an approach to Paul seems out of place (perhaps so totally out of place that it should be written off out of hand), let it be noted that it falls in line with a principle which is central to a number of major currents of twentieth-century philosophy: the principle that meaning is misconceived wherever it is not conceived as impact. It is indeed a principle that can trace its origins far back into the nineteenth century. It was already quite explicitly championed by Schleiermacher.[38] Upholders of it sometimes appeal to Peirce, for reasons that can be seen from what has been said earlier in the chapter. More often it emanates from the general climate of existentialism.[39] This was so with the New Hermeneutic of Fuchs and Ebeling. A newer boost has been given it by the Deconstructionist approach of Derrida and his followers, who have more than once turned their minds to the Bible.[40]

The later Heidegger placed the poetic word at the centre of his philosophy.[41] For Gadamer it is the aesthetic dimension of philosophy that raises it above natural science.[42] The New Hermeneutic views God's word as being the poetic word par excellence. As a result the word of God is held to reside not in the biblical text as such so much as in what the meaning of the text shows itself to be in the impact it makes. Hence preaching assumes a major role as the agent of impact.[43] The task of biblical scholarship must be to deal with the obstacles which in different ways impede or distort impact. The aim of enquiry must be to make of the text 'what really lets it count'.[44] Perhaps we most effectively make of Paul's argumentation what 'lets it count', when, through our attempt to disentangle it (and even if we fail to do so), we open ourselves to its argumentative intensity. But the New Hermeneutic keeps a very watchful eye on any tendency that leads towards the apotheosis of a contentless intuition.[45] And the irregularities of Pauline argumentation actually stand to receive fuller convalidation from Deconstructionist attitudes, though these set out from a scrupulously agnostic base.

Deconstructionism sees only deceptiveness in the articulate and explicit, and looks for meaning in the very things that regularly thwart our attempts to be scientific. It is especially interested in non-sequiturs, irrelevancies, inconsistencies, the unconscious implications of what we say, not what we think we have said. This stems from its emphasis on the written word (on a 'grammatology' which eschews 'logocentricity'), and on how it is the 'trace' this embodies which is the ground of verbal discourse.[46] 'A deconstructive reading tries to bring out the logic of the text's language as opposed to the logic of its author's claims'; 'to demonstrate how the text simultaneously affirms and undermines itself'.[47] Pauline argumentation would seem to offer much scope for this kind of treatment. Where its enthymematic dimension displays itself at its most clumsy and accidental might well be where most light would result.

Despite the objections of Fuchs to hearing the New Hermeneutic described as 'existentialist', by comparison with Deconstructionism it is characterised above all by its link with existentialism (and in particular with existentialist aesthetics).[48] Fundamentally different principles come into play with Deconstructionism; but Derrida, like Fuchs, relates his ideas to those of Heidegger, and 'logocentricity' looks like just the sort of failure, in our normal assumptions regarding meaning, to escape the 'inauthenticity' which Heidegger saw as the mark of 'average everydayness'.[49] But whereas for the New Hermeneutic meaning lies in the written word as something which becomes *actual* through impact, Derrida knows only its identity with writing's mobile impact as 'trace'.[50] (Hence it is not the author who knows what the meaning of his work really is – a daunting principle indeed if that which is under consideration purports to be the word of God.)[51] If meaning is impact, and has its ground in the 'trace' factor, then meaning is epitomised in reader response. Deconstructionism is a prime generator of Reader Response Criticism.[52] But so also, in its way, is the New Hermeneutic. (Each seems unnecessarily concerned to insist that its attitude towards meaning excludes all others.)[53]

Both, however, are approaches to be reckoned with. They resemble each other in leaving us without any criterion by which to discern right from wrong impact (though for very different reasons).[54] The New Hermeneutic seems to have inherited from Heidegger a kind of presumption that impact, because life-enhancing, is necessarily positive. Or perhaps its view is more that where God's word exercises impact it is a pre-understanding within us that is being activated – a pre-understanding which is the work of the Holy Spirit.[55] For the Deconstructionist there are no objective criteria of understanding and we should not be seeking any. Deconstructionism seems to be an utterly 'open' philosophy; all conclusion is deferred by the '*différance*' which governs signification – according to the mind-twisting principle with which, by means of this ambivalent coining, Derrida revises (or perhaps he would say draws out the true meaning of) Saussure.[56] As a result it does not have even the somewhat obscure concept of action as the criterion of meaning that existentialism did and the New Hermeneutic also virtually does, for in the latter the dynamic from which meaning is deemed inseparable is love (and love is not love which is not experience and exercise of love).[57] The apparent problem of how we identify God's word has to be looked at in the light of the dynamic which governs meaning.

Where a propensity to tie meaning to behaviour tempers the menacing emptiness of the view that can see meaning only as impact, we are back to something very much like the Peirce/Morris approach, which still has followers who see great potential in the way it conceives any given sign as leading only to another and another unless action arrests the regression.[58] The New Hermeneutic, however, carries the implication that God's word is not to be grasped by the faculty of human reason; it is its challenge to human logic that needs to be brought out.[59] If Deconstruction is a counsel of despair as far as determination of meaning is concerned, the New Hermeneutic is a counsel of humility, a call for us to be open to the impact of God's word, to discover what it can make of us, not we of it. Each counsels openness, one to the end that illumination may result, the other because it is the only way that such dim light as is available to us can come.[60]

Both offer special modes of approach to, special scope for appreciation of, the communicatory power of Pauline argumentation, but to suggest that they lead us to uncover its 'clarity', even in a recondite sense, may seem too much like a mere misappropriation of the word. And in fact I do not think this is the best kind of clarity we can claim for Paul's tune; to pursue *logic* further is expedient (cf. *supra*, p. 131).

5.3   Coding in 'fuzzy' perspective. The possible implications for some concepts of Paul's.

A sign, it may be felt, is either clear or not. The sign ✦ might not be instantly understood. However, once it is understood there is no doubt about what it signifies. That is by no means the case with every kind of sign. It is the custom on maps to represent trees in two ways: ♤ and ♀. The distinction could be explained as that which obtains between conifers and other types of tree. It remains unclear, however, which of the many types of either is involved. In particular, ♀ offers no indication as to whether evergreen or deciduous trees are involved. For these reasons neither sign has more than a limited degree of clarity, and a clearer method of representation would be possible. But this again is by no means the case with every kind of sign. Let us return to the area of verbal signification.

If A, on taking leave of B, says, 'We must meet again' (and no more), the meaning is not clear and various implications may be present. The words may represent nothing more than a mechanical politeness. They may, however, be expressive at least of a real desire to seem friendly. On the other hand, they may be intended as envisaging a real possibility. It would make sense – although it might well embarrass – for B to ask, 'Are you just being polite?' or 'What is that meant to convey?' But even where directness is a major priority, precision may not follow. To X's 'I love you', it would be as useless as it would be embarrassing for Y to respond 'Could you be a little more precise?' The word 'love' is not precise in meaning. But it would surely not be appropriate to say that it was not 'clear'. There may be ways of 'clarifying' just what sort of love is involved and how deep it goes. To do this there may sometimes be no other way than practical demonstration in a range of situations the general nature of which we find it fairly easy to sum up, but which it would be exceedingly difficult to list exhaustively. If 'giving one's life' may constitute the only absolute proof, something less would also normally be accounted sufficient.

These wide margins of uncertainty do not arise because the word 'love' is not as clear as it might be or as it ought to be. Admittedly the word is polysemic. It can refer to different kinds of love which can and need to be distinguished and defined. But at every level and in whatever context the question 'Can you be more precise?' will ultimately meet with the impossibility of an answer. And yet it is not because at that point it ceases to be clear what the word 'love' means. It is more that in order to convey what it does convey it cannot go beyond a certain level of precision. And for the kind of concept which the word 'love' conveys I suggest we invoke the term 'fuzzy'. The 'fuzziness' is inherent in the meaning. It is not vagueness; it is not lack of clarity. It is a quality which arises where a concept, in order to be what it is, *depends* on a certain level of irreducibility.

The 'fuzzy' concept belongs to a terminology first proposed by L. Zadeh in an article entitled 'Fuzzy sets' (*Information and Control* 8, 1965), and elaborated further in a contribution to *Fuzzy Sets and their Application to Cognitive and Decision Processes* (1975). He notes how the 'class of beautiful women', and 'the class of tall men', present problems when an attempt is made to apply to them the normal criteria regarding 'sets'. 'When A is a set in the ordinary sense of the term, its membership function can take on only two values 0 and 1 . . . according as x does or does not belong to A'. Instead 'beautiful women', 'tall men' confront us with classes in which exist 'grades of membership'. They constitute sets of a special kind, and Zadeh designates them 'fuzzy sets'. When reasoning involves such sets as these it becomes 'approximate'. 'It is neither entirely exact, nor entirely inexact.' It is, however, possible to furnish an analytical basis for the 'fuzzy logic' involved in 'approximate reasoning' by devising a 'calculus of fuzzy restrictions'. Zadeh does it thus. Take the proposition 'Tosi is young'. 'Let age denote a numerically valued variable which ranges over the interval 0,100. The degree to which a numerical age, say 28, is compatible with the concept of "young" is 0.7, while the compatibilities of 30 and 35 with young are 0.5 and 0.2 respectively.' Zadeh saw his calculus as offering an effective method for bypassing levels of precision to which a given semantic domain precludes attainment.[61]

Reasoning involving the term 'love' will depend not only on what kind of love is being described (that is its polysemic aspect) but also on the degree to which such factors as the readiness shown by an individual to make sacrifices for another have shown his/her attitude to be compatible with the concept 'love'. This belongs to its 'fuzzy' aspect. And alongside it other factors, such as displays and professions of affection, will need to be assigned their rating in a way similar to the ages of 35, 30 etc. in relation to 'young'. If actually to give one's life would rate 1, how would to give up all one's possessions, or to bequeath them all, rate? Would it be 0.8, 0.5, or what? Can the mere profession 'I love you' rate more than 0? Reasoning involving 'love' will be 'true' only insofar as it takes account of such issues, and the extent to which they may or may not be resolvable.

Towards the end of *A Theory of Semiotics*, Eco uses as an illustration of the 'fuzzy concept' a situation such as might arise in relation to working conditions.[62] He envisages two contrasting arguments coming into operation (see diagram 22).[63] It is easy to argue that because productivity is desirable, comfortable heating levels must be maintained. The concept of productivity may seem to decide the issue. But there is also the other argument, that comfortable heating levels increase the risk of fire. The concept of security may seem to claim precedence (as for example it is regularly allowed to do where the immense inconvenience of ubiquitous fire-doors to people in wheel-chairs is the issue and not productivity). Concepts like 'productivity', 'security', 'convenience' seem to be clear. And indeed they are clear, but they depend for their clarity upon the circumstances to which they apply. They are 'fuzzy', and, for rather different reasons from those which obtain in the case of 'love', they have to be 'fuzzy' to perform their particular kind of function. It is as little use saying 'define what you mean by "productivity", "security", "convenience"', as saying 'define what you mean by "love"'. It is only possible to illustrate how such words may apply. In this example, what reasoning needs particularly to take into account is what 'stakes' are involved. A given heating level may rate 0.2 in the

Diagram 22

⌒ Comfortable heating levels ⌒	
promote productivity.	involve a security risk.
It is desirable to promote productivity.	Risk needs to be avoided.

security 'stakes' and 0.9 in the productivity 'stakes'. The variability of rating to which, according to circumstances, such concepts as 'security' and 'productivity' are subject makes their 'fuzziness' extremely treacherous in argument.

Another kind of 'fuzziness' informs 'saving' in the sense of 'thrift'. Not to spend may constitute 'saving' in one set of circumstances and not in another, as the example of the price reductions on carpets which I used earlier (*supra*, pp. 25–6) serves to show. And again uncertainty does not arise because we are not clear what we mean by 'save'. The circumstances, on the other hand, of its use may well leave doubt as to whether it does apply or not. 'They claim I shall save if I buy one of their reduced-price carpets, but shall I?' It would be easy loosely to assume that the word 'save' is vague. But that is wrong. It is 'fuzzy'. Or at any rate the now systematically established usage empowers us also so to designate this particular type of indefinability, to mark its fundamental dissimilarity from polysemy. The question here is, 'Do my circumstances render me an agent for whom course of action α can boast a rating in the "saving" class?' This being the question, it cannot be assumed that if α = to procure something cheaply, then α = to make a saving. Nevertheless, my circumstances could be such that α will rate high in the 'saving' class. They could in fact locate it anywhere at all on the gamut between 0 and 1. 'Save' is polysemic, but the uncertainties we have been discussing have nothing to do with its other range of meaning as 'rescue'.

In urging, as I shall now proceed to do, the relevance to Paul of anatomising imprecision in this way, I aim only to indicate a line of approach which I believe could prove valuable. I shall not, therefore, attempt to justify each individual judgement I make regarding the 'fuzziness', or 'polysemy' of given Pauline usages. It is clear that a much more careful analysis would be necessary to substantiate what I here put forward essentially in the spirit of 'kite flying'. Much of my analysis of Paul's use of the enthymeme has been taken up with the study of the different senses in which the key terms in his argumentation can be taken. Typical examples of this are πίστις

Diagram 23

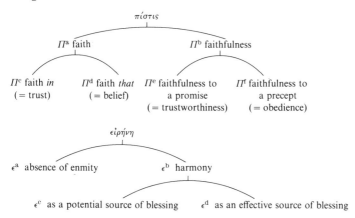

Diagram 24

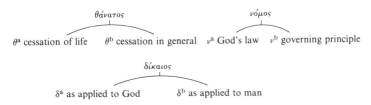

and εἰρήνη. To chart their semantic range as in diagram 23 is only to reveal the bare bones of their polysemic potential (as reference back to more fully worked-out analyses earlier in this study will show). But it is not all polysemy; at various points distinctions arise through 'fuzziness'. For example, πίστις divides into $Π^a/Π^b$ by way of polysemy; so does $Π^a$ into $Π^c/Π^d$. But $Π^b$ divides into $Π^e/Π^f$ by way of 'fuzziness'. 'Faithfulness' ($Π^b$) can only be understood one way. The two outcomes are the result of its application to two different objects. (This remains true even though one of the outcomes – $Π^f$ – happens to be such that it amounts to polysemy.) Turning to εἰρήνη, we find that $ε^b$ retains (like 'love') an indefinable residue to which $ε^c$ merely points more clearly, whilst $ε^d$ covers what *is* definable.

Similar contrasts seem to present themselves with θάνατος, νόμος and δίκαιος (see diagram 24). $θ^b$ and $ν^b$ present a 'fuzziness' which contrasts with $θ^a$ and $ν^a$. Instead the pattern is reversed in the case of δ.

It would be worthwhile to examine in detail the twists of Paul's argumentation in relation to these distinctions between polysemy and 'fuzziness', and to assess to what extent their argumentative validity is affected by this inter-relationship. It can surely be said, however, that a full appreciation of the second factor must do much to mitigate what in terms of the first would seem unpardonable exploitation of semantic ambivalence. But I seem to see something more radical happening, which – if I am right – is of even more interest and importance. As I see it, by virtue of the way Paul handles δίκαιος, νόμος and θάνατος all three terms undergo drastic shifts of semantic orientation which confer on them a strictly Pauline fuzziness.

In Paul's hands, δίκαιος becomes a term which has now, when applied to man, what it formerly had only when applied to God: a depth which precludes definition. When we say 'God is righteous', there is no way we can answer the request 'Could you be more explicit?' any more than in the case of 'I love you'. Through Christ it is the righteousness of God which becomes ours. Paul excludes the possibility of our righteousness being any other than God's. With the exclusion of any earlier definition of human righteousness as law-obedience, it has become indefinable. It has acquired, however, infinite depth. And it is on that which its clarity now depends, just as it is the indefinability due to depth that gives clarity to the word 'love'. A question which the application of the fuzzy calculus to the Pauline view of righteousness would force us to face is: What membership rating in the 'righteous' class would a perfect adherence to the law represent? Would it be 0 or 1? Another question would be: Does his view (in particular his concept of the 'obedience of faith') require us to ascribe to 'faith' an automatic rating of 1? At least it might then emerge more clearly which are the questions we cannot answer, which – that is – are the really uncomfortable areas of his argument.

In Paul's hands, νόμος becomes a term which, like 'security' or 'productivity', designates a factor which can be harmful or beneficial according to the context of its operation. Its meaning now lies precisely in this special kind of indefinability which it has acquired. (As 'a set of laws to be obeyed' it is seen to corrupt.) It is ἅγιος where it convicts us of sin and discloses the magnitude of God's gift of forgiveness; it kills where it is thought of as an instrument of privilege or of salvation. When Paul speaks of the law of faith, does he mean the Torah, or not? The fact that we find this question difficult to answer shows how dependent νόμος has now become for meaning on the opposing contexts of its operation. Law is thus seen no longer as a domain in which a straightforward character of prescriptiveness clarifies its parameters. It is now characterised in terms of the compatibility levels obtaining with regard to such classifiers as (a) 'salvific', (b) 'revelatory', (c) 'condemnatory', (d) 'deleterious'. (c) scores 1. Must (d) too rate 1? (b) is not 0. Does (a) rate 0? or should it be broken down into (i) 'directly salvific' and (ii) 'indirectly salvific', with only (i) scoring absolute 0, and (ii) scoring, say, 0.2 (for a small but crucial indirect role)?

In Paul's hands, θάνατος becomes a term like 'thrift', in that where it applies depends no longer on the process involved (which is always the same), but on what or who are the entities to which it applies. If I am a person in desperate need of a new carpet I save in taking advantage of a price reduction. If my carpet is good for a long time yet, I do not. The new carpet which I desperately need, if I buy it at bargain price, is a saving. The new carpet that I do not need, though I may buy it at a bargain price, is the opposite of a saving. If dying is 'a dying to sin' then it is applicable to the believer. Likewise if it is a dying 'in Christ' it is applicable to the believer. If, on the other hand, it is the effect of law, if it is the penalty of sin, then it is not applicable to the believer. However, it is applicable in exactly the reverse manner where it is the non-believer that is involved. For the believer, dying is not (and must not be) the definable concept that it was. Once 'to live' is Christ, 'death' as 'cessation' becomes irretrievably relative and problematical; Paul is doing far more than just taking that meaning and exploiting it figuratively. This 'more' is something the 'fuzzy' calculus helps to identify. Within the ambit of 'death' construed as a negative factor, the death of the believer rates 0. But where 'death' is seen as a sharing of the death of Christ and a dying to sin, the rating of the believer's experience within its ambit immediately jumps to 1.

It is in the tangles into which Paul's argument leads him, for reasons inherent in his semiological position, that these concepts are thus forged anew, beaten (as it were) into an all-pervasive 'fuzziness' – a property (as I hope to have demonstrated by now) not incompatible with systematic analysis. J. D. McCawley, in the section 'Many-valued and fuzzy logic' in his *Everything that Linguists have Always Wanted to Know about Logic*, gives examples of the kinds of difficulties in deductive logic that the application of a fuzzy calculus helps to sort out. One of them illustrates how the proposition 'All

Diagram 25

	fat	jolly
Kissinger	0.3	0.2
Brando	0.9	0.2

fat persons are jolly' is affected by the existence of the individuals Kissinger and Brando, whose group-membership ratings are as in diagram 25. McCawley adopts (p. 372) a method of applying the fuzzy calculus which would produce the following conclusion: 'The existence of Kissinger would be consistent with "All fat persons are jolly" having a truth value as high as 0.97, whereas the existence of Brando would mean that it could only have at most the truth value of 0.37.' Let me take a cue from this in order to explore how such a technique might work if applied to the deductive logic of Paul.

Take the proposition 'the law is destructive'. What happens if we try to assess its truth value against the scorings I suggested in my paragraph just now on νόμος? Making discretionary allowances for the uncertainties of those fuzzy scorings, I reach a truth value for that proposition of something like 0.5. This is tied in with my being obliged to ascribe to the opposite proposition 'the law is constructive' a truth value of at least 0.5. Such is the taut equilibrium in which the truth values of Paul emerge in this area; but rather than a stance whereby we see the matter in terms of contradiction to be acknowledged or else resolved, the principles of 'fuzzy' logic counsel another approach. As they lead us to regard things, Paul's network of ideas surrounding the law is inherently such that it precludes all reasoning except that which – to revert to Zadeh's terms – is 'neither entirely exact nor entirely inexact'; and we cannot analyse Paul's perception of the truth concerning the relative destructiveness or constructiveness of the law except as dependent on 'approximate reasoning'. What we can do, by means of the 'calculus of "fuzzy" restrictions', is to keep track of the approximate factor. All the ways in which apparently conflicting statements in Romans 1–8 have seemed either to defy or admit resolution take on a new complexion (and indeed need reconsidering) once we recognise 'fuzziness' as something distinct from vagueness or polysemy, something which makes analysis futile unless the extent and nature of the constraints it places on argument are expressly and methodically assessed. Thus probed, however, Paul's logic displays the peculiar value of its being 'approximate', and narrowed access has the effect of affording fuller admission to where clarity is effectively located.

This illustration offers – I hope and believe – a glimpse of how the issues in the enthymematic arguments I have sought to unravel in Chapters 2–4 of this study may be probed more analytically if 'fuzziness' is distinguished from polysemy, and the former systematically measured. It is a glimpse which I would truly like to see those with appropriately specialised skills pursue. It opens up a perspective in which the enthymeme, which may have seemed difficult to reconcile with 'clarity', emerges as the natural friend of the 'fuzzy concept'. The margin of uncertainty it involves parallels the indefinability to which the meaningfulness of such concepts is bound.

If what I am saying is valid, then the irregularity of enthymematic argumentation so apt to be disquieting in Paul may not only be something for which the adjectives 'welcome' and 'exciting' are not exaggerated, but something for which they are too weak; and it is rather as excelled than confirmed, I feel, that they now justify my proceeding to that aspect peculiar to the enthymematic argument in Romans on which I would let the spotlight of my attention finally rest: its office as an agent of encouragement. I thus reach the *reader-benefit issue* (cf. *supra*, p. 131), piloted towards it by the potency of a further phenomenon which plays a key role in semiosis: isotopy. This has to do with the way in which the decoding of any unit of signification depends on how we locate it within a wider unitary frame, or relate it to a wider thematic unit.

5.4   Interpretation and Isotopy. The value of isotopical analysis. An application to Romans on the basis of 1:12.

In *A Theory of Semiotics* Eco introduces the term at the end of the section in which he proposes the semantic model on which depends his theory of codes.[64] His working out of this is characterised by his distinction between denotative and connotative types of signification, and the consequent need to analyse the sign in terms of encyclopaedia rather than dictionary.[65] Noting that 'for a zoologist "whale" is a hierarchically and univocally organised sememe in which secondary properties depend on primary ones', he starts out by illustrating this in a table of the exemplary form seen in diagram 26. He continues: 'For the medieval author of a bestiary, "whale" may have had the same formal semantic structure, except that the content of the properties differed: whale was a fish and not a mammal, and among the secondary properties he would have put a lot of allegorical connotations.' This state of affairs Eco represents as in diagram 27, in which 'd' represents denotative and 'c' connotative meanings. To this he compares the fact that 'for a modern layman "whale" is probably a very disconnected sememe in which such properties as "fish" and "mammal" coexist and its semantic spectrum should probably be a network of superimpositions of possible readings in which the contextual selections are not very well established'. He attempts accordingly to chart a model that would allow for 'a contradictory sememe considering both the medieval, the scientific and the popular system of units' (diagram 28). Thus we have passed from dictionary to encyclopaedia as the basis of our semantic analysis. However, 'should every virtual property be taken into account . . . the reader would be obliged to outline, as in a sort of vivid mental picture, the whole network of interrelated properties that the encyclopaedia assigns to the corresponding sememe'.[66] In fact, though 'they are *virtually* present in the encyclopaedia, that is, they are socially *stored* . . . the reader picks them up from the semantic store only when required by the text'.[67] Contextual pressure actuates part only of the encyclopaedic possibilities. This pressure comes 'either (a) from the identification of a theme or *topic* and, consequently, from the selection of a path of interpretation or *isotopy*; or (b) from the reference to *frames*, which permit us to establish not only what is being talked about, but also under what profile, to what ends, and with what in view, it is being talked about'.[68]

If I say 'I have had a whale of a time', it at once establishes 'enjoyment' as the topic and locates the meaning of 'whale' far down the sequence beginning as in diagram 29, where the size of the whale has enabled its name to be conventionalised into an adjectival unit offering a heightened substitute for 'great' in 'I've had a great time'. Just as the topic thus determines the meaning of an individual word, it can determine the meaning of a sentence, or of any significant element or factor. If I say 'I went to the supermarket to get myself a loaf of bread' the topic 'day-to-day shopping' prevents all but a very small area of the semantic potential of 'supermarket' from coming into play.

Subsequent to my considerations relating to diagram 28 my quotations have been no longer from *A Theory of Semiotics* but from *The Role of the Reader* and *Semiotics and the Philosophy of*

Diagram 26

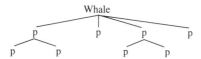

Diagram 27

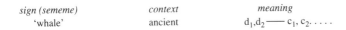

Diagram 28

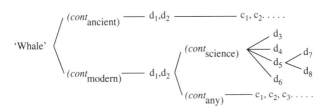

Diagram 29

$(cont_{any})$ ————— $c_1, c_2, c_3. \ldots \ldots \ldots$

Language. In a section of the latter devoted expressly to 'isotopy' Eco explains the relation of 'topic' to 'isotopy' thus: 'The topic is a pragmatic device, whereas the isotopy is a level of possible semantic actualisation of the text.'[69] Of isotopy he says further: 'Isotopy refers almost always to constancy in going in a direction that a text exhibits when submitted to rules of interpretive coherence.'[70] What rules of interpretative coherence would bring out 'constancy in going in a direction' in the letter to the Romans? We cannot understand the meaning of the argumentative factor in that letter except in relation to a conscious or unconscious choice of isotopies.

In the process of getting launched into his letter Paul says (1:11–12):

> ἐπιποθῶ γὰρ ἰδεῖν ὑμᾶς, ἵνα τι μεταδῶ χάρισμα ὑμῖν πνευματικὸν εἰς τὸ στηριχθῆναι ὑμᾶς, τοῦτο δέ ἐστιν συμπαρακληθῆναι ἐν ὑμῖν διὰ τῆς ἐν ἀλλήλοις πίστεως ὑμῶν τε καὶ ἐμοῦ.

If the many arguments that arise in what follows arise because Paul is impelled to argue, and because – in spite of the difficulties he encounters – he does not doubt that arguing fulfils a vital purpose, should we not see what he shares with his hearers already in presenting them with these arguments as at least one vital source of upbuilding and encouragement? The source of his argument in explicative necessity rather than choice on his part,[71] the vital role its inevitable complications serve in uncovering the depth and peculiarity of the concepts on which the gospel message depends,[72] help to cast it in the role of encouragement and indeed as a gift from which he and they all benefit (one which he offers them with the same confident boldness as that with which he proclaims the gospel itself). I will not suggest that we necessarily envisage his argumentation as finding its context in the topic of 'imparting a spiritual gift' – the semantics of 'spiritual gift' in Paul's discourse are too tricky.[73] I will, however, suggest that to *be mutually encouraged by one another's faith* and to *share the arguments that articulate and confirm the gospel message* are topics isotopically interpretative of each other.

5.5   Problems and advantages of the foregoing application. Its interaction with my general thesis.

The 'whale' in 'a whale of a time' is interpreted through the topic of 'enjoyment'. The 'encouragement' in the συμπαρακληθῆναι of Romans 1:12 does not admit of so isotopically uncontroversial an interpretation.

To begin with, there is uncertainty about the meaning of the verb. It can be used in the sense of 'comfort' and 'exhort' as well as 'encourage'. (It seems possible that it could simply refer to 'being brought together'.)[74] Moreover, whereas it has been usual to understand the encouragement as shared between Paul and the Romans, Dunn understands the 'mutual encouragement' to be 'mutual' among the Romans, it is thus only the faith which engenders it that is seen as something which he and they all share.[75] Dunn does this because he is inclined to see a dependence of their being encouraged on the proper understanding of spiritual gifts which Paul's presence among them will make sure of. But there is no agreement among commentators as to whether the χάρισμα πνευματικόν is anything other than the general kind of blessing which Paul's preaching – or indeed just his presence among them – would represent.[76]

Furthermore, to suggest that the συμπαρακληθῆναι of Romans 1:12 may be interpreted through the topic of 'argumentation' – and more particularly through that area of argumentation which is most problematical and which involves the frequent occurrence of enthymemes – is to disturb the hornet's nest of controversy relating to the purpose of Romans. Why the letter goes to such lengths to expound and defend the gospel remains a question. There has been an increasing tendency to seek to explain this in terms of some very specific end. The results, however, can take sharply contrasting forms. It was in order to engage the support of the Roman congregation for travel to Jerusalem and Spain (see Wedderburn, *The Reasons for Romans*). Or it was to urge the addressees themselves to pursue some very definite course of action such as F. Watson argues in *Paul, Judaism and the Gentiles*. Not all scholars even now, however, feel it necessary to see its purpose as anything but more generally pastoral. Much depends on the extent to which exordium and peroration are foregrounded, and on whether chapter 16 is considered integral to the letter. A wide variety of isotopies and referrals to different unitary frameworks is thus involved.[77]

My case for interpreting συμπαρακληθῆναι through the topic of 'argumentation' is based entirely on elements internal to the argumentative material itself, notably:

(1) the importance which, by its pervasiveness in Romans, argumentation shows itself to have in Paul's approach to the gospel and its understanding;

(2) the semiotic situation in which, by virtue of its having the Crucifixion as its object, the argumentation originates and operates;

(3) the nature of the 'light' and 'excitement' to which, through the particular patterns of reasoning prompted by (2), argumentation here gives rise.

In this chapter, where I have been trying to articulate what I believe to be the principal insights of this study, the illustration of the third of these elements has constituted the leading thread (a thread which has led me, via a review of factors of possible relevance such as the aesthetic, to see the richest potential as lying in solid argumentative substance). It is because my study points to 'light' and 'excitement' as qualities substantially ascribable to Pauline argumentation that this argumentation admits of 'mutual encouragement' being taken as a topic that lends to it directional constancy. And it is precisely because this is so that I suggest that, in its turn, such argumentation be seen as isotopically interpretative of συμπαρακληθῆναι.

> . . . πῶς γνωσθήσεται τὸ αὐλούμενον ἢ τὸ
> κιθαριζόμενον; . . .

The 'clarity' of the tune being piped or plucked out by the Pauline enthymeme, any excitement, any impact, which the trumpeting of Pauline calls upon reason may provoke, are of a kind which at one and the same time represents and generates encouragement.

Different isotopies do not necessarily exclude one another. 'Argumentation' would only provide one interpretation of συμπαρακληθῆναι. Nor would *its* meaning be confined to that with which the 'encouragement' framework provides it. It may, however, be impossible for some isotopies to be entertained concurrently, and my approach is clearly incompatible with the isotopical implications of a number of the approaches I was just now alluding to. But I will not set about investigating that matter any further; it would take me beyond the scope of what I am wanting to say, either at this point in particular, or as my overall thesis. I am more than satisfied if the sum of all I have managed to say comes within the terms of the assessment with which I will now conclude. And its terms are set by the following aim: to clarify and reiterate how I am led to assert what remains essentially a preliminary: any attempt to analyse or assess Pauline argumentation which fails to take account of the particular nature of its semiological origination lacks an important prerequisite for the penetration of its logical substance. That is to say, it is because the semiological mode of Recognition both requires of Paul deductive thinking, and at the same time limits the freedom with which he can apply it, that his argument appears erratic as well as consistent, though the extent of its cogency can be shown to reach further than non-'fuzzy' logical analysis would have suggested. With these terms marking the range of my assessment, my formulations will attempt to meet the exigencies of technical precision without losing the advantages of a more directly communicative phraseology.

CONCLUSIONS REACHED; THEIR SCOPE ASSESSED

In spite of, or perhaps because of, the vast amount of attention Paul, and above all Romans, has attracted and continues to attract, a reliable guide through the perplexities that his writing generates seems to become more and more elusive. The perplexity to which his enthymematic mode of argumentation gives rise is only one among the many; but it is a major one, owing, above all, to the frequent tendency for the vigorous persistence of his reasoning to seem ill-matched by the solidity, or at any rate the lucidity, of his logic. It is my contention in this study that semiological theory offers principles which provide some explanation of this phenomenon and something like a basis for orientation – less a compass, perhaps, than a guide to appreciation of the tune Paul is playing. If, in the area of Paul's use of the enthymeme in Romans 1–8, I make any attempt to affirm οὕτως γνωσθήσεται τὸ λαλούμενον, it is on the basis of a definition of his tune as one of encouragement: encouragement arising from the way in which the semiotic dynamic of the Crucifixion, playing tricks with the inherited terminology of Judaism, constrains such standard lexemes as 'law', 'righteousness' and 'death' to *express* the innovatory *content* of the Pauline εὐαγγέλιον.

Paul has to spell out his experience of that mode of semiosis which is Recognition. The content of his recognition (that the crucified Christ is risen and lives forever, with all that that entails) has no parallel. Reason is both indispensable to the task of explication and a source of embarrassment (owing to tensions inherent in the operational dynamics of this mode of semiosis). The patterns of verbal expression which are generated, though they may involve an undeniable measure of confusion and inconsistency, involve also a high degree of creativity, the conceptual depth of which the 'fuzzy' calculus seems peculiarly well fitted to probe. This is the direction of possible future enquiry which I see as offering the greatest promise.

At the same time I do not, of course, wish to exaggerate what it can be expected to account for.

In at least one sense this creative dimension is akin to the 'invention' which characterises aesthetic communication. In that context, a sympathetic inventiveness is required in the recipient. What training and sensibility may or may not ensure there, the spiritual experience of the recipient may or may not ensure in the Pauline context. However, whilst the artist works relatively safely within the semiological boundaries of his art, Paul works precariously on the treacherous edges of the realm of logicality, and the spirituality required in the recipient of the Pauline message is not a decoding agent that simply bypasses the hazards which lie in the way of reason.

In the circumstances it is no surprise if the champion of the εὔσημος λόγος seems to be playing a tune it is not easy to place. The framework in which obscurities arise in Romans 1–8 leads me to suggest that the tune becomes clearer when it is understood as one of encouragement; but I am also taking it for granted that its full and ultimate identity is such that it must always stretch the capabilities of the human ear to where it will elude them. However richly endowed by the Holy Spirit the human capacity for understanding may be, the instruments of semiosis through which understanding occurs remain those with which the limited world of our perceptions provides us. Nor, of course, did Paul, for all his confidence in deductive reasoning, consider that the channels of our present experience, through which the Spirit imparts messages to our human minds, could ever furnish more than a shadowy anticipation of the seeing 'face to face' where love would finally render every other agent of recognition irrelevant.

NOTES

1. Enthymematic semiosis in Paul

1 U. Eco, *A Theory of Semiotics*, p. 224. This appeared first in Italian (1975) under the title *Trattato di semiotica generale*, then in English (1976). I shall preface my page references by *TS* when they refer to the English edition and by *TSG* if to the Italian edition. The focal feature is Table 39 (*TS*, p. 218), which strives to present a comprehensive 'Typology of Modes of Sign Production'.

2 Eco, *TS*, p. 218. These four modes explicate 'the *physical labor* needed to produce expressions' (ibid., p. 217). 'Expressions' are the 'elements of a conveying system'. Through the apportioning of these to the elements of a 'conveyed system' the latter become the 'content' of the former (ibid., p. 48). The Act of Recognition is the 'physical labour' needed for the footprint to become the 'expression' of a 'content'.

3 *TS*, p. 217.

4 Opinions vary concerning this, as over whether the term 'semiotics' or 'semiology' is preferable. For both issues see respectively G. Lepschy's review of Eco's *La struttura assente* (*Linguistics* 62, 1970, p. 109) and his very recent *La linguistica del '900*, p. 140.

5 'A sign-function arises when an expression is correlated to a content' (*TS*, p. 48). Hjelmslev had said of 'expression' and 'content' that they are 'designations of the functives that contract the function in question, the sign-function' (*Prolegomena*, p. 48).

6 These include: (a) signs 'from which a receiver infers something about the situation of the sender even though this sender is unaware of sending something to somebody'; (b) 'phenomena that do not have a human emitter, provided that they do have a human receiver' (*TS*, p. 16). According to Eco, 'The human addressee is the methodological . . . guarantee of the existence of a signification' (ibid.), but he recognises the controversial nature of his position on this matter (ibid.).

7 *TS*, p. 221.

8 Ibid.

9 'Ostension occurs when a given object or event produced by nature or human action (intentionally or unintentionally and existing in a world of fact as a fact among facts) is "picked up" by someone and *shown* as the expression of the class of which it is a member' (*TS*, pp. 224–5).

10 Paul, of course, does not have a concrete and visible object which he can

161

show to those to whom he is speaking, such as Crusoe had in the footprint and could have shown to a fellow castaway. What he has to show them is a historical fact (the crucifixion of Jesus of Nazareth), as must frequently, indeed usually, be the case where the object of Ostension is an event.

11 'Ostension may suggest an entire discourse' (*TS*, p. 225).

12 *TS*, pp. 227–8; *TSG*, p. 297.

13 Music, for example, is a species of sign-production the meaning of which cannot be articulated in words. Eco (*TS*, pp. 228ff.) notes and discusses the 'fallacy' behind observations of Lévi-Strauss on 'the "linguistic" properties of paintings, tonal [but not atonal] music', etc.

14 'Codes provide the rules which *generate* signs as concrete occurrences in communicative intercourse' (*TS*, p. 49).

15 The phonemes and morphemes of verbal discourse (i.e. the smallest distinctive sound units and the smallest units conveying meaning) are 'expressions' which employ 'a continuum' (i.e. raw material) 'completely alien to their possible referents, and arbitrarily correlated to one or more content-units' (*TS*, p. 228). See notes 2 and 5 *supra* for 'expression'/ 'content' terminology.

16 Hence they are referred to by Eco as 'combinational units' or 'unità combinatorie' (*TS*, pp. 227ff.; *TSG*, pp. 297ff.).

17 This kind of analysis has its origins in the work of Hjelmslev, who says on p. 45 of his *Prolegomena*: 'When we attempt to analyse sign-express-ions . . . there comes a stage in the analysis of the expression when the entities yielded can no longer be said to be bearers of meaning and thus no longer are sign-expressions.' To such 'non-signs' as thus 'enter into a sign system as parts of signs' he applies (p. 46) the term 'figurae', and notes: 'a language is so ordered that with the help of a handful of figurae and through ever new arrangements of them a legion of signs can be constructed'.

18 In *Semiotics and the Philosophy of Language* (pp. 169ff.), Eco designates this type of code an 's-code', saying, 'The distinctive features which make up phonemes are elements of a mere system of mutual positions and oppositions, pure paradigm.' In fact 'a phoneme is distinguished from another by the presence or absence of one or more among the features that form the phonological system'. In *Il segno* (pp. 72–3) he had criticised the use of the term 'code' at this level, recommending 'system' instead. 'S-code' is a compromise (but see his comments on this term in *TS*, p. 38).

19 Eco has incurred much criticism for his stretching of the term 'code' to include circumstantial frames of reference (see *infra*, n. 77).

20 So at any rate thinks Hengel (*The Pre-Christian Paul*, p. 83).

21 Taken thus, however, it raises the question of whether the emphasis on the Cross in 1 Corinthians 1 and 2 contrasts with that on the Resurrec-tion in 15. Beker worries greatly over this (*Paul the Apostle*, pp. 173–5), accepting a real distinction in Paul's mind between '*the* gospel' in general and his particular gospel to the Corinthians (ibid., p. 385, n. 77). Conzelmann, on the other hand, sees no problem. The Cross was the permanent focus of Paul's teaching, a focus, however, which depends

invariably on the relation of Cross to Resurrection (*1 Corinthians*, p. 54). Senft puts this point very clearly (*La Première Épitre aux Corinthiens*, p. 46).

22 How far we are safe in doing this is variously assessed: witness the commentaries on Galatians of Longenecker (p. 31), Fung (p. 64), Bruce (p. 89) and Bligh (pp. 131–3), and that on 1 Corinthians of Fee (p. 395); also the studies on Paul's conversion by Ralston and Räisänen, and, most negative of all, that of J. T. Sanders in 1966.

23 For the issue in question see Mussner, *Der Galaterbrief*, p. 85 (discussing O. Betz); Patte, *Paul's Faith and the Power of the Gospel*, p. 239; Bornkamm, 'The revelation', and Kim, whose *The Origin of Paul's Gospel*, pp. 69–70, draws on the views of Baird ('What is Kerygma?') and Wegenast (*Das Verständnis*).

24 *TS*, p. 228.

25 . . . as his appearing alive in front of me proves (the 'Son of God' being God's specially chosen instrument for our salvation).

26 *Gorgias*, pp. 451–5b (Steph).

27 For how the real Gorgias rates it, see J. De Romilly, *Magic and Rhetoric in Ancient Greece*.

28 See A. Michel, *Rhétorique et philosophie chez Cicéron*, p. 90.

29 G. A. Kennedy, *Classical Rhetoric and its Christian and Secular Tradition*, p. 4.

30 Ibid., pp. 5–6.

31 Ibid., p. 4.

32 See Kessler, 'A methodological setting for rhetorical criticism', for a general review of the situation.

33 Kennedy discusses this factor: see *Classical Rhetoric*, p. 130, and *NT Interpretation through Rhetorical Criticism*, pp. 7–8.

34 J. Muilenberg, 'Form criticism and beyond'.

35 Ibid., p. 8. He accordingly defines its task as essentially twofold: (1) to define the limits and scope of the literary unit; (2) to recognise the structure of the composition and discern the configuration of its parts (pp. 8–11).

36 W. Wuellner, 'Where is rhetorical criticism taking us?', pp. 451–3.

37 Ibid., p. 449.

38 The full exposition of the theory is undertaken in C. Perelman and L. Olbrechts-Tyteca, *La Nouvelle Rhétorique*. The reference by Perelman to its original presentation is to be found in *The New Rhetoric and the Humanities*, p. 31.

39 Zyskind in the introduction to Perelman, *The New Rhetoric*, p. ix.

40 Ibid., p. 50.

41 These points are spread over pp. xiii–xx of Zyskind's introduction ibid. (Interesting comments on the *Phaedrus* are made by G. Kennedy in *The Art of Persuasion in Greece*, p. 79.)

42 The bracketed quote is from Zyskind's introduction (p. xi).

43 The contributions of Standaert and H. D. Betz to the 1986 volume *L'Apôtre Paul*, edited by Vanhoye, both, in different ways, highlight the problem. Its complexities may explain why so much of the pioneering work in modern rhetorical criticism of the NT focussed on the Synop-

tics, e.g. Wilder, *Early Christian Rhetoric*; Kennedy, 'An introduction to the rhetoric of the gospels'.

44 See R. Schäfer, 'Melanchthons Hermeneutik', p. 219. Melanchthon's breakdown of Romans 1:8–5:11 may be of doubtful validity, but it illustrates the principle to which he held, that to understand Paul we must use the same tools as he used in making himself understood.

45 See *De Doctrina Christiana*, IV.vii.11, 12. Gibson, 'Lanfranc's Commentary on the Pauline Epistles', p. 103, notes Lanfranc's doubts.

46 Betz, *Galatians*, p. xiv.

47 Ibid., pp. 1–23, of which 16–23 are taken up with detailed illustrative analysis.

48 Ibid., pp. 24–8.

49 Ibid., pp. 28–30.

50 Ibid., p. 25.

51 The last part of Betz's introduction (pp. 30ff.) anticipates what is to be the main task of the commentary itself, tracing the overt reasoning of Paul the theologian as he argues from experience, scripture, baptism, friendship, ethics.

52 Wuellner, 'Where is . . .', pp. 455ff. Kennedy's model prescribes five stages and Wuellner discusses each in turn: (1) the definition of the rhetorical unit; (2) the identification of the rhetorical situation; (3) the identification of the rhetorical disposition or arrangement; (4) the identification of rhetorical techniques or style; (5) the identification of rhetorical criticism as a synchronic whole. Cosby, 'Paul's persuasive language', applies the same technique to Romans 5.

53 Wuellner, 'Paul's rhetoric of argumentation in Romans', p. 335. He takes the axiom thus formulated from Perelman and Olbrechts-Tyteca, *Nouvelle Rhétorique*.

54 How far and to what different kinds of advantage this tendency is in effect eluded can be observed in studies like those of Schüssler Fiorenza, Snyman, Aletti, Standaert, Vouga (see my bibliography). New angles on interpretation characterise some such recent work on Romans (McDonald, Penna). The purposes behind the letter focus the rhetorical analyses of Jewett ('Romans as an ambassadorial letter') and Crafton ('Paul's rhetorical vision'), as they build on Wuellner.

55 And there are other factors. See M. F. Wiles, *The Divine Apostle*, pp. 16–19.

56 Norden recapitulates in *Die antike Kunstprosa* (1971 edn), pp. 479–92.

57 Deissmann's work, originally published in 1908, appeared in English in 1910 as *Light from the Ancient East*. The points I have summarised figure mainly on pp. 224–34 of the latter edition.

58 See Norden, *Antike Kunstprosa*, pp. 492–506.

59 Ibid., p. 509.

60 Bultmann, *Der Stil*, p. 108.

61 Ibid., p. 4.

62 *The NT in its Literary Environment*. Aune takes into account the work by Stowers on the diatribe.

63 J. L. White, 'St Paul', p. 437; see also Stirewalt, 'Form and function'.

64 Kennedy, *NT Interpretation*, p. 93.
65 Ibid., p. 113.
66 Ibid., p. 159. Not purely formal, at least one of Kennedy's school (Levison) urges.
67 Bultmann, *Der Stil*, pp. 105–6.
68 As being a 'heavenly letter' in the case of Galatians (*Galatians*, p. 25).
69 F. Young and D. F. Ford, *Meaning and Truth*, p. 55.
70 Kennedy, *NT Interpretation*, p. 17.
71 Detweiler, 'What is a sacred text?', p. 213.
72 Ibid., pp. 223–4.
73 The words are those of N. Hadjinicolaou and are quoted by L.-J. Calvet in his book *Roland Barthes. Un regard politique sur le signe*, p. 149.
74 Eco analyses it in *TS*, pp. 283ff.
75 Compare the example in Barthes, *Mythologies*, pp. 34–5. For the semiotic structure responsible for such 'mythologies' see ibid., pp. 191ff., and his *Éléments de Sémiologie*, Section IV. That they arise from factors inherent in semiosis itself was clearly anticipated by Saussure (*Cours*, ed. de Mauro, p. 34). 'Inside every historical sign system there exists a hierarchy of cultural codifications' says M. Corti, *An Introduction to Literary Semiotics*, p. 19. If semiotics is seen thus, code-switching must figure as very deeply rooted in human intercourse. Eco brings up code-switching under the heading of rhetorical semiosis; but though the views I have just been discussing are reflected there (*TS*, pp. 276–8) he has reservations (see *I limiti*).
76 He focusses on it at the very height of his discourse on rhetorical code-switching (*TS*, p. 277).
77 I appreciate that this is controversial. Segre (*Semiotics and Literary Criticism*, p. 40) deprecates 'the semiotics of the codified so dear to Eco'. I am working throughout this study on the basis that there are advantages in Eco's view.
78 Eco (as Segre acknowledges, *Semiotics*, p. 40) shows uncertainty about the status of the semiotic codes to which he refers, and in *La struttura assente* (p. 148) considers a different nomenclature. Also, in *TS* (p. 136), affirming that 'overcoding proceeds from existing codes to more analytic subcodes while undercoding proceeds from non-existent codes to potential codes', he admits that 'this double movement, so easily detectable in various cases . . . is frequently intertwined in most common cases of sign production and interpretation, so that in many instances it seems difficult to establish whether one is over or undercoding'. In *Semiotics and the Philosophy of Language* (pp. 164–5) he addresses head-on the issue of whether the 'old' concept of code should be deemed 'metaphorical' and replaced, and suggests on the contrary that it holds promise of 'undiscovered fruitfulness'.
79 The process will be elucidated more fully in my closing chapter.
80 Unless this point is emphasised, we miss the complexity of Paul's epistemological position, and the full diversity of its aspects (as brought into view by Theobald, 'Glaube und Vernunft', and Baasland, 'Cognitio Dei').

2. Varieties of enthymematic effect in Romans 1–4

1 Problems surround Aristotle's distinction between the inference which is immediate (ἄμεσος) and that which is not. They are discussed by Reade, *The Problem of Inference*, pp. 11ff. It is sufficient for our present purpose to relate it to the number of premises involved.

2 Joseph, *An Introduction to Logic*, p. 352. The principle is one which we find spelt out for instance in Quintilian (see Lausberg, *Handbuch*, §371). On syllogism see *infra*, n. 19. Its presence in Paul was noted by Lanfranc (see Gibson, 'Lanfranc's Commentary', p. 102). Enthymemes in Galatians claim the attention of Hansen, *Abraham in Galatians*, pp. 88–9, 117. Vinson, 'A comparative study', notes them in the synoptics.

3 Barker comments (*The Elements of Logic*, p. 297): 'Sometimes the arguer has a premise fairly definitely in mind but regards it as common knowledge and so does not bother to state it. Other times the arguer has not thought of the unstated premise at all, but would embrace it if it were pointed out.'

4 Indeed this contingency explains the reason for the term: τὰ δὲ ἐνθυμήματα ὠνόμασται ... ὅτι προσενθυμεῖσθαι τοῖς δικασταῖς, εἴ τι ἐλλείποι, καταλείπει – as Minucian states (see Lausberg, *Handbuch*, §371).

5 'That a tight logical argument is not effective in rhetoric, which is addressed to a popular audience' is an attitude already perceptible in Aristotle (see Kennedy, *Classical Rhetoric*, p. 71). To the enthymeme rhetoric owes its 'body' (see Mainberger, *Der Leib der Rhetorik*, esp. pp. 72–6).

6 This is part of the pursuit of that which will be readily accepted – 'des publikumsentsprechenden *credibile*' (Lausberg, *Handbuch*, §371).

7 The equivocal character of the enthymeme as depicted by Eco (as I note in Chapter 1, p. 26) is already normative for Quintilian.

8 Barker, *Elements of Logic*, p. 378. An arguer's known view may fix such principles (Walton, *Informal Logic*, p. 115).

9 See, for example, Jevons, *Elementary Lessons in Logic*, pp. 153–4, or Wolf, *Textbook of Logic*, p. 110. Enthymemes of the third order can be motivated by the very precise aim of giving emphasis to an inference by leaving it unsaid (see Jevons, *Elementary Lessons*, p. 154). The result – as Stebbing observes (*A Modern Introduction to Logic*, p. 83) – will have the character of *innuendo*.

10 Although it should not be assumed that the classification of enthymemes into orders reflects their relative importance (or extension), it is true that enthymemes of the first order are by far the most common.

11 The expedient was put forward by Philoponus (see Kneale and Kneale, *The Development of Logic*, p. 71).

12 See ibid., p. 69.

13 Jevons, *Elementary Lessons*, pp. 154–5: 'Even a single proposition may have a syllogistic force if it clearly suggest to the mind a second premise which thus enables a conclusion to be drawn.'

14 Copi, *An Introduction to Logic*, pp. 205–7.

15 Joseph gives a detailed account in *An Introduction*, p. 350, n. 1. See also Keynes, *Studies and Exercises in Formal Logic*, pp. 367–8.

16 Kennedy, *Classical Rhetoric*, p. 80.

17 Hamilton, *Discussions on Philosophy*, p. 156.

18 Schipper and Schuh, *A First Course in Modern Logic*, pp. 155ff. I shall not apply this extended use to Paul.

19 Joseph, *An Introduction*, p. 256. He continues: 'The major premise is the premise in which the major term occurs, and the minor premise that in which the minor term occurs. Thus in the syllogism: "All organisms are mortal – Man is an organism – so: Man is mortal", the major term is *mortal*, and the major premise *all organisms are mortal*; the minor term *man*, and the minor premise *man is an organism*; the middle term, *organism*. It will be noticed that each term in a syllogism appears twice: the major and minor terms each in its respective premise and in the conclusion, the middle in both premises but not in the conclusion. In giving examples of syllogism, it is usual to write down the major premise first; but in ordinary life and conversation, no particular order is observed.' The structure of the syllogism can be indicated diagrammatically as in diagram 30. The positioning of the terms in the premises varies, and the possible permutations produce the four 'figures' (σχήματα) of the syllogism. The positioning shown here is that of the first figure; for the rest (and the 'moods') see Strawson, *Introduction to Logical Theory*, p. 158.

Diagram 30

		Terms		RELATIONSHIP
		(subject)	(predicate)	
Premise	{ *Major*	Middle	Major	
	{ *Minor*	Minor	Middle	
Conclusion		Minor	Major	

20 Cf. *supra*, n. 4.

21 Dunn, CR, p. 45. Cf. Vuilleumier and Keller, *Michée, Nahoum, Habacuc, Sophonie*, p. 159, but also Brownlee, *The Midrash Pesher of Habakkuk*, p. 129.

22 Ziesler, CR, pp. 71–2. Koch, in his exhaustive survey of the textual complications involved ('Der Text von Hab. 2:4b . . .'), doubts whether the MT gives us the original meaning, a position which Fitzmyer's probings have not disposed him to endorse: CR, p. 264.

23 Dunn, CR, p. 46.

24 Dunn (ibid.) indicates how the major commentators stand aligned on this matter. Cranfield's (CR, p. 101) remains a very balanced and steady discussion of the subject, and, though he recognises many weighty arguments to the contrary, he concludes that ἐκ πίστεως should almost certainly be connected with δίκαιος. This was the view argued by Feuillet in one of the most extensive studies of the question ('La citation d'Habacuc 2:4'). The matter continues to elicit comment and debate (e.g. Robertson, 'The "justified (by faith)"'; Cavallin, 'The righteous

shall live by faith'; Moody, 'The Habakkuk quotation'; Fitzmyer, CR). The implications of Paul's use of the same quotation in Galatians 3:11 have to be considered, of course, but are difficult to assess in view of the different nature of Paul's concerns in that letter – *and*, as Moody aptly adds ('The Habakkuk quotation', p. 207), the 'different treatment of similar matters'.

25 Dunn, CR, p. 44. The Midrashic principle involved is lucidly summed up in *DBI*, p. 457.

26 Dunn, CR, pp. 43, 44. The background to this he has dealt with on pp. 40–2: 'In Hebrew thought *zedeq/zdaqah* is essentially a concept of *relation*. Righteousness is not something which an individual has on his or her own, independently of anyone else; it is something which one has precisely in one's relationships as a social being. People are righteous when they meet the claims which others have on them by virtue of their relationship . . . God is "righteous" when he fulfils the obligations he took upon himself to be Israel's God, that is, to rescue Israel and punish Israel's enemies . . . It is clearly this concept of God's righteousness which Paul takes over . . . What marks Paul's use of the concept off from that given to him in his Jewish heritage, however, is precisely his conviction that the covenantal framework of God's righteousness has to be understood afresh in terms of faith.'

27 And Dunn is not in the least bothered if it does. 'In the tradition of Jewish exegesis Paul would not necessarily want to narrow the meaning to *exclude* other meanings self-evident in the text forms used elsewhere, so much as to *extend* and broaden the meaning to include the sense he was most concerned to bring out. The various rules of interpretation already current in Pharisaic circles at the time of Paul . . . were designed to draw out as much meaning as possible from the text. In this case the fuller meaning would include the possibility of taking the ἐκ πίστεως with both ὁ δίκαιος and ζήσεται.' Indeed Paul does not expect a reader to opt one way or the other. Thus Dunn, CR, pp. 43–6. However, it is all very well to see Paul as entertaining more than one meaning as he speaks; but he cannot really do that *and* engage in deductive reasoning at the same time, at any rate not without a messy result. The build-up of scholarship (as seen for example in Fitzmyer, 'The use of explicit OT quotation' or Longenecker, 'Paul and the OT') has led Dunn a long way from the mood ascribed to Paul by Ellis in *Paul's Use of the Old Testament*.

28 Joseph, *Introduction to Logic*, p. 579.

29 Fitzmyer, *Pauline Theology. A Brief Sketch*, p. 64.

30 Käsemann, CR, p. 30. (All page references to Käsemann, CR, apply to the ET (1982 edn) unless otherwise indicated.) Schlier (CR, p. 44) also takes particular note of the fact that the righteousness of God referred to is such that the gospel *reveals* it. Williams, 'The "righteousness of God" in Romans', p. 256, raises some pertinent questions in this connection.

31 'Käsemann's quite proper and influential understanding of divine right-eousness as a gift which has the character of power, because God is savingly active in it' Dunn (CR, p. 42) calls it, in affirming its legitimate derivation from the understanding of righteousness as relationship. But

there are complications: see Soards, 'Käsemann's "Righteousness" re-examined'.

32 As Sanders sees Paul's righteousness terminology, it is not used with '*any one* meaning. It may be used as the equivalent of salvation and life; or it may refer to acquittal in the present for past transgressions, or to future vindication in the judgement' (*PPJ*, p. 495) – *contra* Käsemann, 'The righteousness' and Stuhlmacher, 'The apostle Paul's view of righteousness'.

33 Cranfield examines in detail the long-standing controversy concerning the first issue, defining it (CR, p. 96) as 'whether δικαιοσύνη refers to an activity of God or to a status of man resulting from God's action'. But in Dunn's opinion (CR, p. 41) this is still to see the matter as an either–or which 'allows nothing for the dynamism of relationship which can embrace both senses' (a new relevance for the either/or, however, is discovered by Güttgemanns: '"Gottesgerechtigkeit" und strukturale Semantik'; and Fitzmyer, CR, p. 262, urges we speak afresh in terms of 'subjective' construal). Regarding the πιστεύοντι of 1:16, Käsemann says: 'the Greek sense, "regard something as true", plays no role for Paul, just as the OT sense "trust" or, derived from it, "become part of a new relationship with God" is still not decisive. The verse speaks of faith only as decision' (CR, p. 23). Cranfield echoes this ('faith . . . can exist only as response to the gospel', CR, p. 90), but is also concerned both to emphasise how often faith for Paul is "fides qua" (see pp. 66–7) and yet also to acknowledge the indispensability of the "fides quae" dimension (see p. 312), going even so far as to affirm 'it is in fact upon the "belief that" that the "belief in" is based'.

34 Murray (CR, p. 30) and Leenhardt (CR, p. 56) both saw a false dichotomy as arising from this tendency, and tried to correct it.

35 I limit myself to saying 'admits of' for reasons that emerge in the next note.

36 I am taking the εἰς τὸ εἶναι of 1:20 as introducing a consecutive clause. Some commentators have taken it to be final: Michel (CR) and Barrett (CR) are notable examples. If it is taken thus, then what I am saying does not hold. But Käsemann (CR, p. 42) argues: 'The declarative sense of the accusation can be maintained only if it is understood as consecutive.'

37 Controversy regarding just what ἀδόκιμος νοῦς and man's being 'handed over' must be understood to entail (see Cranfield, CR, pp. 120–1) leads to different assessments of Paul's precise position, but only affects the logic of this enthymeme if it places in doubt the universality of condemnation.

38 For the awkwardness involving διό compare 2Cor 4:16; 5:9; and for somewhat similar cases with a following ἵνα, Phil 2:9; 2Cor 12:7.

39 Which commentators subscribe to how much of such a reading is of less importance than the fact that since the days (c. 1973) when Cranfield referred to the 'weighty reasons' there were for identifying the referent of ὁ κρίνων as the Jew (see CR, p. 138), the tendency has been predominantly to find yet weightier reasons for doing so.

40 Leenhardt, CR, p. 74.

41 Watson, *Paul, Judaism and the Gentiles*, pp. 109ff.

42 Ziesler says (CR, p. 81): 'Whether or not we can say that this was originally a synagogue sermon, there is much in it that would have been at home in such a setting, and virtually nothing that would not.' For Sanders's defence of this theory and the use to which he puts it see *Paul, the Law and the Jewish People*, pp. 129–32.

43 See Cranfield, CR, p. 141. The Jewish relevance is further probed by Carras, 'Romans 2:1–29: a dialogue of Jewish ideals'.

44 Dunn, CR, p. 79.

45 Ziesler, CR, p. 18. Cf. Drane, 'Why did Paul write Romans?'; of a different mind: Minear, *The Obedience of Faith*; Watson, *Paul, Judaism . . .*; Elliott, *The Rhetoric of Romans*.

46 That the 'Kampfthesen' of 2:27–8 work against what is now the argumentative drift is noted by Michel (CR, p. 137).

47 Could it, for example, mean 'not altogether'? See Cranfield, CR; Davies, *Faith and Obedience in Romans*.

48 For example, 'Are we Jews excelled?' (Fitzmyer, CR), or 'How do I defend myself?' (O'Neill's choice in *Paul's Letter to the Romans*), or even 'Am I ascribing priorities?', as Synge proposes in 'The meaning of προεχόμεθα'.

49 There are a number of textual variants. Juggling with the punctuation opens up another range of options. Dahl sets it all out in full in 'Romans 3.9. Text and meaning'.

50 Dunn (CR, p. 147) gives considerable credence to a solution proposed by Dahl (favouring the variant omitting οὐ πάντως). Ziesler (CR, p. 102) thinks the interpretation represented by the RSV, 'Are we Jews any better off? No, not at all' had best be accepted. Cranfield preferred that which understands οὐ πάντως as 'not altogether' (CR, p. 190). As Dodd notes (CR, p. 47), it irks one to credit Paul with 'direct self-contradiction within a few verses'. Davies, *Faith and Obedience*, follows Cranfield.

51 It is an issue where the traditional bounds of the discussion have been vigorously challenged in recent times. Watson (*Paul, Judaism . . .*, pp. 115–22) provides an illustration. See also Räisänen, *Paul and the Law*, pp. 101–9, and, for earlier debate on the subject, Riedl, 'Die Auslegung von Röm 2:14–16'.

52 The extent to which Paul is here proclaiming a doctrine of mankind's bondage to evil and the relation of this to his sources and to contemporary Jewish thought are all succinctly surveyed by Ziesler (CR, pp. 102–3).

53 διότι is capable of meaning 'therefore', and is so rendered here not only in the AV but also in the NIV. But Sanday and Headlam (CR, p. 42) affirm that it never has that meaning in the NT. Neither Cranfield nor Dunn even considers the possibility. See also BDF, §451(5).

54 Cranfield (CR, p. 143) notes parallel usage in Romans 3:19, 8:28 and 1Tim 1:8, which would confirm this to be Paul's tone here.

55 See Dunn, CR, pp. 152–3.

56 That is probably all the *yizdaq* in Psalm 143 (LXX 142):2 originally meant. Ziesler (*The Meaning of Righteousness in Paul*, pp. 190–1) insists

on the importance of taking 3:20 in conjunction with 3:10–18. 'The impossibility of justification is consequent upon the non-existence of law-righteousness.' Schreiner takes the same view in '"Works of Law" in Paul'. Tobin, 'Controversy and continuity in Romans 1:18–3:20', has an interesting slant.

57 For some critical coverage of what these are see Ziesler, CR, p. 105. It emerges in more detail in Schreiner, '"Works of Law"', and in Cosgrove, 'Justification in Paul'.

58 Both Cranfield (briefly, CR, p. 198) and Wilckens (at some length, CR, I, pp. 176–82) warn against the mistake of premature anticipation of concepts not developed until later in the letter when interpreting 3:20.

59 Ziesler (CR, p. 106) links 20a to 20b via the concept of role: 'The law cannot justify; its role is only to reveal sin.' I have purposely here avoided broaching the question I am about to allude to in my next paragraph, namely whether the ἔργα νόμου, misguidedly associated with being adjudged righteous, belong to law-observance conceived as a boundary-marker or as intrinsically meritorious.

60 'The pattern is based on election and atonement for transgressions, it being understood that God gave commandments in connection with the election and that obedience to them, or atonement and repentance for transgression, was expected as the condition for remaining in the covenant community. The best title for this sort of religion is "covenantal nomism".' Thus Sanders defines the key term in the study which effected what has come to be known as the 'Sanders revolution', *Paul and Palestinian Judaism* (see p. 236).

61 Räisänen, *Paul and the Law*, p. 168.

62 Ibid., pp. 187–8.

63 Sanders, *PPJ*, p. 497.

64 See Dunn, CR, pp. lxviii–lxxix.

65 Watson, *Paul, Judaism . . .*, p. 120.

66 Ibid., p. 119.

67 A variety of grounds for varying degrees of doubt appear in Jewett, 'Major impulses in the interpretation of Romans'; Hooker, 'Paul and covenantal nomism'; Moo, 'Paul and the law in the last ten years'; Beker, 'Paul's theology: consistent or inconsistent?'; Westerholm, *Israel's Law and the Church's Faith*; Martin, *Christ and the Law in Paul*.

68 E.g. just since 1980: Piper, 'The righteousness of God in Rom. 3:1–8'; Hall, 'Romans 3:1–8 reconsidered'; Stowers, 'Paul's dialogue with a fellow Jew'; Räisänen, 'Zum verständnis'; Cosgrove, 'What if?'; Penna, 'La funzione strutturale'; Achtemeier, 'Romans 3:1–8: structure and argument'.

69 Doeve, 'Some notes with reference to τὰ λόγια'; also Barth and others.

70 This is the range of opinion which emerges in Manson's 'Appendix on λόγια'.

71 Watson's exposition occupies pp. 124–31 of his *Paul, Judaism and the Gentiles*. The 'oddities' of Romans 3:2–8 have led to much affirmation and denial: affirmation and denial that parody is involved (that Paul is parodying at least the ideas of his adversary is the view favoured by Michel, CR); affirmation and denial that there is any real adversarial

dynamic at all (Stowers is confident that the Socratic model is reflected – see 'Paul's dialogue').

72 This premise, in the context, is not the platitude it might otherwise seem. That the Jew is *not* a man as other men are was axiomatic to the Jew's conception of his identity as a member of God's chosen people.

73 I appreciate that Watson's understanding of 3:19–20 (and of 20b in particular) cannot leave room for what I am positing.

74 The meaning of δικαιούμενοι here cannot be considered independently of δικαιωθέντες in 5:1. It is closely connected with the revelation of God's righteousness in 1:17. Everything it means here may already have been in Paul's mind in the δικαιωθήσεται of 3:20, but a simpler meaning *suffices* to cover its usage there. The crucial factor is that as a result of the process involved in men being δικαιούμενοι they are saved from what would otherwise be the consequences of their unrighteousness, or perhaps more accurately (in view of the διὰ τῆς ἀπολυτρώσεως) from being its prisoners. It is sufficient for the argument I am positing as proleptically implicit in Paul's reasoning from the opening of Romans 3 that what man receives 'cost-free' is this freedom, though down-playing 6:21–6 as theodicy (see e.g. Campbell, *The Rhetoric of Righteousness in Romans 3:21–26*) gives an extra boost to δωρεάν.

75 Dunn, CR, pp. 129–30.

76 Ibid., p. 185. The 'hot breath of debate' – as Jeremias ('Zur Gedanken-führung in den paulinischen Briefen', p. 270) called it!

77 Käsemann's understanding of καύχησις in 3:27 is very different (see CR, pp. 102–3). He sees the whole section 3:27–31 as expressive of Paul's 'militant' doctrine of justification by grace. It neither draws inferences nor sums up; it attacks. The 'principle of achievement' fostered by the law 'throws a person back upon himself' promoting 'self-confidence, and unceasing self-assurance'. To such self-glorifying, to such boasting, faith puts an end. As Käsemann sees the section it is not relevant for my purposes. With my construal of καύχησις it harks back to unresolved problems created by the conflicting inferences that have preceded it. Cf. Thompson, 'Paul's double critique of Jewish boasting'; Lambrecht, 'Why is boasting excluded?'; Davies, *Faith and Obedience*, pp. 127ff.

78 Clearly the most radical challenge to the *sola fide* view is that represented by those who claim that Paul saw faith in Christ as a special means by which the Gentiles were brought into the ambit of God's promises of salvation, one stage only in the fulfilment of which had been accomplished in his relations with Israel. See the arguments of Gaston, *Paul and the Torah*, and also Gager, *The Origins of Anti-Semitism*. A less extreme approach would define Paul's view as the recognition that in Christ the promises were fulfilled, a preliminary stage (but only a preliminary stage) in the fulfilment of which was accomplished in the giving of the law to Israel. As Thielman says: 'Christ's death and the sending of the Spirit meant that the curse of the Torah had ceased, sin had been forgiven, and the law could now be kept' (*From Plight to Solution*, p. 119).

79 All are views – as can be seen from my illustration of them in the

previous note – that reduce the antithesis between Paul's teaching and that of Judaism. The more of Paul's teaching that we perceive to have been already present in Judaism, the more it is natural to say that the Jews both do and do not have an advantage over Gentiles.
80 Ziesler, CR, p. 120. In Malherbe ('μὴ γένοιτο in the Diatribe and Paul') 3:31 figures as the exception (proving the rule).
81 The textual difficulties are reviewed in some detail by Cranfield (CR, pp. 226–7) and Wilckens (CR, I, pp. 260–1). The latter pays particular attention to the syntactical puzzle.
82 Ziesler, CR, p. 119.
83 It is the view favoured by Cranfield (see CR, pp. 224, 226, 227).
84 The view behind this, namely that 'Paul's concept of the function of the law is the negative one of revealing sin' – and only that (cf. Ziesler, *supra*, n. 59) – can be considered as endorsed in Rom 7 (the quote being in fact from the 'actantial' analysis of Rom 5–8 by Lindars, p. 139).
85 They arise as a result of the slant in this view adopted by Elliott in *The Rhetoric of Romans* (see esp. pp. 67, 95), just one very recent example on the focus which Eichholz, twenty years ago, played a major role in bringing to prominence (see *Die Theologie des Paulus im Umriss*).

3.   Ways in which enthymemes arise in Romans 5–7

1 It involves construing Paul's meaning as 'We are justified; therefore we have peace with God.' Alternative construals are: 'We are justified, and in addition (hence without prejudice to any further factors that may be involved) we have peace with God', or 'We are justified, which is equivalent to saying "we have peace with God".' And there may be others. To the extent that δικαιωθέντες is felt to be metaphorical the inferential factor is likely to be compromised or weakened, if not eliminated. There is also the variant reading ἔχωμεν. For the method used in the diagrams which follow, see my explanation on pp. 85–6.
2 Cranfield, CR, p. 258. The point is a relevant one but not often made, despite regular reference to the 'forensic' dimension of δικαιόω: a dimension which, though primarily due to aspects of its original Greek application, is confirmed (if also radically modified) through its having to represent *zadaq* in the LXX. The full panorama is displayed by Ziesler in *The Meaning of Righteousness in Paul*.
3 It did not, of course, need Paul to introduce the theocratic dimension. The tribunal of God is the background to virtually every use of the verb δικαιόω/*zadaq* in the OT, although it is generally the relation of human judgements to God's justice that occasions its use. The sections of particular relevance in Ziesler are *Meaning of Righteousness*, pp. 18–22 and 48–58.
4 Cranfield, CR, p. 258. A human judge (it might be added) does not normally 'confer the status of righteousness', if this means 'to hold innocent one who is not'. Such an action, moreover, is not one which δικαιόω/*zadaq* ever attributes to the divine judge in the OT, while 'acquitting the wicked' figures as an abomination (Prov 17:15, Isa 5:23), which God disowns as fiercely as he condemns it (Ex 23:7).

5 I am taking it that in Paul's view both the forensic and relational dimensions are essentially real, and his terms not such as might justly be called 'picture language'.

6 Dunn (CR, p. 20) sums up the characteristically Hebrew understanding of peace as 'something visible, including the idea of a productively harmonious relationship between people'. And Wolter (*Rechtfertigung und zukunftiges Heil*, pp. 102–3) alludes to the ease with which the sense of εἰρήνη current in Paul's world could cover the God/man rapport.

7 'Personal' but not only 'individual'. Here g and h cover 'absence of enmity among members of the collectivity' or 'between God and the collectivity'.

8 In English we may speak of 'enjoying' a circumstantial factor like 'good health' where no specific perception of the benefit may be involved. That could certainly be the way in which we might characterise the peace arising out of justification as distinct from that which may arise out of reconciliation (with peace there involving awareness).

9 With 'manifested' I have in mind peace which is a harmony involving reciprocity of feeling productive of tangible effects such as (most notably) obedience to God's will on the part of man.

10 Where i is concerned we would have to consider a possible range of enjoyment extending from little or nothing more than *awareness* of the peace being 'enjoyed' (in the weak sense) to exulting in it.

11 See Dunn, CR, p. 247. The 'specifically spiritual attitude of inward peace' is not explicitly to be found there, Von Rad affirms (*TDNT*, II, p. 406).

12 Dunn, ibid. For a selective critique of work on 'peace' in the NT see Klemm, *Εἰρήνη im neutestamentlichen Sprachsystem*, pp. 69–70.

13 Dunn, CR, p. 259.

14 Ziesler, CR, p. 136.

15 Barrett (CR, p. 108) says plainly: 'Justification and reconciliation are different metaphors describing the same fact.'

16 It is not, however, the case that Cranfield, in steering clear of Barrett's conclusion, is therefore led to see reconciliation as dependent on justification; he prefers to say 'justification involves reconciliation' (Cranfield, CR, p. 258). Martin (*Reconciliation*, in particular at pp. 139–40), Dupont (*La Réconciliation*) and Goppelt ('Versöhnung durch Christus') all in different ways see these two concepts as separable; how significantly separable Marshall ('The meaning of "Reconciliation"', p. 124) feels is measured by the fact that Paul can say in 2Cor 5:20 'be reconciled', but never 'be justified'.

17 For example, the ἀπό of ἀπὸ τῆς ὀργῆς is balanced by the ἐν of ἐν τῇ ζωῇ αὐτοῦ in the interest of the *qal vahomer* pattern of which it is part, and for which see SB, III, §§223–6, and Müller, 'Der rabbinische Qal-Wachomer-Schluss'.

18 An argument for the analysis of which see my discussion on p. 79.

19 'Being at peace' in the sense of enjoying peace circumstantially, to recall the terminology of my branching diagram 5.

20 And that this is what it does is still the rock to which many modern

Pauline critics hold fast, for all the variety of theories they confront us with: whether, like Bornkamm, *Paul*, they still see δικαίωσις as occupying the central place in Pauline theology that the reformers ascribed to it, or whether, in the wake of Wrede, they see it as a 'secondary, juridical-rabbinic crater' (see Beker, *Paul the Apostle*, p. 67) used 'only rhetorically' to lead to conclusions of an essentially different order (see Sanders, *PPJ*, p. 500).

21 Bornkamm, *Paul*, pp. 151–2. For the shadow of Trent, see Wilckens, CR, I, p. 302.

22 On p. 186 of *The Meaning of Righteousness* Ziesler comes to the subject of Romans, and I employ the phraseology he adopts in interpreting Romans 1:17. This is the product of the thesis to which his exhaustive analysis of the linguistic background has led him, and which he outlines thus on his opening page: 'The heart of the present study is the contention that the verb "justify" is used relationally, often with the forensic meaning "acquit," but that the noun, and the adjective δίκαιος, have behavioural meanings, and that in Paul's thought Christians are both justified by faith (i.e. restored to fellowship, acquitted), and also righteous by faith (i.e. leading a new life in Christ).' Cf. Reumann *et al.*, *Righteousness in the New Testament*, p. 85: 'δικαιοσύνη includes "walk"'.

23 'What worse relation of subject and predicate subsists between either of two terms and a common third term, with which both are related and one at least positively so – that relation subsists between the two terms themselves.'

24 Ziesler, *The Meaning of Righteousness*, p. 189: 'God's saving righteousness does two things for men and does them inseparably: it restores their relationship with God, and it makes them new (ethical, righteous) beings.' See Byrne's comments in 'Living out the righteousness of God', p. 576.

25 For this see Sanders, *PLJP*, p. 14.

26 Sanders, *PPJ*, pp. 198–205.

27 'Justified,' Sanders argues, 'conveys to most English speakers the meaning of "be declared or found innocent".' Instead, whether that *is* the meaning is the very question to which the variations in Paul's usage prevent us from having a standard answer.

28 E.g. Cranfield, CR, pp. 154–5; Ziesler, *The Meaning of Righteousness*, p. 190.

29 See Ziesler, *The Meaning of Righteousness*, pp. 197–200.

30 Käsemann, CR, p. 138. Reconciliation highlights how ('Some thoughts on the theme "The doctrine of Reconciliation"', p. 63).

31 Cranfield, CR, p. 257, n. 1. Not all major commentators have rejected ἔχωμεν. It is the best-attested reading. Porter ('The argument of Romans 5', p. 662) has very recently upheld it. Wilckens quotes Origen's defence of it (CR, I, p. 289).

32 Cranfield, CR, p. 258. Compare and contrast Dinkler, *Der urchristliche Friedensgedanke*.

33 See Dunn, CR, p. 258; Cranfield, CR, pp. 266–7. Ziesler differs (see CR,

p. 142). There is reluctance in some quarters to see the wrath from which we are saved (5:9) as entailing 'hostility' (see Hanson, *The Wrath of the Lamb*, p. 89; Hofius, 'Sühne und Versöhnung', p. 29).

34 Ziesler, CR, p. 142. He has just said, 'The enmity was on the human side, not the divine.'

35 Käsemann, CR, p. 138. Stuhlmacher (CR, p. 76) notes the relevance of Romans 8:15: from being God's enemies, we are now his beloved children.

36 Dunn (CR, p. 248) glosses 'grace' in 5:2 as 'a sphere or state (a secure area) into which one enters'. Ziesler (CR, p. 137) says: 'It is almost the condition in which those who have received God's kindness now exist, and is thus close in meaning to peace' (and the range of meaning he envisages for 'peace' I have noted).

37 Käsemann, CR, p. 133. Here, as Käsemann sees it (p. 134), we are very much in the throes of eschatological tension: 'The δόξα τοῦ θεοῦ is the fulfilment of the righteousness already given and is anticipated in the righteousness in such a way that hope still waits for the remaining fulfilment and yet is certain of it beyond the gift already received.' Cf. Kertelge, *'Rechtfertigung' bei Paulus*, p. 284: δικαίωσις is eschatological truth.

38 According to Käsemann (CR, p. 133) 5:2 is already very much part of the argument. But he notes Michel's differing views regarding the doxological factor.

39 Dunn, CR, p. 249.

40 Cranfield, CR, p. 260.

41 Dunn, CR, p. 252.

42 See Joseph, *Introduction to Logic*, p. 354.

43 Dunn, CR, p. 254: 'The γάρ serves to link the new sequence of thought back to the preceding sequence: vv. 6–8 provide further justification for the hope of vv. 3–5.'

44 Ibid., p. 267.

45 My phrase 'in which we exult' incorporates the content of 5:11 into the argument. It depends on a controversial construal of the syntactical relationship between vv. 10 and 11.

46 See Bruce, CR, pp. 67–8; Dunn, CR, p. 271.

47 Obviously, if hope is seen as the central motive of Romans (as it is by Heil, *Romans*), 5:12–21 will ultimately serve to add weight to the argument for hope. Gaugler, CR, dubs 5:1–21 'die durchgreifende Hoffnung'.

48 Barrett, CR, p. 110.

49 Cranfield, CR, p. 271, n. 1. See also his earlier 1969 study, 'On some problems in the interpretation of Rom 5:12'.

50 Leenhardt, CR, p. 140. Wolter discusses the issue at some length (*Rechtfertigung*, pp. 214–15).

51 That is Paul's point, though he refers only to the situation where law was wanting. Cranfield, CR, p. 282: 'Only in comparison with what takes place when the law is present can it be said that, in the law's absence, sin οὐκ ἐλλογεῖται . . .'

52 'The law by showing men that what they are doing is contrary to God's

will gives to their continuing to do it the character of conscious and wilful disobedience' (Cranfield, CR, p. 293). *At least* in this sense the law makes sin abound/increase, whether or not Paul means that it puts new kinds of wickedness into man's head, as he seems to in 7:7ff.

53 Dunn sees a difference in the way the diatribe style figures here and how it figures earlier in the letter. In his view (CR, p. 305) it is resumed here by Paul 'not so much to argue with querulous fellow-countrymen, more as a device for exhorting his Roman audiences'.

54 That 6:1 is not merely rhetorical is stated with increasing confidence as a result of the increasing amount of attention being given to the purpose of Romans in its historical setting (see Stuhlmacher, 'The purpose of Romans', p. 240; Campbell, 'Romans 3 as a key', p. 261). However, the tone which Paul adopts at such moments as this (and discussion continues concerning the propriety of the term 'diatribe style') raises a threefold uncertainty which no amount of critical research can dispose of. Does Paul introduce knock-down arguments (a) because they represent serious objections that *need* intrinsically to be raised (or even way-out objections that nevertheless *might* be raised), or (b) because *someone is actually raising them* (in which case they might be such as merit serious consideration or they might be merely preposterous), or (c) not because of either (a) or (b) but to focus attention on the incontrovertibility of what they *enable to be presented* as a contradiction of the patently outrageous?

55 Dunn, CR, p. 323.

56 Ibid. The resurrection of Jesus as 'Korporativpersönlichkeit' indicates irreversibly the eschatological culmination of the believer's life (Frankemölle, *Das Taufverständnis des Paulus*, p. 95).

57 Dunn, CR, p. 321.

58 Ibid. Rising he broke death's power to cut man off from God (Osten-Sacken, *Römer 8 als Beispiel paulinischer Soteriologie*, p. 319).

59 Noted by Ziesler, *The Meaning of Righteousness* , p. 200, n. 2, where he comments on the difficulty in seeing how Christ can be justified from sin; Scroggs ('Romans 6:7') does not address it.

60 Cranfield, CR, p. 311.

61 CR, p. 314. Baptism is into Christ 'en tant qu'il a subi la mort' (i.e. 'as having undergone death'), Légasse, 'Etre baptisé dans la mort du Christ'.

62 CR, p. 157. And in this sense the dying is final: Schnackenburg, *Baptism in the Thought of St Paul*, p. 43.

63 Sanday and Headlam, CR, p. 153.

64 CR, p. 307. This is compatible with a death which is final (cf. *supra* n. 62).

65 The formula 'Communication Unit' (CU) can be applied to units of any size (see its implementation by Beekman, Callow and Kopesec, *The Semantic Structure of Written Communication*). In the context of such an enquiry as this, I felt it would avoid the confusion that might arise if I used 'proposition' or 'sentence' as terms.

66 It should be noted, however, that HEAD–support relationships are essentially two-way affairs. For example, where a HEAD–cause relationship is indicated it is obvious that the HEAD stands in relation to cause

as 'result'. Which of the two the analyst denotes as 'HEAD' is justified by an evaluative judgement concerning where the emphasis of the discourse falls. The surface pattern of its syntax is not always the best guide to this. See Cotterell and Turner, *Linguistics and Biblical Interpretation*, pp. 209–10.

67 Most of all if the believer is construed as unable to sin.

68 Some, however – see Zeller's 'Der Zusammenhang von Gesetz und Sünde im Römerbrief' on Wilckens, and N. M. Watson's 'Justified by faith, judged by works' – would see contextual 'disentanglement' ('Entfechtung') as obviating the relevance of distinguishing.

69 Ziesler, CR, p. 164.

70 Käsemann, CR, p. 174 (= p. 166, 1980 German edn). See in this connection particularly Bultmann, *Theology*, I, pp. 332–3.

71 Käsemann notes the pull of this perspective outside the limits of Bultmann's own school.

72 CR, p. 175. He sees the 'become-what-you-are' formula as symptomatic of an anthropological orientation which must be revised (cf. 'On Paul's anthropology').

73 Ibid., p. 163 (= p. 155, 1980 German edn). Barth (he registers) takes this view.

74 Ibid.

75 Dunn, CR, p. 339. He sees κυριεύσει, however, as a temporal future, not hortative – as it could be (BDF §362), and as Moffatt took it to be ('The interpretation of Romans 6:17–18').

76 Ziesler, CR, p. 165. A view not unlike that of Furnish, *Theology and Ethics in Paul*, or Tannehill, *Dying and Rising with Christ*.

77 Käsemann, CR, p. 176; Dunn, CR, p. 339. Malan, 'Bound to do right', sees the balance as very subtle.

78 Cranfield, CR, pp. 318–19. He seeks to avoid the conclusion (whilst not categorically excluding the possibility) 'of Paul's having been illogical', though he rejects the imperatival construal of κυριεύσει, which would fit most easily with βασιλευέτω (he does in fact recognise its attractiveness).

79 See *supra*, n. 63. Cranfield (CR, p. 298) finds their treatment so perfunctory as to make it 'hard to understand how they can . . . speak of Paul's "profound and original argument"'. Yet their statement (p. 153) 'Sin is a direct contradiction of the state of things which baptism assumes' closely anticipates Käsemann's concept of sin-avoidance as 'verification' of the outcome of baptism.

80 Cranfield, CR, p. 319. For an attempt, instead, to reinterpret v. 12, see Marcus, '"Let God arise and end the reign of sin"'.

81 Käsemann, CR, pp. 175–6 (= pp. 167–8, 1980 German edn). Thus Käsemann resolves the dictum of Windisch ('Das Problem des paulinischen Imperativs', p. 280) that the Christian's sinlessness is gift and task 'Gabe und Aufgabe').

82 Michel, CR, renders 'Sollen wir (weiter) sündigen . . .', making the two exactly identical in meaning. Both can be explained as deliberative subjunctives (see Zerwick and Grosvenor, *A Grammatical Analysis of the Greek New Testament*, pp. 471–2) and the aorist tense of the

ἁμαρτήσωμεν as inceptive (Zerwick, *Biblical Greek*, §251). Maillot (CR, p. 168) focusses on the shifting motivational perspective in which Paul sets the reiterated question.

83 The change, as Dunn points out (CR, p. 341), is more than a simple variation. Cf. Maillot, CR.

84 'The question of a Man's being free in the sense of having no master at all simply does not arise', notes Cranfield (CR, p. 323), and finds a way to seeing the fact in a highly positive light, for to imagine one is free is a delusion – it is to be at the service of one's own ego; Paul is right that the alternative is an exclusive one. The syllogistic structure here involved is noted by Lanfranc (cf. *supra*, Chapter 2 n. 2).

85 Dunn, CR, pp. 347, 355. For the freedom side, see Jones, '*Freiheit*', pp. 110ff.

86 Ziesler, CR, p. 169; Wilckens, CR, II, pp. 38–9. Ziesler comments that the language of slavery is 'not naturally appealing . . . In the minds of many of his readers, the language might well have had deeply unpleasant associations.' However, the institution of slavery in antiquity did not have purely negative connotations (as D. B. Martin has recently pointed out in *Slavery as Salvation*).

87 Barth, CR, pp. 224, 216.

88 Käsemann, CR, p. 183. This is for Bouttier ('La vie du chrétien', p. 155) a fact as 'irremediable' as passing from death to life.

89 Watson, *Paul, Judaism . . .*, p. 224, n. 19.

90 See Ziesler (CR, pp. 173–4), who refers to the thorough exploration of the matter by Gale, *The Use of Analogy in the Letters of Paul*. Cranfield (CR, pp. 334–5), following Kümmel ('Römer 7 und die Bekehrung des Paulus'), takes a different view and sees 7:2–3 as illustrating 7:1: 'Verse 4 is the conclusion drawn from vv. 1–3 as a whole, that is, from v. 1 as clarified by vv. 2–3.' For some very recent thoughts see Earnshaw, 'Reconsidering Paul's marriage analogy in Romans 7:1–4'.

91 Dunn (CR, p. 378) notes the insensitivity displayed by some commentators to 'the rhetorically shaped sharpness of Paul's question'.

92 Hübner, *Law in Paul's Thought*, p. 71. Cf. Sloan, 'Paul and the law', p. 49: 'The good law of God . . . becomes sin's agent.'

93 Hübner, *Law in Paul's Thought*, pp. 74ff.

94 Dunn, CR, p. 385. Lyonnet, 'L'histoire du salut', believed the explanation of the problematical pericope 7:14–25 to depend on its being linked closely with the Genesis foundation. Cf. Watson, *Paul, Judaism . . .*, pp. 151–5. All illustrate what Fitzmyer would consider 'eisegesis' (CR, p. 464).

95 Hübner, *Law in Paul's Thought*, p. 75. Outside Christ such is always the impact of God's demand (Deidun, *New Covenant Morality in Paul*). Fitzmyer's unpersuadedness and Hübner's meticulousness show some tendency to converge.

96 Cranfield, CR, p. 352.

97 Dunn, CR, p. 383.

98 Ziesler, CR, pp. 188–9. Sloan sees it as redemptively sinister ('Paul and the law', p. 57).

99 Barrett, CR, p. 146. Some commentators take 7:13–21 as the unit for

discussion, among them Michel, Cranfield, Wilckens and Stuhlmacher. Barth, Dunn and Ziesler do not do this (they take it as 7:14–21), and Dunn speaks (CR, p. 387) of Paul as 'beginning' an argument at this point. It is, however, an argument 'clearly intended' as 'clarification and elaboration' (p. 403).

100 And it is possible to say this, and even to epitomise his problems in the questions 'What was God up to before Christ? What was the point of the law? How can one hold together the history of Israel?' – as Sanders does (*PLJP*, p. 79) – without ascribing the level of incoherence to Paul in Romans 7 that he (and Räisänen even more so) would wish to do. (For the latter 7:14 is just 'glaring self-contradiction', see *Paul and the Law*, p. 142.) It is often harder to know how substantial the elements of orderliness which some (often with remarkable ingenuity, e.g. Rolland, 'L'antithèse de Rm 5–8') uncover in Paul's discourse really are – a nettle which is in fact (momentarily) grasped by a firm advocate of such effort, Aletti, in 'La *dispositio* rhétorique dans les épîtres pauliniennes', pp. 398–9. Boers, 'The foundations of Paul's thought', contests that contradiction in Paul precludes coherence; so, virtually, does Luciani, 'Paul et la loi'.

4. How enthymematic argument stands in Romans 8

1 Doubt has, however, been created here too by those who believe we should correct the order of 8:1 and 2 by reversing it. See Cranfield (CR, p. 373) for some reference to this. The difficulties of thought sequence which have prompted recourse to this expedient lead Keck ('The law of the "law of sin and death"', p. 42) to see all inferential connections involving 8:1 as compromised. (See also Schmithals, *Die theologische Anthropologie des Paulus*, p. 82.)

2 Dunn (CR, p. 414) notes the preference frequently accorded at one time to μέ.

3 I am discounting the possibility of any order inversion being apposite (see n. 1 *supra*).

4 I will not, initially, broach the question of the sense in which Paul is using the word 'law' and whether the sense changes from A to B. I come to that on p. 105. It is necessary to clarify how the logic works if we assume that the semantic value of 'law' is constant throughout the syllogism, before considering the effect on the argument that a shifting use of it would have.

5 Sanday and Headlam, CR, p. 190.

6 Dodd, CR, p. 119. Though in 7:6 Paul had 'contrasted the Spirit with the written code of the Mosaic Law', here the law in view is that of 7:23 – as Dodd sees it.

7 Dunn, CR, p. 419.

8 Ibid., p. 417. He follows Lohse: see 'ὁ νόμος . . .', pp. 284–5 (also 'Zur Analyse und Interpretation von Röm 8:1–17', pp. 137ff.).

9 Dunn, CR, pp. 416–17. The contrast with 7:6 and even more seriously with Gal 3:21 is undeniable; Dunn faces this squarely, whilst drawing attention, at the same time, to a group of mitigating factors.

10 Hübner, *Law in Paul's Thought*, p. 144.
11 Ibid., p. 145.
12 Räisänen, however, whilst recognising all this, contests the identity of νόμος τοῦ πνεύματος with Torah. For his reasons see 'Das "Gesetz des Glaubens"', pp. 114ff. Osten-Sacken, Keck, Deidun, Zeller, all debate the issue. Fitzmyer calls the phrase 'oxymoron' (CR, p. 482), a ploy which the flexible 'narrative' analyses of Wright leave little occasion for, marginalising the whole debate as they do (see *The Climax of the Covenant*, p. 209).
13 It may help to line up the relevant sections of the text so that the parallels can be clearly observed. See diagram 31.

Diagram 31

		Chap 7				Chap 8 vv1–2
v5	v6	v14	v23	vv24–25a	v25b	
	κατηργήθ.			με ρύσεται		**Segment A** οὐδὲν κατάκριμα
	ἀπὸ τοῦ νόμου			διὰ 'I X		**Segment B** τοῖς ἐν X 'I
	δουλεύειν	ὁ νόμος			δουλεύω νόμῳ	**Segment C** ὁ νόμος
	ἐν καινότ. πνεύματος	πνευματικός			θεοῦ	**Segment D** τοῦ πν. τῆς ζωῆς ἐν X 'I
	κατηργήθ.			με ρύσεται		**Segment E** ἠλευθέρωσέν σε
τὰ παθήμ. τῶν ἁμαρτ. τὰ διὰ τοῦ νόμ. ἐνεργ. ἐν τοῖς μέλ. ἡμῶν εἰς τὸ	ἀπὸ τοῦ νόμου		με ἐν τῷ νόμῳ τῆς ἁμαρτίας	ἐκ τοῦ σώμ.	νόμῳ ἁμαρτίας	**Segment F** ἀπὸ τοῦ νόμου τῆς ἁμαρτίας
καρποφορ. τῷ θαν.				τοῦ θαν. τούτου		**Segment G** καὶ τοῦ θανάτου

14 Dunn (CR, p. 415) questions whether, when ἄρα is coupled with νῦν and not οὖν, anything very direct is established in the way of connection with what precedes. The problem begins with the oddity of the thought sequence in 7:24–5. It is the strong feeling that those two verses need reversing that has generated the proposal that 8:1 and 2 also be reversed (see *supra*, n. 1). Stuhlmacher (CR, pp. 104–5) feels that the impulse to reverse 7:24–5 is misconceived, the thought sequence having a well-established OT pedigree. But he no more sees 8:2 as proof of 8:1 than those who posit sequence irregularities (cf. n. 1 *supra*).
15 It is Cranfield's view (CR, p. 373) that 8:1 makes sense as grounds for what has gone before 'provided we recognize that it connects neither

with 7:25a nor with 7:25b but with 7:6'. Dunn (CR, p. 415), however, considers that 'if in 8:1 the thought skips back to 7:6 . . . it does not stop there'. As Wilckens sees it, in fact (CR, II, p. 119), 8:1 refers back to 5:18.

16 And it is, in fact, the sweep that Wilckens' perspective sees it as encompassing (see previous note).

17 Torah 'as A' being the life-giving force it was meant to be; Torah 'as B' being the instrument of condemnation to death which sin had made it into.

18 The latent CU displays that I have formulated relating to the two laws can be set alongside each other and joined into a single display by means of a linking section presenting the factor responsible for the transformation: see diagram 32. (The vertical presentation of elements originally ranged horizontally will not – I hope – cause perplexity.) Italics and dotted lines distinguish the areas of the display which correspond to my earlier probings of the content of 8:2 from the central area which, extrapolating from the content of 8:3–4, links the opposing foci of those probings.

Diagram 32

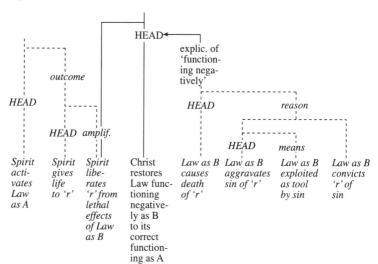

19 Dunn, CR, p. 436.

20 Factors whose interaction with one another has here to be worked out – namely that exemption from condemnation to death arises from victory over the power of sin – are more strikingly and succinctly brought together in 1Cor 15:56–7.

21 'The strong consensus of modern commentators', Dunn (CR, p. 431) calls it. Ziesler lists its main adherents (CR, p. 212, fn. r). He himself, in *The Meaning of Righteousness* (p. 204), had taken πνεῦμα here as

referring to the human spirit. Dunn (CR, p. 431) calls that the 'older view' and remarks on the fact that 'modern translations have not kept up' with what he considers to be the only view compatible with the dominant co-textual emphasis on the Holy Spirit.

22 I am purposely very guarded in the wording of my paraphrase. I use the formulation 'according to the Spirit' to match κατὰ πνεῦμα. The expression ἐν πνεύματι does not occur until 8:9, though its occurrence there may well justify our taking κατά in the preceding verse as equivalent to ἐν. I speak of the fulfilment of the just demands of the law being 'made effective' in us to avoid committing myself to whether we are being seen by Paul strictly as the 'location' of the fulfilment or whether the ἐν carries the sense of 'by' ('durch', 'bei' or 'unter uns', but not 'in uns' is Schlier's verdict, CR, p. 243). Deidun has argued that what Paul here means is that 'the law's demand is accomplished (by God) previous to any περιπατεῖν on the part of the Christian', a view which Dunn (CR, p. 424) considers 'wholly unconvincing' (unlike Fitzmyer, CR, pp. 487–8). The other extreme, which sees the law as *fulfilled* precisely in the Christian's sinlessness, he considers equally uncalled-for. It is 'the direction, the set, of our lives' which according to Cranfield (CR, p. 385) constitutes the fulfilment (cf. Thompson, 'How is the Law fulfilled in us?'). That δικαίωμα might mean other than 'the law's just requirement' is a contingency I have not allowed for, though there is not perfect unity regarding that either (as Ziesler notes in *The Meaning of Righteousness*, p. 204, n. 1, and Cranfield in CR, p. 384, n. 1). Sandt's findings and views on this are discussed by Keck, 'The law of the "law of sin and death"', pp. 52–3.

23 See Dunn, CR, p. 431. Paulsen (*Überlieferung und Auslegung in Röm 8*, pp. 72–3) lists six reasons for favouring this view, but neither he nor Dunn detail the implications as explicitly as H. G. C. Moule did (CR, pp. 214–15): '*If Christ is,* thus by the Spirit, *in you,* dwelling by faith in the hearts which the Spirit has "strengthened" to receive Christ (Eph 3:16–17) – *true* (μέν) *the body is dead, because of sin,* the primeval sentence still holds sway *there*; the body is deathful still, it is the body of the Fall; *but the Spirit is life,* he is in that body, your secret of power and peace eternal, *because of righteousness,* because of the merit of your Lord, in which you are accepted, and which has won for you this wonderful Spirit-life. Then even for the body there is assured a glorious future, organically one with this living present.'

24 See Dunn, CR, p. 431; Ziesler, CR, p. 211. It is the second half of the statement (τὸ πνεῦμα ζωὴ διὰ δικαιοσύνην) that Ziesler suspects Paul of having wanted to balance too neatly in the first half (τὸ σῶμα νεκρὸν διὰ ἁμαρτίαν).

25 It fades, for example, in inverse proportion to the extent of the adversative tone which is read in the affirmation of Outcome 1. ('If Christ is in you, in spite of Outcome 1, Outcome 2 follows.')

26 Ziesler, CR, p. 211. Aune ('Romans as a *Logos Protreptikos*', p. 293) does not treat it as 'unlikely'.

27 It would raise the Platonic spectre of the body as the prison of the soul, of the principle enunciated by his Socrates that it is the business of the

philosopher to kill the body, and in this sense to die. Wilckens, noting these matters (CR, II, p. 135), insists it is precisely *as* bodily life that Paul sees human life to be most 'wesenhaft', thus salvation as somatically based (Jewett, *Paul's Anthropological Terms*, p. 457).

28 The way this complicates the interpretation of 8:10 was given special prominence by Sanday and Headlam (CR, pp. 197–8).

29 'About the most negative use of σῶμα in Paul', Dunn terms it (CR, p. 449): he admits he would have expected σάρξ. Cranfield clarifies (CR, p. 395): 'It is not the body's activities (which include such things as sleeping and walking) which are intended, but the activities or schemings of the sinful flesh' ('die Machenschaften des Leibes', as Wilckens does not scruple to translate πράξεις τοῦ σώματος, CR, II, p. 118). For the negative thrust, however, σῶμα alone is responsible: see Kuss, CR, p. 598).

30 'Denn alle, die vom Geiste Gottes getrieben werden, die sind Söhne Gottes' (CR, p. 257), 'Getrieben werden' seems a proper match for ἄγονται. The otherwise almost universal inclination to prefer the notion of 'being led' needs perhaps to be questioned. Dunn (CR, p. 450) discusses at some length the expression ἄγεσθαι πνεύματι, and notes that its 'most natural sense' here is 'that of being constrained by a compelling force', in spite of his own opting (on balance) for 'led'.

31 Michel, CR, p. 259. Cranfield notes (CR, pp. 400–1) that whilst Dodd sees Paul as turning away with 8:14 from the ethical area into which 8:13 had launched him, Barth sees 8:15 as stating 'in principle' all that there is to be said about ethics.

32 There has been controversy over whether Paul intends any distinction between τέκνον and υἱός (see Cranfield, CR, p. 396, n. 1; Dunn, CR, pp. 454–5), and over whether we need to be careful to see υἱοθεσία as indicating 'sonship' only in the special sense of 'adoption' (see Cranfield, CR, p. 398, n. 1; Dunn, CR, pp. 460–1). But all these words are merely images (just like δοῦλος and δουλεία). Byrne (*'Sons of God' – 'Seed of Abraham'*, p. 126) points out that in 8:23 υἱοθεσία = resurrection; Hester ('Paul's Concept of Inheritance', p. 115) observes how, outside the context of *Heilsgeschichte*, the inheritance which sonship secures is without content.

33 Amid what is made explicit at once, unit h is notable for appearing here without its bearing on the argument having been anticipated by anything since the now-distant derivation of hope from tribulation in 5:3–4 – anything, that is, other than the concept of our 'dying with Christ'; and Cranfield, at least, is categorical in denying that this is what the συμπάσχομεν of 8:17 refers to. It refers to 'that element of suffering which is inseparable from faithfulness to Christ in a world which does not yet know him as Lord' (CR, p. 408).

34 Concerning this additional factor and its place in the logic, see note 33 above.

35 See Cranfield, CR, pp. 405–7.

36 He sees it as not the less 'extraordinarily' effective for being subject to the inevitable limitations of imagery (CR, p. 407). This is above all due to its locating in our relation to God, in 'his having claimed us for his own', the basis for the confidence of our expectations.

37 It *is* predictable in the sense that, as Dunn says (CR, p. 449), 'continuity with and fulfilment of the promises to Abraham and Israel is the hidden current which carries Paul's thought forward: the role of the law, the eschatological Spirit, the status of sonship all follow in a natural sequence as topics of an exposition of believers' privileges which is tantamount to the claim that they have entered into the eschatological privileges promised to Israel'.

38 Cranfield is so conscious of this redimensioning that he breaks to a new section with 8:17 (not, as is usual, with 8:18), commenting (CR, p. 404): 'Verse 17 by its movement of thought from sonship to heirship makes the transition to the subject of Christian hope, with which this sub-section is concerned. The life which is characterised by the indwelling of the Spirit of God, which is a life in which God's law is established, is a life characterised by hope.'

39 'The παθήματα which Paul has in mind here are no doubt, in view of the συμπάσχομεν in v. 17, those of Christians, though in vv. 19–22 the range of interest is much wider' (Cranfield, CR, p. 409). 'This section takes up and expands the theme of 5:2–4. In their sufferings, which are presumably to be understood in terms of opposition and even persecution, Christians are signs for the whole world that the present universal decay, wickedness, and suffering are but a stage in a divine process which is moving towards freedom and renewal' (Ziesler, CR, p. 218). Despite this widening, the *value* of suffering for the sufferer, the lessons (especially that of hope) to be learned from it, which had been stressed in 5:3–4, are not being lost to view, as the imminent resumption of the 'hope' theme in 8:24 demonstrates.

40 'The Spirit is simply an earnest and pledge of what is to come' (Käsemann, CR, p. 231).

41 Käsemann (CR, p. 239) sees here a polemical shaft against the 'pneumatics, who no longer see that their place is beneath the cross'. Paul is making it clear that 'if disciples are no longer on the road they have no more to say and give either to themselves or the world'.

42 'Reverent defiance' is Barth's expression (*Church Dogmatics* II/2, p. 493). Paul 'has no other reason for this defiance than the consolation of Jesus. But it is the consolation of Jesus which makes this defiance necessary.'

43 'Contra' – as Luther puts it (quoted by Barth, CR, p. 326) – becomes 'an altogether scandalous and disgraceful preposition'.

44 The area of enthymematic implication that is of real moment is that which supplies the grounds that enable us to say that God is for us.

45 This time we have also a πρὸς ταῦτα. If πρὸς ταῦτα = 'in view of these things' (and Moule, *Idiom Book*, p. 53 says it can), then it strengthens the οὖν. If it merely means 'concerning these things', or even 'with all this in mind' (cf. NEB, noted by Dunn, CR, p. 499), it does not strengthen the deductive implications of οὖν, but the ταῦτα generates concern to identify precisely where the οὖν is pointing (the issue around which Fiedler builds his analysis of 8:31–9 in 'Röm 8:31–39 als Brennpunkt paulinischer Frohbotschaft').

46 Dunn and Cranfield, focussing on the content of ταῦτα, see that as extending to the whole epistle so far (or at least chapters 6–8). To do this

weakens the deductive dynamic, and seems to go against the mood of the τί οὖν ἐροῦμεν type of rhetorical question (though admittedly the πρὸς ταῦτα may be a signal that the reference is wider than usual).

47 After what has been said in 8:28–30, Barth (CR, p. 326) asks: 'Is it not inevitable that anything we say must be said "about" or "in addition to" or "contrary to" what God has said?' However, at once he adds: 'Must not our silence also, quite as much as our speech, obscure the truth concerning the knowledge of love?' Cranfield ('Rom 8:28 . . .'); Hiebert, 'Romans 8:28–29 and the assurance of the believer'; Leaney, 'Conformed to the image of his son'; Grayston, 'The doctrine of election in Rom 8:28–30'; and Kürzinger, 'συμμόρφους τῆς εἰκόνος', all opt for speech.

48 Käsemann (CR, p. 231) stresses the nature of 8:19–27 as a 'counter-thrust' to 8:18 and 8:28ff. and the importance of the 'tension' it creates.

49 The relevant section of the CU display on p. 124 may assist consideration of these issues (CUs 1–8 can easily be isolated from what follows).

50 This proposition, which in the dilemma of saying more and keeping silent (see n. 47 *supra*) Barth identifies as the 'final' truth (CR, p. 327), is subjected to subtle scrutiny by Schwartz, 'Two Pauline allusions'. Claims concerning the relevance of Gen 22:16 he views with reserve. (For these claims see Segal, '"He who did not spare his own son"'; Dahl, 'The Atonement'; Le Déaut, 'La présentation targumique'.)

51 It is possible to take the σὺν αὐτῷ so that the meaning of χαρίσεται τὰ πάντα σὺν αὐτῷ becomes 'give us all in giving us Christ'. This is the understanding preferred by Michel (CR, p. 280, n. 5), and followed by Wilckens (CR, II, p. 173, n. 775), as also Schlier (CR, p. 277), who is not content to take χαρίζεσθαι merely as 'schenken'. It is 'gnädig gewähren'. And the 'Gnade' factor causes equal emphasis to fall on what we already experience of God's gift in Christ and what we have yet to experience.

52 Both Cranfield (CR, p. 436) and Wilckens (CR, II, p. 173) discuss this. It has this meaning in Paul (2Cor 2:7, 10).

53 Christ's having died for us while we were still sinners 'carries with it everything else . . . victory over anything that threatens our ultimate well-being . . . First, there is the fact of our sin' (Dodd, CR, p. 143).

54 They celebrate what Käsemann calls (CR, p. 247) 'the triumph of the assaulted'. As he sees things, this is not to say *more* about God's love, since his love in his 'being for us' – and to say that is at once to say all (as Barth affirmed, CR, pp. 516–17). However, the content of πάντα would transcend 'the triumph of the assaulted' if the totality of gifting is seen on the scale Wilckens thinks it must be seen (CR, II, pp. 173–4). 'Salvation' itself does not represent this totality: it is *included* in it. See also Beker: 'Suffering and triumph in Paul's letter to the Romans'.

55 What I refer to here as 'plain speaking', I just now referred to as 'spelling-out'. 8:37 is a verse in which Leenhardt (CR, p. 238) notes the complete absence of rhetoric. Dunn (CR, p. 506) explains the aorist in ἀγαπήσαντος ἡμᾶς as 'referring to God's love expressed in the gift of his son'.

56 What is crucial for Fiedler ('Röm 8:31–39 als Brennpunkt') is that *through* Christ the suffering is *bearable*.

57 See Cranfield, CR, p. 440, and his comments on the ἐν τούτοις of 8:37, where he notes – but does not favour – the view that the meaning is 'in spite of all these things'. Fiedler, and likewise Schrage ('Leid, Kreuz und Eschaton') and Kleinknecht (*Der leidende Gerechtfertigte*) work on it as locative.

58 Dunn, CR, p. 506. Kleinknecht (*Der leidende Gerechtfertigte*, p. 349) sees the experience of sonship as the key.

59 Leenhardt, CR, p. 239. In Güttgemanns, *Der Leidende Apostel und sein Herr*, transmitted witness is primal.

60 Dodd, CR, p. 147.

61 Käsemann, CR, p. 250.

62 Cranfield, CR, p. 441, n. 5. Nothing that might influence Paul to deny the fact can alter the truth of our inseparability from God's love.

63 Barrett, CR, p. 174.

64 Bruce, CR, p. 181.

65 To what extent this is seen to be Paul's tone depends on how far the 'personal' nature of the τίς of 8:35 is seen to filter down right through v. 38 to the τίς of 8:39 (and the τις κτίσις made retro-active throughout v. 38). Pelagius reads each item in the tenfold list of 8:38–9 (θάνατος to κτίσις ἑτέρα) strictly in terms of an omnipresent implicit 'quis'.

66 The certainty is characterised by Moule (CR, p. 241) as 'the eternal embrace wherein the Father embosoms the Son, and, in the Son, all who are at one with him'. However much out of line it may be with the sobriety expected of today's commentator to recall – as Moule does – reading the end of Romans 8 by moonlight in the Colosseum (pp. 242–3), the fact remains that nothing focusses our minds on the limitations of argument in determining the certainty of belief more powerfully than the blood of martyrs.

67 Cranfield, CR, p. 444.

68 For instance, when enthymematic argument arises in the contexts I designated (a) and (b) in chapter 3.6.

69 Be it associated with heuristic mutability as in Romans 8 (as I noted in 4.2 and 3) or the more devious kind seen in Romans 5–7 (arising in contexts of the type designated (a) in 3.6).

70 A point constantly commented on by Ziesler (CR), when in reviewing some proposed interpretation of a problematical verse he remarks that if that is indeed what Paul had been wanting to say he certainly failed to make it clear.

71 This came up, for example, in Romans 3 where I referred particularly to Dunn's highlighting of it (see chapter 2.5). Tangled argument is often a pointer. Contexts of the kind I have designated (c) in chapter 3.6 readily give rise to it.

72 Käsemann, CR, p. 247.

73 See chapter 1.5, in particular p. 29. I extrapolate from what I said there: 'Recognition is governed by explicability ... Spelling-out is only spelling-out if it remains within the boundaries of what has been recognised. Explication is in this sense subservient to Recognition ...

never more so than where the code governing the recognition is experiential.'

74 The logic by virtue of which the Cross signifies God's unbounded love to Paul also forces him to decide whether that love is belittled if we say those who obey God's commandments please him more than those who do not – an example among several which I included in chapter 1.5, p. 31.

5.   Knowing what tune Paul is playing

1 At the head of *TSG* he himself wryly recalls Pascal's plea: 'Let no one say I have said nothing new: I have rearranged the subject matter.'

2 The Guiraud references which follow are to the 1975 English edition of his *Semiology*, first published in French (*La Sémiologie*) in 1971. For Prieto, see *infra*, n. 11.

3 Guiraud, *Semiology*, pp. 6–21. He points to McLuhan as the source of the 'hot' and 'cool' terminology: pp. 16–17.

4 Ibid., pp. 24–9. Usage is a factor which both erodes and promotes precision of codification.

5 Ibid., p. 14. 'Communion' is the emotional side of the dimension of which the practical side is 'collaboration'.

6 A view which of course results in its nature being a matter of perpetual redetermination. Denial of the possibility of correct interpretation or a theory of 'necessary error' may ensue (as Knapp and Michaels note, 'Against theory', pp. 11, 25, n. 17). Corti theorises soberly (*Introduction to Literary Semiotics*, p. 33): 'The universe of the addressees of a literary work is the product of ongoing and often uncontrollable relations with the text.'

7 'Reception' and 'Reader Response' have separate histories. For the first, see Holub, *Reception Theory*. That the pursuit of authorial intention is a totally inadequate basis for literary history was the 1970 protest of the theory's founder, Jauss. For the second, see the studies assembled in *Reader Response Criticism* (1980). The idea that the gospel message has its reality in what it means for each individual believer has helped, on this front, to generate a school of biblical application. *Reader Response Approaches to Biblical and Secular Texts* (*Semeia* 31, 1985) displays some of its fruits.

8 Hobbes (*Leviathan*, Blackwell 1946, p. 337) is referring more particularly to Paul's reasoning from the authority of Scripture. But his axiom is equally valid, and even more significant, where Paul's reasoning claims the authority of logical necessity.

9 Fee notes various theories (*The First Epistle to the Corinthians*, p. 681, n. 34) and proposes his own (p. 682). Cf. Conzelmann, *1Cor*, p. 242, and Héring, *The First Epistle of St Paul to the Corinthians*, pp. 152–3.

10 This is the focus of his concern with 'tongues' prior to 14:13. It is the focus again from 14:26 onwards.

11 Prieto had made a variety of innovatory contributions by the end of the 1960s, notable particularly for the complexities of 'l'acte sémique' they bring to the fore.

12 *Messages et signaux*, p. 34.

13 Ibid., p. 37.
14 Ibid., p. 35.
15 Each ascribes the sign to a code which determines for him the range of possibilities which apply within either of the two fields.
16 See in particular Hervey (*Semiotic Perspectives*, p. 72ff.), who examines an exhaustive range of examples of the different kinds of mismatching which Prieto's analysis of semiosis embraces.
17 The co-text of the verse seems consistent with two interpretations: either 'if, through (i.e. as a result of) speaking in tongues, you do not utter meaningful words', or 'if, by means of tongues (i.e. through the medium of tongues) you do not etc.', the first implying that tongues are not meaningful, the second implying that they can be.
18 This could be said to be the case if we were to take the meaning as 'recognise what is being played as constituting a tune – as making musical sense'.
19 Lepschy, *Survey*, p. 50.
20 Peirce understood the sign as triadic (see diagram 33). As he saw it, 'anything which can be isolated, then connected with something else and "interpreted" can function as a sign' (Hawkes's wording, *Structuralism and Semiotics*, p. 128).

Diagram 33

21 Morris, on pp. 27–8 of *Signs, Language and Behaviour*, first published in 1946, the quote being from Peirce's *Collected Papers*, v, para. 476.
22 The remaining four are (1) the designative, (2) the appraisive, (3) the identificative, and (5) the formative.
23 The disposition to engage in battle being the 'interpretant' – cf. Morris's dog conditioned to go for food on hearing buzzer (discussed by Hervey, *Semiotic Perspectives*, p. 48).
24 'Communion' demands relaxation of 'attention'. They are therefore inversely proportional: Guiraud, *Semiology*, p. 14.
25 He links with 'hermeneutics' the semiosis which occurs in 'poetic' as distinct from 'technical' discourse (ibid., p. 41).
26 The prelude to Eco's principal writings had a strong aesthetic bias, as the titles of the first publication he lists, *Il problema estetico in Tommaso d'Aquino*, 1956, and the volume *La definizione dell'arte*, containing material from 1955 to 1963, indicate.
27 See *La struttura assente*, p. 77.
28 This isomorphosis can perhaps best be understood when seen as the process by virtue of which the expression aspect of the sign assumes the role of the content aspect (Eco, *TSG*, p. 335; *TS*, p. 268). Music best illustrates 'formal' meaning: as I noted in chapter 1.4, p. 27.
29 A period during which translation extended its accessibility.
30 Mukařovský, *The Word and Verbal Art*, p. 6.
31 'Closing statement', p. 377. The essential agents of the re-evaluation are

identified by Stankiewicz ('Linguistics and the study of poetic language', p. 77). That the briefest fragment is quite adequate to serve as an illustration is envisaged by Mukařovský (*Il processo motorio in poesia*, p. 28).

32 'Defamiliarisation' is, of course, an effect of art which was among the first to be focussed upon by the Russian Formalists.

33 *TS*, p. 250.

34 Aesthetic impact is no more surely guaranteed by Mary's μακαριοῦσίν με πᾶσαι αἱ γενεαί (Luke 1:48) riding the waves of eloquence generated by her 'poem', than it is by the *kol-hashomea yizhaq-li* (Genesis 21:6) which clinches the laconic aphorism of Sarah.

35 It is hard to think of Paul viewing argument as an elegant epistolographical device, if not so hard to see him using it more to give colour to his assertions than to prove them.

36 A very wide gulf has existed from the start between modern 'aesthetics' and the theory of art as earlier ages approached it. The dependence of art on form is no longer seen as inseparable from orderliness, it may well be the reverse.

37 *Structure, Sign and Function*, p. xxxi.

38 Gadamer discovers in him a programme very closely akin to that which I have just outlined (see *Truth and Method*, especially pp. 187–9).

39 Indeed, only in the context of an existentialist distinction between authentic and inauthentic existence can it be other than inane to maintain that in ordinary conversation there is no understanding. Examples of how, against an existentialist background, it can be done are hardly necessary, but for an illustration see Weinsheimer, *Gadamer's Hermeneutic*, pp. 217–18. My use of the word 'impact' may seem inadequate and unclear. Compelled to over-simplify for the sake of brevity, I allude with it to the focal factor underlying that heroic miscellany of verbal ambiguities involving 'immediacy', 'intuition', 'feeling', 'happening', 'actuality', 'defamiliarisation', 'existentiality' (and their non-English prototypes and counterparts) to which thinkers have variously resorted in their unequal struggles with the unobjectifiable.

40 *Semeia* 23 (1982), entitled *Derrida and Biblical Studies*, provides both illustration and evaluation of such work. As does Ward, 'Why is Derrida important for theology?' (1992).

41 A succinct account of this and the disparate body of Heidegger's writings that witness to it is given by Thiselton in *The Two Horizons*, pp. 327–42.

42 See his 'Afterword' added to *Truth and Method* (p. 563; German edn p. 526).

43 In Fuchs 'the distinctively Protestant definition of the church in terms of the preaching of the word has been restated in terms of the new hermeneutic's understanding of language': Robinson, 'Hermeneutic since Barth', p. 58.

44 Ibid., p. 68. Ebeling's attitude is now the object of attention (*Theologie und Verkündigung*, p. 15).

45 Comments of Heidegger's regarding Zen Buddhism bear witness to this risk (see Thiselton, *The Two Horizons*, pp. 341–2). Some would argue

that it is a risk the New Hermeneutic cannot claim to have averted: e.g. Wilder, 'The word as address and meaning', p. 213.

46 See n. 56 *infra*. The highly idiosyncratic terminology of Deconstructionism grows out of Derrida's critique of Saussure.

47 I have combined two quotes from different contributors to *Modern Literary Theory* (ed. Jefferson and Robey), pp. 110 and 131. An example of Derrida doing just what is thus described is his treatment of Saussure, summarised below in n. 56.

48 Fuchs protests in this matter in his 'Response to the American discussion', p. 242.

49 Derrida's professed aim was to conduct a critique of language as radical as Heidegger's concerning being (but not taken far enough concerning language).

50 But it is very difficult to make such comparisons without falsifying the tenets of Deconstructionism. The first target of Derrida's *De la grammatologie* is the very science of signs itself.

51 There is, however, a sense in which Derrida's redimensioning of the human author actually leaves more room for the divine. See, in *Semeia* 23, Crossan, Schneidau, Derrida himself, and Leavey. For a recent stocktaking, see Ward, 'Why is Derrida important for theology?'

52 Without Barthes and Derrida 'reader criticism in its present form would hardly exist': Tompkins, 'An introduction to Reader-Response Criticism', p. xxvi. It has, however, also been shaken by it (see *Against Theory* – a volume expressly designed to highlight the crisis which has arisen – and, for the repercussions in biblical studies, *Orientation by Disorientation*).

53 The more or less overtly aesthetic bias which informs the terms in which both of them explain language could be seen either as an endorsement of this exclusiveness or the reverse.

54 See Thiselton's comments (*The Two Horizons*, p. 353). It is a problem of which the New Hermeneutic was quite aware (see Ebeling, *Word and Faith*, p. 314).

55 Fuchs says: 'Only the faith of the hearer makes evident as the word of God the word that is proclaimed to him' (*Studies of the Historical Jesus*, p. 214).

56 Every verbal element exists only by virtue of not being another, but the full scope of the 'being another' which it is not is in a perpetual state of incomplete emergence. Saussure could (says Derrida) fittingly have said 'grammatologie' where he refers to 'sémiologie'. And to prove the point Derrida tries it out (see *De la grammatologie*, Pt I, ch.2, sec. 2)!!

57 See Fuchs, 'Response . . .', p. 241; Ebeling, *Introduction*, p. 200.

58 Eco is one of these. See *The Role of the Reader*, pp. 191ff. Nevertheless, how Peirce is rightly to be understood remains controversial. See Wykoff, 'Semiosis and infinite regress'.

59 Ebeling relates this to Luther's dictate that the word of God comes to us as our adversary (see Thiselton, *The Two Horizons*, p. 356).

60 How 'dim' it is is evident from Derrida's *De la grammatologie*, p. 142: 'Penser, c'est ce que nous savons déjà n'avoir pas encore commencé à faire' (Thinking is what we know we haven't begun to do yet).

61 It has proved so effective in computer science that via fuzzy grammar and fuzzy artificial languages a whole new branch of technology has developed which is being exploited above all in Japan.

An article in *The Guardian* of 28 February 1991 reviewed the 'wonders' it has produced, from fuzzy lifts and fuzzy trains to fuzzy washing machines and fuzzy cameras, the characteristic superiority of all of them being their capacity to adapt automatically to a far wider range of situational variables than their non-fuzzy equivalents can do.

62 See Eco, *TS*, pp. 292ff.

63 Eco uses a series of diagrams to clarify what I here try to condense into one.

64 See Eco, *TS*, p. 142.

65 See ibid., p. 112ff. In each of the diagrams which follow I have omitted certain complexities of which I cannot here enter into sufficient explanation.

66 I am now quoting from *The Role of the Reader*, p. 23.

67 Ibid.

68 With this quote I have switched to *Semiotics and the Philosophy of Language*, pp. 117–18.

69 Ibid., p. 189.

70 Ibid., p. 201.

71 The theme of my opening chapter.

72 One aspect of which was the theme of section 3 of this chapter.

73 *Infra.*, n. 76.

74 This latter meaning is found in Xenophon (see LSJ). In NT lexicons (as by NT commentators) it has normally (e.g. UCr, MM, BAGD, BA, LN) been disregarded (though WGTh noted it). Presumably juxtaposition with στηριχθῆναι is seen as excluding it.

75 In fact he translates (CR, p. 26) 'that there may be mutual encouragement among you'; whilst Cranfield (CR, p. 74) has 'in your midst to be comforted together with you'.

76 See Dunn, CR, pp. 30–1; Cranfield, CR, pp. 78–9; both discuss the variety of opinion among commentators; neither favours the view (particularly linked with Michel) that Paul is anticipating a display of 'gifting' that will legitimise him in the eyes of Roman πνευματικοί. That the blessing may be especially associated with preaching is Käsemann's view. Though Dunn would not be too restrictive about it, he favours something special as a referent. Cranfield thinks the benefit of Paul's presence is as far as we need look.

77 A recent wide-ranging review of theories is to be found in Ziesler, CR, pp. 3–16. He considers a mixture of motives on Paul's part to be perfectly feasible. Too recent to have come under Ziesler's scrutiny: Guerra, 'Romans: Paul's purpose and audience'; Crafton, 'Paul's rhetorical vision' (using as a basis Lampe, *Die stadtrömischen Christen*); Haacker, 'Der Römerbrief als Friedensmemorandum'; Jarvis, *The Purpose of Romans*.

BIBLIOGRAPHY

Achtemeier, P. J. 'Romans 3:1–8: structure and argument', *ATRSS* 11 (1990), pp. 77–87.

Against Theory. Literary Studies and the New Pragmatism, ed. W. J. T. Mitchell, Chicago and London, Chicago UP, 1985.

Aletti, J.-N. 'L'argumentation paulinienne en Rom 9', *Bibl* 68 (1987), pp. 41–56.

'La *dispositio* rhétorique dans les épîtres pauliniennes', *NTS* 38 (1992), pp. 385–401.

'La présence d'un modèle rhétorique en Romains: son rôle et son importance', *Bibl* 71 (1990), pp. 1–24.

L'Apôtre Paul. Personnalité, Style et Conception du Ministère, ed. A. Vanhoye, Louvain, Louvain UP, 1986.

Art and Meaning in Biblical Literature, ed. D. J. A. Clines, Sheffield, JSOT, 1982.

Aune, D. E. *The NT in its Literary Environment*, Cambridge, Clark, 1988.

'Romans as a *Logos Protreptikos*', in *The Romans Debate* (q.v.), pp. 278–96.

Baasland, E. 'Cognitio Dei im Römerbrief', *SNTU* 14 (1989), pp. 185–218.

Baird, W. 'What is Kerygma?', *JBL* 76 (1957), pp. 181–91.

Barker, S. F. *The Elements of Logic*, NY, McGraw Hill, 1985.

Barnwell, K. *Introduction to Semantics and Translation*, Horsley's Gn., SIL, 2nd edn 1980.

Barrett, C. K. *A Commentary on the Epistle to the Romans* (BNTC), London, Black, 2nd edn 1962.

Barth, K. *Church Dogmatics II: The Doctrine of God*, Edinburgh, Clark, n.d.

The Epistle to the Romans (ET from the 6th edn by E. C. Hoskyns), Oxford UP, 1968.

Barthes, R. *Éléments de sémiologie*, Paris, Seuil, 1964.

Mythologies, Paris, Seuil, 1957.

Battesimo e Giustizia in Rom 6 e 8, ed. L. de Lorenzi, Rome, Abbazia S. Paolo, 1974.

Beekmann, J., Callow, J. and Kopesec, M. *The Semantic Structure of Written Communication*, Dallas, SIL, 5th edn 1981.

Beker, J. C. *Paul the Apostle. The Triumph of God in Life and Thought*, Edinburgh, Clark, 1980.

'Paul's theology: consistent or inconsistent?', *NTS* 34 (1988), pp. 364–77.

'Suffering and triumph in Paul's letter to the Romans', *HBT* 7 (1985), pp. 105–19.

Betz, H. D. *Galatians. A Commentary on Paul's Letter to the Churches in Galatia* (HCHC), Philadelphia, Fortress, 1979.

'The literary composition and function of Paul's letter to the Galatians', *NTS* 21 (1975), pp. 353–79.

'The problem of rhetoric and theology according to the Apostle Paul', in *L'Apôtre Paul* (q.v.), pp. 16–48.

Betz, O. 'Die Vision des Paulus im Tempel von Jerusalem – Apg. 22:17–21, als Beitrag zur Deutung des Damaskuserlebnisses', in *Verborum Veritas* (q.v.), pp. 113–23.

Bligh, J. *Galatians. A Discussion of Paul's Epistle*, London, St Paul, 1969.

Boers, H. W. 'The foundations of Paul's thought: a methodological investigation. The problem of the coherent centre of Paul's thought', *ST* 42 (1988), pp. 55–68.

Bornkamm, G. *Paul* (ET by D. M. G. Stalker), London, Hodder and Stoughton, 1971.

'The revelation of Christ to Paul on the Damascus road and Paul's doctrine of justification and reconciliation. A study in Gals 1', in *Reconciliation and Hope* (q.v.), pp. 90–103.

Bouttier, M. 'La vie du chrétien en tant que service de la justice pour la sainteté: Romains 6:15–23', in *Battesimo e Giustizia* (q.v.), pp. 127–54 (–176).

Brownlee, W. M. *The Midrash Pesher of Habakkuk*, Ann Arbor, Scholars, 1979.

Bruce, F. F. *The Epistle to the Galatians. A Commentary on the Greek Text* (NIGTC), Exeter, Paternoster, 1982.

The Epistle of Paul to the Romans. An Introduction and Commentary (TNTC), London, Tyndale, 1971 (1st edn 1963).

Bultmann, R. *Der Stil der paulinischen Predigt und die kynisch-stoische Diatribe*, Göttingen, Vandenhoeck and Ruprecht, 1910.

Theology of the NT (ET), London, SCM, 1951.

Byrne, B. 'Living out the righteousness of God: the contribution of Rom 6:1–8:13 to an understanding of Paul's ethical presuppositions', *CBQ* 43 (1981), pp. 557–81.

'Sons of God' – 'Seed of Abraham'. A study in the idea of the sonship of God of all Christians in Paul against the Jewish background (AnBib 83), Rome, PIB, 1979.

Calvet, L.-J. *Roland Barthes. Un regard politique sur le signe*, Paris, Payot, 1973.

Campbell, D. A. *The Rhetoric of Righteousness in Romans 3:21–26* (JSNT SS 65), Sheffield, JSOT, 1992.

Campbell, W. S. 'Romans 3 as a key to the structure and thought of the letter', in *The Romans Debate* (q.v.), pp. 251–64.

Carras, G. P. 'Romans 2:1–29: a dialogue of Jewish ideals', *Bibl* 73 (1992), pp. 183–207.

Cavallin, H. C. C. 'The righteous shall live by faith', *ST* 32 (1978), pp. 33–43.

Conzelmann, H. *1 Corinthians. A Commentary on the First Epistle to the Corinthians* (HCHC) (ET by J. W. Leitch), Philadelphia, Fortress, 1985.

Copi, I. M. *An Introduction to Logic*, London/NY, Macmillan, 1953.

Corti, M. *An Introduction to Literary Semiotics* (ET of *Principi*), Bloomington, Indiana, 1978.

Principi della comunicazione letteraria, Milan, Bompiani, 1976.

Cosby, M. R. 'Paul's persuasive language in Romans 5', in *Persuasive Artistry* (q.v.), pp. 209–26.

Cosgrove, C. H. 'Justification in Paul: a linguistic and theological reflection', *JBL* 106 (1987), pp. 653–70.

'What if some have not believed? The occasion and thrust of Romans 3:1–8', *ZNW* 78 (1987), pp. 90–105.

Cotterell, P. and Turner, M. *Linguistics and Biblical Interpretation*, London, SPCK, 1989.

Crafton, J. A. 'Paul's rhetorical vision and the purpose of Romans: toward a new understanding', *NovT* 32 (1990), pp. 317–39.

Cranfield, C. E. B. *A Critical and Exegetical Commentary on the Epistle to the Romans* (ICC), Edinburgh, Clark, I, 1987 (1st edn 1975); II, 1986 (1st edn 1979).

'On some problems in the interpretation of Rom 5:12', *SJT* 22 (1969), pp. 324–41.

'Romans 8:28', *SJT* 19 (1966), pp. 204–15.

Crossan, J. D. 'Difference and Divinity', *Sem* 23 (1982), pp. 29–40.

Dahl, N. 'The Atonement – an adequate reward for the Aqedah? (Rom 8:32)', in *Neotestamentica et Semitica* (q.v.), pp. 15–29.

'Romans 3:9. Text and meaning', in *Paul and Paulinism* (q.v.), pp. 184–204.

Davies, G. N. *Faith and Obedience in Romans. A Study in Romans 1–4* (JSNT SS 39), Sheffield, JSOT, 1990.

Déaut, R. Le 'La présentation targumique et la sotériologie paulinienne', in *Studiorum Paulinorum* (q.v.), pp. 563–74.

Deidun, T. J. *New Covenant Morality in Paul* (AnBib 89), Rome, PIB, 1981.

Deissmann, A. *Light from the Ancient East* (ET by L. R. M. Strachan), NY, Doran, 1927 (1st edn 1910).

De Romilly, J. *Magic and Rhetoric in Ancient Greece*, Harvard UP, 1975.

Derrida, J. *De la grammatologie*, Paris, Minuit, 1967.

'Of an apocalyptic tone recently adopted in philosophy', *Sem* 23 (1982), pp. 63–97.

Derrida and Biblical Studies, ed. R. Detweiler, = *Sem* 23 (1982).

Detweiler, R. 'What is a sacred text?', in *Reader Response Approaches* (q.v.), pp. 213–30.

Dinkler, E. *Der urchristliche Friedensgedanke*, Heidelberg, Winter, 1973.

The Divine Helmsman (Silberman FS), ed. J. L. Crenshaw and S. Sandmel, NY, Ktav, 1980.

Dodd, C. H. *The Epistle of Paul to the Romans* (MNTC), London, Hodder and Stoughton, 1947 (1st edn 1932).

Doeve, J. W. 'Some notes with reference to τὰ λόγια τοῦ θεοῦ in Rom 3:2', in *Studia Paulina* (q.v.), pp. 111–23.

Drane, J. W. 'Why did Paul write Romans?', in *Pauline Studies* (q.v.), pp. 208–27.

Dunn, J. D. G. *Romans 1–8* (WBC 38A), *9–16* (WBC 38B), Dallas, Word, 1988.

Unity and Diversity in the NT, London, SCM, 1977.

Dupont, J. *La Réconciliation dans la théologie de St Paul* (ALBO 2.32), Louvain, Louvain UP, 1953.

Earnshaw, J. D. 'Reconsidering Paul's marriage analogy in Romans 7:1–4', *NTS* 40 (1994), pp. 68–88.

Ebeling, G. *Introduction to a Theological Theory of Language* (ET by R. A. Wilson), London, Collins, 1973.

Theologie und Verkündigung, Tübingen, Mohr, 1963.

Word and Faith (ET), London, SCM, 1963.

Eco, U. *La definizione dell'arte*, Milan, Mursia, 1968.

Le forme del contenuto, Milan, Bompiani, 1971.

I limiti dell'interpretazione, Milan, Bompiani, 1990.

Il problema estetico in Tommaso d'Aquino, Milan, Bompiani, 2nd edn 1970.

The Role of the Reader. Explorations in the Semiotics of Texts, Bloomington and London, Indiana UP, 1979.

Il segno, Milan, ISEDI, 1973.

Semiotics and the Philosophy of Language, London, Macmillan, 1988.

La struttura assente, Milan, Bompiani, 4th edn 1987 (1st edn 1968).

A Theory of Semiotics, Bloomington, Indiana UP, 1976.

Trattato di semiotica generale, Milan, Bompiani, 10th edn 1987 (1st edn 1975).

Eichholz, G. *Die Theologie des Paulus im Umriss*, Neukirchen, Neukirchener, 1972.

Elliott, N. *The Rhetoric of Romans. Argumentative Constraint and Strategy and Paul's Dialogue with Judaism* (JSNT SS 45), Sheffield, JSOT, 1990.

Ellis, E. E. *Paul's Use of the Old Testament*, Edinburgh, Oliver and Boyd, 1957.

Fee, G. D. *The First Epistle to the Corinthians* (NICNT), Grand Rapids, Eerdmans, 1987.

Feuillet, A. 'La citation d'Habacuc 2:4 et les huit premiers chapîtres de l'Epître aux Romains', *NTS* 6 (1959–60), pp. 52–80.

Fiedler, P. 'Röm 8:31–39 als Brennpunkt paulinischer Frohbotschaft', *ZNW* 68 (1977), pp. 23–34.

Fitzmyer, J. A. 'Habakkuk 2:3–4 and the New Testament', in Fitzmyer, *To Advance the Gospel* (q.v.), pp. 236–46.

'Paul and the Law', in Fitzmyer, *To Advance the Gospel* (q.v.), pp. 186–201.

Pauline Theology. A Brief Sketch, Englewood Cliffs, Prentice Hall, 1967.

Romans. A new translation with introduction and commentary (Anchor Bible), London, Doubleday, 1993.

To Advance the Gospel. New Testament Studies, NY, Crossroad, 1981.

'The use of explicit Old Testament quotation in Qumran literature and in the New Testament', in Fitzmyer, *Essays on the Semitic Background of the New Testament*, London, Chapman, 1971, pp. 3–58.

Frankemölle, H. *Das Taufverständnis des Paulus. Taufe, Tod und Auferste-hung nach Röm 6* (StB 47), Stuttgart, Katholisches Bibelwerk, 1970.

From Jesus to Paul (Beare FS), ed. P. Richardson and J. C. Hurd, Water-loo, Laurier, 1984.

Fuchs, E. 'Response to the American discussion', in *The New Hermeneutic* (q.v.), pp. 232–43.

Studies of the Historical Jesus (ET), London, SCM, 1964.

Fung, R. Y. K. *The Epistle to the Galatians* (NICNT), Grand Rapids, Eerdmans, 1988.

Furnish, V. P. *Theology and Ethics in Paul*, Nashville, Abingdon, 1968.

The Future of Our Religious Past (Bultmann FS), ed. J. M. Robinson, London, SCM, 1971.

Fuzzy Sets and their Application to Cognitive and Decision Processes, ed. L. A. Zadeh, King-Sun Fu, Kokichi Tanaka and Masamichi Shimura, NY, Academic Press, 1975.

Gadamer, H.-G. *Truth and Method* (ET by J. Weinsheimer and D. G. Marshall), London, Sheed and Ward, 2nd edn 1989.

Wahrheit und Methode, Tübingen, Mohr, 3rd edn 1972.

Gager, G. *The Origins of Anti-Semitism. Attitudes towards Judaism in Pagan and Christian Antiquity*, NY, Oxford UP, 1985.

Gale, H. M. *The Use of Analogy in the Letters of Paul*, London, West-minster, 1964.

Gaston, I. *Paul and the Torah*, Vancouver, British Columbia UP, 1987.

Gaugler, E. *Der Römerbrief*, I, Zürich, Zwingli, 1st edn 1945.

Gibson, M. 'Lanfranc's Commentary on the Pauline Epistles', *JTS* 22 (1971), pp. 86–112.

Goppelt, L. 'Versöhnung durch Christus', in Goppelt, *Christologie und Ethik. Aufsätze zum Neuen Testament*, Göttingen, Vandenhoeck and Ruprecht, 1968, pp. 147–64.

Grayston, K. 'The doctrine of election in Rom 8:28–30', *SE* 2 (1964), pp. 574–83.

Grönbech, V. *Paulus Jesu Christi Apostel*, Copenhagen, 1940.

Guerra, A. J. 'Romans: Paul's purpose and audience with special attention to Romans 9–11', *RB* 97 (1990), pp. 219–37.

Guiraud, P. *La Sémiologie*, Paris, PUF, 1971.

Semiology (ET), London, Routledge and Kegan Paul, 1975.

Güttgemanns, E. '"Gottesgerechtigkeit" und strukturale Semantik. Linguistische Analyse zu δικαιοσύνη θεοῦ', in Güttgemanns, *Studia Linguistica Neotestamentica. Gesammelte Aufsätze zur linguistischen Grundlage einer Neutestamentlichen Theologie* (BETh 60), Munich, Kaiser, 1971, pp. 59–98.

Der Leidende Apostel und sein Herr. Studien zur paulinischen Christologie, Göttingen, Vandenhoeck and Ruprecht, 1966.

Haacker, K. 'Der Römerbrief als Friedensmemorandum', *NTS* 36 (1990), pp. 25–41.

Hall, D. R. 'Romans 3:1–8 reconsidered', *NTS* 29 (1983), pp. 183–97.

Hamilton, W. *Discussions on Philosophy and Literature, Education and University Reform*, London, Longmans, 1853.

Hansen, G. W. *Abraham in Galatians*, Sheffield, JSOT, 1989.

Hanson, A. T. *The Wrath of the Lamb*, London, SPCK, 1975.

Hawkes, T. *Structuralism and Semiotics*, London, Methuen, 1977.

Heil, J. P. *Romans: Paul's Letter of Hope* (AnBib 112), Rome, PIB, 1987.

Hengel, M. *The Pre-Christian Paul* (ET by J. Bowden), London, SCM, 1991.

Héring, J. *The First Epistle of St Paul to the Corinthians* (ET by A. A. Heathcote and P. J. Allcock), London, Epworth, 1962.

Hervey, S. *Semiotic Perspectives*, London, Allen and Unwin, 1982.

Hester, J. D. *Paul's Concept of Inheritance* (*SJT* Occasional Papers 14), Edinburgh, Boyd, 1968.

Hiebert, D. E. 'Romans 8:28–9 and the assurance of the believer', *BS* 148 (1991), pp. 170–83.

Hjelmslev, L. *Prolegomena to a Theory of Language*, Wisconsin UP, 1963.

Hofius, O. 'Sühne und Versöhnung: zum paulinischen Verständnis des Kreuzestodes Jesu', in *Versuche, das Leiden und Sterben Jesu zu verstehen* (q.v.), pp. 25–46.

Holub, R. C. *Reception Theory. A Critical Introduction*, London and NY, Methuen, 1984.

Hooker, M. D. 'Paul and covenantal nomism', in *Paul and Paulinism* (q.v.), pp. 47–56.

Hübner, H. *Law in Paul's Thought. A Contribution to the Development of Pauline Theology* (ET by J. C. G. Greig), Edinburgh, Clark, 2nd edn 1986.

Jakobson, R. 'Closing statement. Linguistics and Poetics', in *Style in Language* (q.v.), pp. 351–77.

Jarvis, L. A. *The Purpose of Romans* (JSNT SS 55), Sheffield, JSOT, 1991.

Jauss, H. R. *Literaturgeschichte als Provocation*, Frankfurt, Suhrkamp, 1970.

Jeremias, J. 'Zur Gedankenführung in den paulinischen Briefen', in Jeremias *Abba. Studien zur neutestamentlichen Theologie und Zeitgeschichte*, Göttingen, Vandenhoeck and Ruprecht, 1966, pp. 269–72.

Jevons, W. S. *Elementary Lessons in Logic*, London, Macmillan, 1903.

Jewett, R. 'Major impulses in the interpretation of Romans since Barth', *Int* 34 (1980), pp. 17–31.

Paul's Anthropological Terms, Leiden, Brill, 1971.

'Romans as an ambassadorial letter', *Int* 36 (1982), pp. 5–20.

Jones, F. S. *'Freiheit' in den Briefen des Apostels Paulus* (GTA 34), Göttingen, Vandenhoeck and Ruprecht, 1987.

Joseph, H. W. B. *An Introduction to Logic*, Oxford, Clarendon, 2nd edn 1916.

Käsemann, E. *An die Römer* (HNT 8A), Tübingen, Mohr, 4th edn 1980 (1st edn 1973).

Commentary on Romans (ET by G. W. Bromily), London, SCM, 2nd edn 1982.

'On Paul's anthropology', in Käsemann, *Perspectives on Paul*, London, SCM, 1971, pp. 1–31.

'"The righteousness of God" in Paul', in Käsemann, *NT Questions of Today*, London, SCM, 1969, pp. 168–82.

'Some thoughts on the theme "The doctrine of Reconciliation in the NT"', in *The Future of our Religious Past* (q.v.), pp. 49–64.

Keck, L. E. 'The law of "the law of sin and death" (Rom 8:1–4): reflections on the spirit and ethics in Paul', in *The Divine Helmsman* (q.v.), pp. 41–57.

Keller, see Vuilleumier.

Kennedy, G. *The Art of Persuasion in Greece*, Princeton UP, 1963.

Kennedy, G. A. *Classical Rhetoric and its Christian and Secular Tradition*, London, Croom Helm, 1980.

'An introduction to the rhetoric of the gospels', *Rhet* 1 (1983), pp. 17–31.

NT Interpretation through Rhetorical Criticism, North Carolina UP, 1984.

Kertelge, K. *'Rechtfertigung' bei Paulus. Studien zur Struktur und zum Bedeutungsgehalt des paulinischen Rechtfertigungsbegriffs*, Münster, Aschendorff, 1967.

Kessler, M. 'A methodological setting for rhetorical criticism', in *Art and Meaning in Biblical Literature* (q.v.), pp. 1–19.

Keynes, J. N. *Studies and Exercises in Formal Logic*, London, Macmillan, 4th edn 1906.

Kim, S. *The Origin of Paul's Gospel*, Tübingen, Mohr, 1981.

Kleinknecht, K. T. *Der leidende Gerechtfertigte* (WUNT 2.13), Tübingen, Mohr, 1984.

Klemm, M. Εἰρήνη *im neutestamentlichen Sprachsystem*, Bonn, Linguistica Biblica, 1977.

Knapp, S. and Michaels, W. B. 'Against theory', in *Against Theory* (q.v.), pp. 11–30.

Kneale, W. and Kneale, M. *The Development of Logic*, Oxford UP, 1962.

Koch, D.-A. 'Der Text von Hab 2:4b in der Septuaginta und im Neuen Testament', *ZNW* 76 (1985), pp. 68–85.

Kümmel, W. G. 'Römer 7 und die Bekehrung des Paulus', in Kümmel, *Römer 7 und das Bild des Menschen im Neuen Testament. Zwei Studien*, Munich, Kaiser, 2nd edn 1974, pp. ix–160.

Kürzinger, J. 'συμμόρφους τῆς εἰκόνος τοῦ υἱοῦ αὐτοῦ (Röm 8:29)', *BZ* NF 2 (1958), pp. 294–9.

Kuss, O. *Der Römerbrief. Übersetzt und erklärt*, ii, Regensburg, Pustet, 1959.

Lambrecht, J. 'Why is boasting excluded? A note on Rom 3:27 and 4:2', *ETL* 61 (1985), pp. 365–9.

Lampe, R. *Die stadtrömischen Christen in den ersten beiden Jahrhunderten. Untersuchungen zur Sozialgeschichte*, Tübingen, Mohr, 1987.

Lausberg, H. *Handbuch der literarschen Rhetorik*, München, Hüber, 2nd edn 1973.

Law and Religion. Essays on the Place of the Law in Early Christianity, ed. B. Lindars, Cambridge, Clark, 1988.

The Law of the Spirit in Rom 7 and 8, ed. L. de Lorenzi, Rome, St Paul's Abbey, 1976.

Leaney, A. R. 'Conformed to the image of his son (Rom 8:29)', *NTS* 10 (1963–64), pp. 470–9.

Leavey, J. P. 'Four protocols: Derrida, his deconstruction', *Sem* 23 (1982), pp. 43–57.

Leenhardt, F. J. *The Epistle to the Romans. A Commentary* (ET), London, Lutterworth, 1964.

Légasse, S. 'Être baptisé dans la mort du Christ; Étude de Romains 6:1–14', *RB* 98 (1991), pp. 544–59.

Lepschy, G. *La Linguistica del Novecento*, Bologna, Mulino, 1992.

A Survey of Structural Linguistics, London, Deutsch, 1982.

Review of U. Eco: *La struttura assente*, *Linguistics* 62 (1970), pp. 105–10.

Levison, J. R. 'Did the spirit inspire rhetoric?', in *Persuasive Artistry* (q.v.), pp. 25–40.

Lindars, B. 'Romans 5–8: an actantial analysis', in *Law and Religion* (q.v.), pp. 126–40.

Lohse, E. 'Zur Analyse und Interpretation von Röm 8:1–17', in *The Law of the Spirit* (q.v.), pp. 129–46.

'ὁ νόμος τοῦ πνεύματος τῆς ζωῆς. Exegetische Anmerkungen zu Röm 8:2', in *Neues Testament* (q.v.), pp. 279–89.

Longenecker, R. *Galatians* (WBC 41), Dallas, Word, 1990.

'Paul and the OT', in Longenecker, *Biblical Exegesis in the Apostolic Period*, Grand Rapids, Eerdmans, 1975, pp. 104–23.

Luciani, D. 'Paul et la loi', *Nouvelle Revue Théologique* 115 (1993), pp. 40–68.

Lyonnet, S. 'L'histoire du salut selon le chapître 7 de l'épître aux Romains', *Bibl* 43 (1962), pp. 117–51; also in Lyonnet, *Études sur l'Épître aux Romains*, Rome, PIB, 1989, pp. 203–30.

McCawley, J. D. *Everything that Linguists have Always Wanted to Know about Logic – but were ashamed to ask*, Oxford, Blackwell, 1981.

McDonald, P. M. 'Romans 5:1–11 as a rhetorical bridge', *JSNT* 40 (1990), pp. 81–96.

Maillot, A. *L'Épître aux Romains. Épître de l'oecuménisme et théologie de l'histoire*, Paris, Centurion, 1984.

Mainberger, G. K. 'Der Leib der Rhetorik', *LB* 52 (1982), pp. 71–86.

Malan, F. S. 'Bound to do right', *Neot* 15 (1981), pp. 118–38.

Malherbe, A. J. 'μὴ γένοιτο in the Diatribe and Paul', *HTR* 73 (1980), pp. 231–41.

Manson, T. W. 'Appendix on λόγια', in Manson, *Studies in the Gospels and Epistles*, Manchester UP, 1962, pp. 87–104.

Marcus, J. '"Let God arise and end the reign of sin". A contribution to the study of Pauline parenesis', *Bibl* 69 (1988), pp. 386–95.

Marshall, H. 'The meaning of "Reconciliation"', in *Unity and Diversity* (q.v.), pp. 117–32.

Martin, B. L. *Christ and the Law in Paul* (NovTS 62), Leiden, Brill, 1989.

Martin, D. B. *Slavery as Salvation. The Metaphor of Slavery in Pauline Christianity*, Yale UP, 1990.

Martin, R. P. *Reconciliation. A Study of Paul's Theology*, Atlanta, John Knox, 1981.

Michel, A. *Rhétorique et philosophie chez Cicéron*, Paris, PUF, 1960.

Michel, O. *Der Brief an die Römer* (MKEK 4), Göttingen, Vandenhoeck and Ruprecht, 5th edn 1978 (1st edn 1955).

Minear, P. S. *The Obedience of Faith. The Purposes of Paul in the Epistle to the Romans*, London, SCM, 1971.

Modern Literary Theory. A Comparative Introduction, ed. A. Jefferson and D. Robey, London, Batsford, 1982.

Moffatt, J. 'The interpretation of Romans 6:17–18', *JBL* 48 (1929), pp. 233–8.

Moo, D. J. 'Israel and Paul in Romans 7:7–12', *NTS* 32 (1986), pp. 122–35.
'Paul and the law in the last ten years', *SJT* 40 (1987), pp. 287–307.

Moody, R. M. 'The Habakkuk quotation in Romans 1:17', *ExT* 92 (1980–81), pp. 205–8.

Morris, C. W. *Signs, Language and Behaviour*, NY, Prentice Hall, 1950.

Moule, C. F. D. *An Idiom Book of New Testament Greek*, Cambridge UP, 2nd edn 1959.

Moule, H. G. C. *The Epistle of St Paul to the Romans* (EB), London, Hodder and Stoughton, 2nd edn 1894.

Muilenberg, J. 'Form criticism and beyond', *JBL* 88 (1969), pp. 1–18.

Mukařovský, J. *Il processo motorio in poesia* (AP 15), Palermo, CISE, 1987.
Structure, Sign and Function. Selected Essays, New Haven and London, Yale UP, 1978.
The Word and Verbal Art. Selected Essays, New Haven and London, Yale UP, 1977.

Müller, H. 'Der rabbinische Qal-Wachomer-Schluss in paulinischer Typologie. Zur Adam-Christus-Typologie in Röm 5', *ZNW* 58 (1967), pp. 73–92.

Murray, J. *The Epistle to the Romans* (NICNT), I, Grand Rapids, Eerdmans, 1960.

Mussner, F. *Der Galaterbrief* (HTKNT 9), Freiburg, Herder, 1977 (1st edn 1974).

La Narration. Quand le récit devient communication (LT 12), ed. P. Bühler and J. F. Habermacher, Geneva, Labor et Fides, 1988.

Neotestamentica et Semitica (Black FS), ed. E. E. Ellis and M. Wilcox, Edinburgh, Clark, 1969.

Neues Testament und Christliche Existenz (Braun FS), ed. H. D. Betz and L. Schottroff, Tübingen, Mohr, 1973.

The New Hermeneutic (New Frontiers in Theology II), ed. J. M. Robinson and J. B. Cobb, NY, Harper and Row, 1964.

Norden, E. *Die antike Kunstprosa*, Darmstadt, Wissenschaftliche Buchgesellschaft, 1971.

Nygren, A. *Commentary on Romans* (ET), Philadelphia, Fortress, 1988 (1st edn 1949).

O'Neill, J. C. *Paul's Letter to the Romans*, London, Penguin, 1975.

Orientation by Disorientation. Studies in Literary Criticism and Biblical Literary Criticism (Beardslee FS), ed. R. A. Spencer, Pittsburg, Pickwick, 1980.

Osten-Sacken, P. von der *Römer 8 als Beispiel paulinischer Soteriologie* (FRLANT 112), Göttingen, Vandenhoeck and Ruprecht, 1975.

Patte, D. *Paul's Faith and the Power of the Gospel. A Structural Introduction to the Pauline Letters*, Philadelphia, Fortress, 1983.

Paul and Paulinism (Barrett FS), ed. M. D. Hooker and S. G. Wilson, London, SPCK, 1982.

Pauline Studies (Bruce FS), ed. D. A. Hagner and M. J. Harris, Grand Rapids, Eerdmans, 1980.

Paulsen, H. *Überlieferung und Auslegung in Röm 8* (WMANT 43), Neukirchen, Neukirchener, 1974.

Peirce, C. S. *Collected Papers*, Cambridge, Mass., Harvard UP, 1931–58.

Penna, P. 'La funzione strutturale di 3:1–8 nella lettera ai Romani', *Bibl* 69 (1988), pp. 507–42.

Perelman, C. *The New Rhetoric and the Humanities* (ET by W. Kluback), Dordrecht, Reidel, 1979.

Perelman, C. and Olbrechts-Tyteca, L. *La Nouvelle Rhétorique. Traité de l'argumentation*, Paris, PUF, 1948.

Persuasive Artistry. Studies in NT Rhetoric (Kennedy FS), ed. D. F. Watson, Sheffield, JSOT, 1991.

Piper, J. 'The righteousness of God in Rom 3:1–8', *TZ* 36 (1980), pp. 3–16.

Porter, S. E. 'The argument of Romans 5. Can a rhetorical question make a difference?', *JBL* 110 (1991), pp. 655–77.

Prieto, L. *Messages et signaux*, Paris, PUF, 1966.

Räisänen, H. 'Das "Gesetz des Glaubens" (Röm 3:27) und das "Gesetz des Geistes" (Röm 8:2)', *NTS* 26 (1979–80), pp. 101–17; also in Räisänen, *The Torah and Christ* (q.v.), pp. 95–118.

Paul and the Law (WUNT 29), Tübingen, Mohr, 1983.

'Paul's conversion and the development of his view of the law', *NTS* 33 (1987), pp. 404–19.

The Torah and Christ, Helsinki, Finnish Exegetical Society, 1986.

'Zum Verständnis von Röm 3:1–8', in Räisänen, *The Torah and Christ* (q.v.), pp. 185–205.

Ralston, T. J. 'The theological significance of Paul's conversion', *BS* 147 (1990), pp. 198–215.

Reade, N. H. V. *The Problem of Inference*, Oxford, Clarendon, 1938.

Reader Response Approaches to Biblical and Secular Texts, ed. R. Detweiler, = *Sem* 31 (1985).

Reader Response Criticism from Formalism to Post-Structuralism, ed. J. P. Tompkins, Baltimore and London, John Hopkins UP, 1980.

Reconciliation and Hope, ed. L. L. Morris and R. Banks, Exeter Paternoster, 1974.

Reumann, J. (*et al.*) *Righteousness in the NT*, Philadelphia, Fortress, 1982.

Rhyne, C. T. *Faith Establishes the Law* (SBLDS 55), Ann Arbor, Scholars, 1981.

Riedl, J. 'Die Auslegung von Röm 2:14–16 in Vergangenheit und Gegenwart' in *Studiorum Paulinorum* (q.v.), pp. 271–81.

Robertson, O. P. '"The justified (by faith) shall live by his steadfast trust"': Habakkuk 2:4', *Presb* 9 (1983), pp. 52–71.

Robinson, J. M. 'Hermeneutic since Barth', in *The New Hermeneutic* (q.v.), pp. 1–77.

Rolland, P. 'L'antithèse de Rm 5–8', *Bibl* 69 (1988), pp. 396–400.

The Romans Debate, ed. K. P. Donfried, Peabody, Hendrickson, 2nd edn 1991 (1st edn 1977).

Sanday, W. and Headlam, A. C. *A Critical and Exegetical Commentary on the Epistle to the Romans* (ICC), Edinburgh, Clark, 5th edn 1902 (1st edn 1895).

Sanders, E. P. *Paul, the Law and the Jewish People*, London, SCM, 1985.

Paul and Palestinian Judaism, London, SCM, 1977.

Sanders, J. T. 'Paul's autobiographical statements in Galatians 1–2', *JBL* 85 (1966), pp. 335–43.

Sandt, H. W. M. van de 'Research into Rom 8:4a. The legal claim of the law', *BTFT* 37 (1976), pp. 361–78.

Saussure, F. de *Cours de linguistique générale* (ed. T. De Mauro), Paris, Payot, 1978.

Schäfer, R. 'Melanchthons Hermeneutik im Römerbriefkommentar von 1532', ZTK 60 (1963), pp. 216–35.

Schipper, E. W. and Schuh, E. *A First Course in Modern Logic*, London, Routledge and K. Paul, 1960.

Schlier, H. *Der Römerbrief. Kommentar* (HTKNT 6), Freiburg, Herder, 3rd edn 1987 (1st edn 1977).

Schmithals, W. *Die theologische Anthropologie des Paulus. Auslegung von Röm 7:17–8:39*, Stuttgart, Kohlhammer, 1980.

Schnackenburg, R. *Baptism in the Thought of St Paul* (ET by G. R. Beasley-Murray), Oxford, Blackwell, 1964.

Schneidau, H. N. 'The word against the word: Derrida on textuality', *Sem* 23 (1982), pp. 5–28.

Schrage, W. 'Leid, Kreuz und Eschaton. Die Peristasenkataloge als Merkmale paulinischer theologia crucis und Eschatologie', *EvTh* 34 (1974), pp. 141–75.

Schreiner, T. R. '"Works of Law" in Paul', *NovT* 33 (1991), pp. 217–44.

Schüssler Fiorenza, E. 'Rhetorical situation and historical reconstruction in 1Cor', *NTS* 33 (1987), pp. 386–403.

Schwartz, D. R. 'Two Pauline allusions to the redemptive mechanism of the Crucifixion', *JBL* 102 (1983), pp. 259–68.

Scroggs, R. 'Romans 6:7 ὁ γὰρ ἀποθανὼν δεδικαίωται ἀπὸ τῆς ἁμαρτίας', *NTS* 10 (1963), pp. 104–8.

Segal, A. F. '"He who did not spare his own son . . .": Jesus, Paul and the Akedah', in *From Jesus to Paul* (q.v.), pp. 169–84.

Segre, C. *Semiotics and Literary Criticism*, Paris, Mouton, 1973.

Senft, C. *La Première Épître de Saint Paul aux Corinthiens*, Neuchâtel, Delacroix and Niestlé, 1979.

Sloan, R. B. 'Paul and the law: why the law cannot save', *NovT* 33 (1991), pp. 35–60.

Snyman, A. H. 'Style and the rhetorical situation of Romans 8:31–39', *NTS* 34 (1988), pp. 218–31.

Soards, M. L. 'Käsemann's "Righteousness" re-examined', *CBQ* 49 (1987), pp. 264–7.

Standaert, B. 'La rhétorique ancienne dans St Paul', in *L'Apôtre Paul* (q.v.), pp. 78–92.

Stankiewicz, E. 'Linguistics and the study of poetic language', in *Style in Language* (q.v.), pp. 69–81.

Stebbing, L. S. *A Modern Introduction to Logic*, London, Methuen, 3rd edn 1942.

Stirewalt, M. L. 'The form and function of the Greek letter-essay', in *The Romans Debate* (q.v.), pp. 147–71.

Stowers, S. K. *The Diatribe in Paul's Letter to the Romans*, Chico, Scholars, 1982.

'Paul's dialogue with a fellow Jew in Romans 3:1–9', *CBQ* 46 (1984), pp. 707–22.

Strawson, P. F. *Introduction to Logical Theory*, London, Methuen, 1966.

Studia Paulina (de Zwaan FS), ed. J. A. Sevenster and W. C. Van Unnik, Haarlem, Bohn, 1953.

Studiorum Paulinorum Congressus Internationalis Catholicus 1961 (AnBib 17–18), Rome, PIB, 1963.

Stuhlmacher, P. 'The Apostle Paul's view of righteousness', in Stuhlmacher, *Reconciliation, Law and Righteousness. Essays in Biblical Theology* (ET), Philadelphia, Fortress, 1986, pp. 68–93.

Der Brief an die Römer. Übersetzt und erklärt (NTD 6), Göttingen, Vandenhoeck and Ruprecht, 1989.

'The purpose of Romans', in *The Romans Debate* (q.v.), pp. 231–42.

Style in Language, ed. T. A. Sebeok, Massachusetts Institute of Technology, 1960.

Synge, F. C. 'The meaning of προεχόμεθα in Rom 3:9', *ExT* 81 (1969–70), p. 351.

Tannehill, R. C. *Dying and Rising with Christ*, Berlin, Töpelmann, 1967.

Theobald, M. 'Glaube und Vernunft. Zur Argumentation des Paulus im Römerbrief', *TQ* 169 (1989), pp. 287–301.

Thielman, F. *From Plight to Solution. A Jewish Framework for Understanding Paul's View of the Law in Galatians and Romans* (NovTS 61), Leiden, Brill, 1989.

Thiselton, A. C. *The Two Horizons*, Exeter, Paternoster, 1980.

Thompson, R. W. 'How is the Law fulfilled in us? An interpretation of Rom 8:4', *Louvain Studies* 11 (1986), pp. 31–40.

'Paul's double critique of Jewish boasting. A study of Rom 3:27 in its context', *Bibl* 67 (1986), pp. 520–31.

Tobin, T. H. 'Controversy and continuity in Romans 1:18–3:20', *CBQ* 55 (1993), pp. 298–318.

Tompkins, J. P. 'An introduction to Reader-Response Criticism', in *Reader Response Criticism* (q.v.), pp. ix–xxvi.

Unity and Diversity in the NT (Ladd FS), ed. R. A. Guelich, Grand Rapids, Eerdmans, 1978.

Verborum Veritas (Stählin FS), ed. O. Böcher and K. Haacker, Wuppertal, Brockhaus, 1970.

Versuche, das Leiden und Sterben Jesu zu verstehen, ed. W. Maas, Munich, Schnell and Steiner, 1983.

Vinson, R. B. 'A comparative study of the use of enthymemes in the synoptic gospels', in *Persuasive Artistry* (q.v.), pp. 119–41.

Vouga, F. 'Romains 1:18–3:20 comme *narratio*', in *La Narration* (q.v.), pp. 145–61.

Vuilleumier, R. and Keller, K. A. *Michée, Nahoum, Habacuc, Sophonie*, Neuchâtel, Delachaux and Niestlé, 1971.

Walton, D. N. *Informal Logic*, Cambridge UP, 1989.

Ward, G. 'Why is Derrida important for theology?', *Theol* 95 (1992), pp. 263–70.

Watson, F. *Paul, Judaism and the Gentiles. A Sociological Approach* (SNTSMS 56), Cambridge UP, 1986.

Watson, N. M. 'Justified by faith, judged by works – an antinomy?', *NTS* 29 (1983), pp. 209–21.

Wedderburn, A. J. M. *The Reasons for Romans*, Edinburgh, Clark, 1988.

Wegenast, K. *Das Verständnis der Tradition bei Paulus und in den Deuteropaulinen* (WMANT 8), 1962, Neukirchen, Neukirchener.

Weinsheimer, J. C. *Gadamer's Hermeneutic*, Yale UP, 1985.

Westerholm, S. *Israel's Law and the Church's Faith. Paul and his Recent Interpreters*, Grand Rapids, Eerdmans, 1988.

White, J. L. 'St Paul and the Apostolic Letter tradition', *CBQ* 45 (1983), pp. 433–44.

Wilckens, U. *Der Brief an die Römer* (EKKNT 6), Zürich, Benziger/Neukirchen, Neukirchener, I, 2nd edn 1987 (1st edn 1978); II, 2nd edn 1987 (1st edn 1980); III, 2nd edn 1989 (1st edn 1982).
'Christologie und Anthropologie im Zusammenhang der paulinischen Rechtfertigungslehre', *ZNW* 67 (1976), pp. 64–82.

Wilder, A. N. *Early Christian Rhetoric. The Language of the Gospel*, London, SCM, 1964.
'The word as address and meaning', in *The New Hermeneutic* (q.v.), pp. 198–218.

Wiles, M. F. *The Divine Apostle. The Interpretation of St Paul's Epistles in the Early Church*, Cambridge UP, 1967.

Williams, S. K. 'The "righteousness of God" in Romans', *JBL* 99 (1980), pp. 241–90.

Windisch, H. 'Das Problem des paulinischen Imperativs', *ZNW* 23 (1924), pp. 265–81.

Wolf, A. *Textbook of Logic*, London, Allen and Unwin, 1930.

Wolter, M. *Rechtfertigung und zukunftiges Heil. Untersuchungen zu Röm 5:1–11* (BZNW 43), Berlin, De Gruyter, 1978.

Wright, N. T. *The Climax of the Covenant. Christ and the Law in Pauline Theology*, Edinburgh, Clark, 1991.

Wuellner, W. 'Paul's rhetoric of argumentation in Romans: an alternative to the Donfried–Karris debate over Romans', *CBQ* 38 (1976), pp. 330–51, also in *The Romans Debate* (q.v.), pp. 128–46.
'Where is rhetorical criticism taking us?', *CBQ* 49 (1987), pp. 448–63.

Wykoff, W. 'Semiosis and infinite regress', *Semiotica* 2 (1970), pp. 59–67.

Young, F. and Ford, D. F. *Meaning and Truth in 2 Corinthians*, London, SPCK, 1987.

Zadeh, L. A. 'Calculus of fuzzy restrictions', in *Fuzzy Sets* (q.v.), pp. 1–39.
'Fuzzy sets', *Information and Control* 8 (1965), pp. 338–53.

Zeller, D. 'Der Zusammenhang von Gesetz und Sünde im Römerbrief. Kritischer Nachvollzug der Auslegung von U. Wilckens', *TZ* 38 (1982), pp. 193–212.

Zerwick, M. *Biblical Greek*, Rome, PIB, 1963.

Zerwick, M. and Grosvenor, M. *A Grammatical Analysis of the Greek NT*, Rome, PIB, 1981.

Ziesler, J. A. *The Meaning of Righteousness in Paul. A Linguistic and Theological Enquiry* (SNTSMS 20), Cambridge UP, 1972.
Paul's Letter to the Romans (TPINTC), London, SCM, 1989.

INDEX OF NAMES

INDEX OF TECHNICAL TERMS